the archaeology of
animal
bones

An Anglo-Saxon horse burial under excavation. Despite the poor state of preservation, a study of these bones will reveal the age, sex and height of the horse, while the deliberate burial shows what it meant to the people.

the archaeology of
animal
bones

Terry O'Connor

SUTTON PUBLISHING

First published in the United Kingdom in 2000 by
Sutton Publishing Limited · Phoenix Mill
Thrupp · Stroud · Gloucestershire · GL5 2BU

British Library Cataloguing in Publication Data
A catalogue record for this book is available from the British Library

ISBN 0 7509 2251 6

Dedication
For Sonia, and anyone else who has to put up with
a zooarchaeologist.

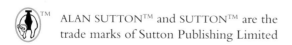
ALAN SUTTON™ and SUTTON™ are the
trade marks of Sutton Publishing Limited

Typeset in 10/13pt Sabon.
Typesetting and origination by
Sutton Publishing Limited.
Printed in Great Britain by
Bookcraft, Midsomer Norton, Somerset.

CONTENTS

PREFACE

Archaeology has rather unfortunately become associated with ancient ruins, Indiana Jones, unique and precious artefacts, and even with pyramid cults and the search for Atlantis. This book is about none of those things. Archaeology is fundamentally about people who lived and died in the past, and the detectable traces that those people, individually and collectively, have left on the world that we live in. At its heart, archaeology is about what it means to be human, even in that foreign country which we call the past.

One important aspect of being human is the range of interactions that we have with other animals. The very ordinary day in which this Preface has been written included eating parts of a sheep; discussing a flock of sheep with one's offspring; discussing one's offspring with various pets; discouraging one household pet from bringing wild rodents into the house; putting out food for wild birds to encourage their presence close to the house; and probably many more unintended and un-noticed interactions. Of all the aspects of past human lives that archaeology can set out to investigate, our involvement with other animals is one of the few that can be explored across all cultures, and throughout the history and prehistory of our species. The archaeological investigation of the surviving evidence of these interactions is termed *zooarchaeology*.

Most of the animals concerned in our past interactions will have been invertebrates: fleas and flies that made life a little more irritating, worms that made agriculture possible, other worms that made digestion uncomfortable. However, most of our deliberate interaction is with vertebrate animals, and it is these that are most closely involved with our economies and cultural frameworks. We find their remains on most archaeological sites throughout the world: scraps of bones, sometimes in great abundance, representing meals and pets and vermin, but also representing that web of relationships that humans make with other vertebrates. And this book is about the means of, and reasons for, studying those scraps of bone.

Our study, then, is ultimately the relationship between past peoples and the animals with which they shared the world. That investigation will lead us into some rather obscure and dusty corners of ancient and modern osteology, but we should not lose sight of the aim. Where necessary, some chapters go into the biological background of archaeological animal bone studies – *vertebrate zooarchaeology* – in some detail, and some delve into the history of the development of particular research areas. In both instances, the intention is to show why vertebrate zooarchaeology has adopted certain practical or interpretative methods. This book is not intended to be a didactic account that explains *how* animal bones ought to be examined and studied. Instead, the aim is to show *why* this field of scholarship is an important one, and to give sufficient detail about the development of methods and ideas to allow the reader to draw informed conclusions about the best way to proceed, or the practical constraints that have limited the scope of published reports and interpretation. Despite not being overtly didactic, the text is often quite opinionated. This is deliberate: a text is more likely to be of educational benefit if there are clearly stated views with which the reader can take issue.

The book deliberately does not set out to be all-inclusive in the range of topics which it covers, and it is written from an individual perspective. This will inevitably weight the importance given to particular topics, though the examples used to illustrate the points being made have been chosen from as wide a geographical distribution as possible. There is something of a bias towards sources published in English, the author's native language, though not necessarily towards sources published in Britain.

The structure of the text is straightforward. A brief introduction shows how one person came to be involved in this research area, and introduces an archaeological assemblage to which the book returns in a number of places. Bone is then introduced as a living tissue, and the structure of the vertebrate skeleton is reviewed. Developed from undergraduate teaching notes, this chapter assumes little prior knowledge, and introduces many of the anatomical terms that feature elsewhere in the text. The next two chapters review the processes of death, burial and decay, and archaeological recovery of bones: the sequence of events by which a live animal becomes an archaeological sample. Six chapters then follow the process of recording and analysis, discussing topics such as identification, quantification, age at death estimation, and skeletal markers of disease and injury. The text then turns from methodology to archaeological interpretation. There is a review of the use of small vertebrates as indicators of past environmental conditions, then a study of the contribution that bone assemblages can make to the study of hunter-gatherer sites, early agricultural settlements, and socially complex sites such as early towns. A brief final chapter offers some views on the future direction of animal bone studies and its relationship with other scientific disciplines. Individual chapters can be read as a critical review of a particular topic, though the book is also intended to have coherence as a single work.

Acknowledgements

Early drafts of various parts of this text were read and commented on by students at the University of Bradford, and it was much improved for being read by Geoff Gaunt. I am grateful to a number of readers for their comments on the text through the editing process, in particular for encouraging me to clear paths through the thickets of detail. Most of all, Rupert Harding was by turns an encouraging and patient editor for Sutton Publishing.

Unless otherwise credited, photographs are by Jean Brown, who is thanked for her skill, patience and good humour. The following are thanked for their permission to use other photographs: James Barrett for Fig 4.3; York Archaeological Trust for Figs 7.4, 11.2 and 14.1; Andrew Jones for Fig. 12.2. I am grateful to Amanda Forster for her work on Figs 2.1–2.7, 7.2 and 7.3: all other line illustrations are by the author.

The author has benefited over the years from the support, encouragement, ideas and criticism of too many colleagues to mention them all here. The late Ian Cornwall set me on the right path with his easy erudition and encyclopaedic knowledge, and I am greatly indebted to Don Brothwell, who encouraged me to ask apparently unanswerable questions, and to find ways of answering them. Above all, Barbara Noddle freely gave of her time over many years, and ensured that I would never forget that dry bones have to be understood as flesh and blood animals. Her death while this book was nearing completion deprived it of its most constructive, incisive and knowledgeable critic. To these three in particular, and many others besides, this book owes whatever merits it may have.

ONE

WHY STUDY A LOT OF OLD BONES?

On reflection, this book has its origins in a basement room at the National Museum of Wales, in Cardiff, over twenty years ago. Even by the standards of academic publishing, twenty years may seem a long gestation, so perhaps I should explain.

Among the clutter in that basement room was a series of boxes containing bones collected during recent excavations at a Roman site called Caerleon. As an impoverished graduate student, I had been offered hard currency in return for studying and recording those bones. Identifying and recording archaeological bones requires a good knowledge of the skeletal anatomy of a wide range of animals, and I had been fortunate enough to have studied with I.W. Cornwall, a particularly influential figure in the development of archaeological bone studies, who taught comparative skeletal anatomy with assurance and skill. The archaeological study of bones also requires a questioning approach, in order to see the significance of small details of anatomy or preservation that might reveal something about the original animals, their involvement with people, and the circumstances of their disposal and burial. My doctoral supervisor was Don Brothwell, well known on both sides of the Atlantic for seeing the important questions before anyone else, and for not accepting received wisdom.

As for the site itself, Caerleon today is an overgrown village close to the town of Newport, in south-east Wales. By the end of the first century AD Caerleon was a booming garrison town serving as a legionary fortress and base for the subjugation of those Welsh tribes who were reluctant to embrace the benefits of Roman civilization. One of those benefits was regular bathing, and the excavations in question had investigated parts of the bath-house and adjacent swimming pool (*natatio*: excavators of Roman sites have a curious aversion to English). Most of the bones had been recovered during the excavation of the *natatio* and other bath structures. Having been constructed on a grand scale, the baths were substantially altered in the late third and fourth centuries. The opportunity was obviously taken to dump garbage into the back-filling, and that garbage included a lot of bones.

Another source of numerous bones was that other icon of Romanization, the drains. Baths need drains, and the assorted civilian administrators and off-duty grunts who used the baths occasionally dropped things into the drains, including coins, items of personal adornment, and the bones from light snacks consumed while enjoying the facilities. The Caerleon bones thus offered a real opportunity to investigate both the general garbage of the fortress and the particular leavings of the bath-house clientele.

And so it proved. Deposits in the *natatio* back-fill and other garbage accumulations around the bath-house complex contained mostly cattle bones, but not just any cattle bones. Some deposits had a preponderance of head and foot bones, arguably the debris from the first stages of slaughter and butchering. Others contained a high proportion of shoulder blades, indicating a pattern of butchery unlike that commonly seen today. Years later, I was to encounter heaps of Roman cattle shoulder blades again, this time in York, another garrison town. By an analysis of body-part distribution for the Caerleon cattle, it was possible to piece together something of the butchering procedure in use at the time, and to suggest that butchering and the disposal of refuse from it became rather less systematic as the civilian influence on life in the fortress increased.

The drains told a different story. Here there were very few cattle bones. Instead, the bones were mostly sheep ribs and vertebrae, and chicken bones. The bath-house catering came to life: pieces of chicken and lamb chops. This must have been a welcome contrast to the unremitting beef indicated by deposits elsewhere on the site.

And there was more. In one of the bath-house buildings, the *frigidarium*, the last surviving floor of Roman date was overlain by a patchy light brown deposit that consisted almost entirely of small bones. There were so many small bones, in fact, that it would have been quite impossible to record each of them individually, forcing me to take decisions about sampling. In the end, I sorted a small sub-sample by body part – a pile of tiny mandibles, a heap of minute shoulder blades – then identified all the skulls and mandibles as precisely as possible. Most proved to be species of rodent, with some shrews, and a few frogs. After the piles of butchered cattle bones, the intellectual challenge of identifying field voles and water shrews was totally absorbing, and so-called 'small mammals' have remained a particular interest. Venturing out of the basement to the elevated marble halls of the Museum one day, I mentioned to the eminent Roman archaeologist George Boon that I had found bones of dormouse. 'The Romans ate dormice, you know,' he observed, and returned to his scrutiny of some particularly enthralling *denarii*. Having grown up at the seaside, I have eaten some fairly improbable things, but surely dormice have more to do with Alice and the Mad Hatter? Some hasty research revealed that the reference to dormice in Roman cookbooks was probably to a much larger southern European relative of the species whose tiny bones I had recognized in the *frigidarium* deposit. However, like the cattle scapulae, Roman dormice were to haunt my subsequent career, and they make a return appearance in Chapter 5.

So why was the *frigidarium* apparently carpeted with piles of tiny bones? Common sense, that most unscientific of things, ruled out deliberate human activity. Even though we zooarchaeologists accumulate the skeletons of assorted animals in our laboratories and homes (yes, I'm afraid we do), we rarely if ever accept that people in the remote past might have collected skeletons entirely out of interest. Besides, the *frigidarium* assemblage represented tens of thousands of individual animals, and nobody needs that many mice. Fortunately, a plausible answer lay in the zoological literature. Many other predators accumulate bones at locations to which they have taken prey in order to eat it. Hyenas are particularly adept at this, though they were clearly not responsible for the Caerleon assemblage. In fact, the range of species in the assemblage nicely matched the prey typical of owls, probably barn owls. These superb nocturnal hunters swallow their furry prey in large lumps, then retire to some favourite perch at which to digest the meal. In due course, a pellet of indigestible bones and fur is regurgitated. Where owls repeatedly use the same perch, many pellets will accumulate, leaving a deposit of many tiny bones. The sheer quantity of bones in the *frigidarium* indicated many owl-years of occupation. That in turn suggested that the building was particularly attractive to owls, a conclusion which in turn fitted neatly with other evidence that the *frigidarium* had remained standing, with roof intact, for many years after its abandonment. The patient identification of minute bones led back to deductions about the survival of a Roman building in subsequent centuries (see Chapter 11).

By the time I had finished with Caerleon, written the report (O'Connor 1986b), and delivered a conference paper on it, many of the themes that are explained and explored in this book had come together. The deceptively simple process of identifying bones (Chapter 5) was made clear to me by the mice and voles: the skulls and teeth could mostly be identified to species level, the pelvic girdles to genus, the limb bones only to family, and the ribs and vertebrae hardly even to Order. Just understanding the accumulation of the bones had led to the literature on bone taphonomy (Chapter 3). The *natatio* fills taught a lesson about the information that body-part analysis can reveal (Chapter 7), and my attempts to express the quantities of cattle bones in numbers brought quantification methods to the fore (Chapter 6). Measurement of some of the more complete bones had given an estimate of the stature of the cattle, and measurements of mouse mandibles had helped to separate two closely related species (Chapter 10). Most of all, when unusual or abnormal specimens had me puzzled, a stroll up the road to Cardiff's University College brought me to the cactus-infested office of Barbara Noddle, who would dispense osteological wisdom with precision, humour, and a rare talent for oblique digression.

Presenting Caerleon as the source of much that follows in this book is, of course, a plot device, a useful hook on which to hang a sometimes highly technical text. However, in the intervening couple of decades, I have studied many (too many!) other bone assemblages, large and small. Some have been a serious challenge in practical terms, while others have led to unexpected deductions. None, I think, has stimulated the critical faculties in quite the way that the Caerleon bones did. While assembling material for this book, I disturbed my Caerleon records from their eternal rest, and soon lost myself in one of those 'That's interesting, I wonder if . . .' moments. Pieces of ancient bone lack the aesthetic appeal of artefacts or the grandeur of ancient buildings, yet they have a complex fascination that arises in part from their zoological origin, as evidence of long-dead animals, and in part from what we can infer from them about past human activities, and about the involvement of people in those animals' lives.

Of necessity, parts of this book are quite technical in their content, requiring patience, if not stamina, of the reader. I think that is unavoidable. In order to understand the potential of archaeological bone studies, we have to understand bone itself, and what can have happened to it before we lift it on to the laboratory bench. Each of the various analytical procedures that we use has some basis in zoology or statistics, and we need to understand that background if we are to use the methods intelligently. The process of interpretation and deduction merits examination, too, with discussion of what we have inferred from animal bone assemblages about our diverse and changing relationship with our helpers, vermin, pets and dinners.

The author's first language is English, and most of the examples cited here are from the English language, though not necessarily from British literature. The emphasis given to certain issues, and the sometimes idiosyncratic choice of illustrative examples, reflects my own interests and those published works that have caught my attention, or that of my students. The aim has been to produce a book that introduces the study of ancient animal bones in some depth, and provides enough sources to allow the enthusiastic reader to pursue the detail. At the same time, the text should be read as an explanation of why animal bones are fascinating, deserving of study, and an important source of information about what people did in the past.

Two

Bone, Bones and Skeletons

Part of the fascination of working with ancient bones is that they are parts of formerly living animals. Unlike potsherds or stone tools, bones have been alive, and their complexity reflects that origin. We need to understand the constituents of bone, and how they are organized, in order to understand how, and whether, bones will survive burial and excavation. Furthermore, we need to understand the basic structure of the vertebrate skeleton if we are to comprehend those excavated fragments as parts of whole animals. The purpose of this chapter is to introduce bone as a tissue, and to outline the structure of the vertebrate skeleton. There is a lot of anatomical terminology in this chapter: subsequent chapters use precise anatomical terms where necessary, and this is the place where they are introduced. Readers who are less concerned with the osteological details, or who find it all too much, may prefer to skip to the summary of this chapter before reading on, and then to return to this chapter as a source of reference as necessary.

Bone Composition

Bone is a living tissue with cells and a blood supply, just like muscle or skin. As an animal grows, so its bones grow and undergo modification and repair. Thus the form of the skeleton at the time of death is one point in a process of continuous change. By the time archaeologists deal with the bone, it is a hard, dead material, much altered since the animal's death. It is important to remember that bone in the living animal is as susceptible to damage or alteration as any other living tissue. An excellent introduction to bone, and especially to its versatility as a skeletal material, is given by Alexander (1994), and Halstead (1974) remains a useful source.

Fresh bone has three main components: a complex protein scaffolding; a mineral which stiffens this scaffold; and a 'ground substance' of other organic compounds. Although proportions vary in different tissues, about half of the weight of fresh bone is mineral, the remainder being organic matter and water.

Of the organic fraction, about 95 per cent is the structural protein *collagen* (Miller & Gay 1982; Linsenmayer 1991), which is unusual in containing high proportions of the amino acids glycine and hydroxyproline. Collagen molecules have few large side-chains and can pack together very closely, bonding at regular intervals. The macromolecules are arranged in a left-handedly spiralling triple helix, which itself spirals to the right about a central axis. The structure is a bit like a traditional hawser-laid rope, and gives collagen its characteristics of being strong under tension yet flexible.

The mineral phase is mainly *hydroxyapatite*. This may be loosely described by the formula $Ca_{10}(PO_4)_6.(OH)_2$, though the Ca ions may be replaced by Sr, Ra, or Pb, the PO_4 ions by CO_3, and the OH groups by F. Other ions, mostly metals, can be attached to the surface of hydroxyapatite crystals by adsorption, which may occur in living bone, but can also occur in dead, buried bone (Lee-Thorp & van der Merwe 1981; Millard & Hedges 1995). It can therefore be difficult to tell whether the chemistry of an ancient bone reflects its chemistry during life, or the burial environment after death.

The ground substance makes up only a very small proportion of fresh bone. It serves as a packing, and probably also regulates hydration, and is composed of a mixture of mucoproteins and aminopolysaccharides.

BONE STRUCTURE

There are numerous detailed texts on bone histology and growth. A useful introduction is given by Davis (1987, 47–53), a little more detail by Alexander (1975, 74–9), and a full account in histology texts such as Bloom & Fawcett (1975). Although an old source, Frost (1973, 3–27) gives a particularly dynamic account of bone growth and remodelling.

Mineralized bone is formed by the secretion of hydroxyapatite by specialized cells (*osteoblasts*), upon and within a framework of interwoven collagen fibrils. The fibrils are roughly aligned to a common axis, determined by the stresses and strains placed upon the growing bone. In some bone, the osteoblasts are distributed throughout the tissue. This is cellular, or endochondral, bone, and is typical of most parts of mammal and bird skeletons. In acellular, or dermal, bone, osteoblasts are organized at the surface of thin laminae of bone, and not distributed throughout. Acellular bone is typical of most parts of the skeleton of the majority of fishes.

The compact bone which makes up the shafts of limb bones of birds and mammals is, at its simplest, a series of lamellae of bone deposited more or less concentrically about the longitudinal axis of the bone, and permeated by large and small channels. The cells (*osteocytes*) which are responsible for the secretion and subsequent remodelling of the bone remain enclosed in voids (*lacunae*) within the bone, which are interconnected by a branching and interdigitating network of fine channels (*canaliculi*), and the system is connected at intervals to blood vessels. This links the osteocytes to the transport system of the rest of the body, and makes bone remarkably porous, albeit on a microscopic scale. Some mammals, and a few birds and dinosaurs, show remodelling of the compact bone to produce secondary osteons. Essentially, an *osteon* is a cylindrical unit of heavily mineralized bone arranged around a longitudinally directed blood vessel. Bone which has largely been remodelled into secondary osteons is sometimes termed dense *Haversian bone* (Fig. 2.1).

A limb bone typically consists of a tube of compact bone capped at each end by strap-like pieces (*trabeculae*) arranged in a stress-bearing and shock-absorbing pattern of arches and buttresses. This is termed *cancellous* bone, or more graphically spongy bone. Other parts of the skeleton, such as ribs and shoulder blades, typically consist of thin surface layers of a form of compact bone, with cancellous bone making up most of the thickness.

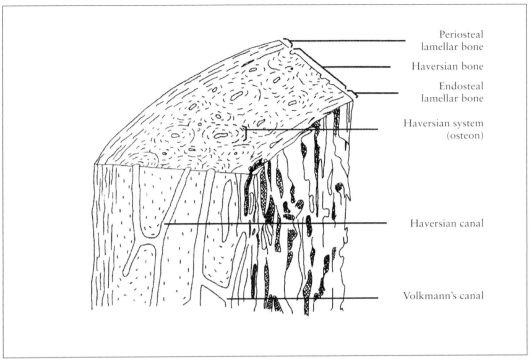

Fig. 2.1. Schematic diagram of the microstructure of mammalian compact bone, to illustrate some of the terms used in the text.

THE VERTEBRATE SKELETON

In evolutionary terms, bone developed as stiffened cartilage, to provide a flexible support through the long axis of the body, support for the gills and jaws, rigid plates to protect the brain and sensory organs, and a jointed structure against which muscles pull in order to move the body. A good review of the vertebrate skeleton from an evolutionary perspective is given by Romer (1970). The earliest vertebrates were fish-like creatures, and very far removed in appearance from modern mammals or birds. None the less, all vertebrates have much the same skeleton, developed or modified to particular functions: one body-plan encompasses mammals, birds, reptiles, and amphibians. Fish also conform to the basic vertebrate plan, but have modifications not seen in land-dwelling vertebrates. In agnathan fish (lampreys, etc.) and the cartilaginous fish (skates, rays, sharks) the skeleton is composed of cartilage, though some stress-bearing elements may be partly mineralized. This is seen, for example, in the jaws of some sharks, and in the vertebrae of some sharks and rays (Wheeler & Jones 1989, 80–1).

In order to describe the vertebrate skeleton, it is necessary to use specific terms of direction and location. These are summarized in Table 2.1. Figs 2.2 to 2.4 show the main skeletal elements of a typical mammal, bird and fish.

Table 2.1   *Terms for Location and Direction*

When trying to describe where you are around the skeleton or on a piece of bone, it is important to be consistent in the use of terms. These are some of the more commonly used terms for describing direction and location around the body.

Dorsal:	towards the back of the body.
Ventral:	towards the underside of the body.
Anterior:	towards the front; i.e the direction in which an animal normally faces.
Posterior:	towards the rear.
Medial:	towards the mid-line of the body.
Lateral:	away from the mid-line of the body.
Proximal:	towards the point of attachment of a limb.
Distal:	away from the point of attachment of a limb.
Cranial:	towards the head.
Caudal:	towards the tail.
Palmar:	the palm of the hand or sole of the foot.
Volar:	the 'back' of the hand or foot.

Thus a limb bone has proximal and distal ends, and has anterior, posterior, medial and lateral surfaces (or 'aspects'). Your knee joint consists of the distal end of the femur and the proximal end of the tibia, plus the patella, which is positioned anterior to the other bones. A vertebral centrum has a cranial surface and a caudal surface. Your navel, should you wish to contemplate it, is on your ventral surface, medial to your hips, and faces anteriorly. The meaning of a manual 'V-sign' depends on whether the palmar or volar aspect of your hand faces anteriorly.

Note also directions around the mouth:

Mesial:	towards the mid-line of the jaws; i.e. where left and right sides meet.
Distal:	away from the mid-line of the jaws.
Buccal:	towards the inner surface of the cheeks.
Lingual:	towards the tongue.
Occlusal:	the 'chewing surface' of a tooth.

(Note: the term *labial* is sometimes used synonymously with *buccal*, though sometimes only to refer to the 'towards the lips' surfaces of canine and incisor teeth. Because of this ambiguity in use, it is best avoided.)

Thus your incisors are positioned mesial to your canines. The mesial surface of LM_2 (lower molar 2) abuts the distal surface of LM_1. The distal surface of LM_3 abuts nothing, as it's the most distal part of the tooth row in a normal mammal. When you smile, you expose the buccal surfaces of your incisors (and canines in a really big grin), but few people apart from the dentist ever see the lingual surfaces. When you close your mouth, the occlusal surfaces of your upper and lower molars and premolars meet.

THE SKULL AND BACKBONE

The most primitive relatives of vertebrates, such as sea-squirts, are stiffened by a simple cartilaginous rod which runs along the length of the body (the *notochord*). In vertebrates this is replaced by a backbone comprising vertebrae which articulate with each other to give limited flexibility and support. Each vertebra comprises a roughly cylindrical structure called the *centrum*, attached to which is the *neural arch*. This arch carries

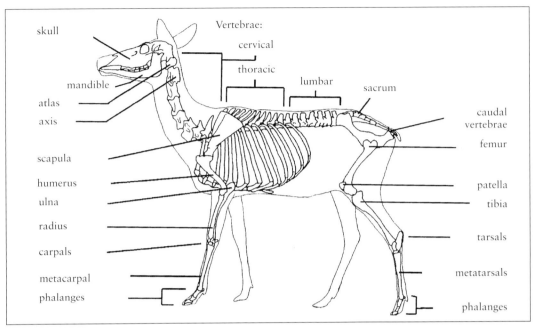

Fig. 2.2. *The essentials of the mammalian skeleton, as illustrated by the skeleton of a red deer.*

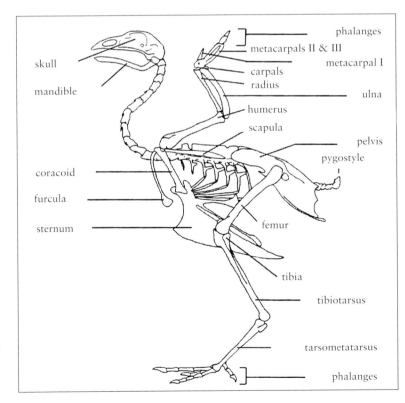

Fig. 2.3. *The skeleton of a domestic fowl as a typical bird. Note in particular the massive sternum, and compare the forelimb with that of a mammal.*

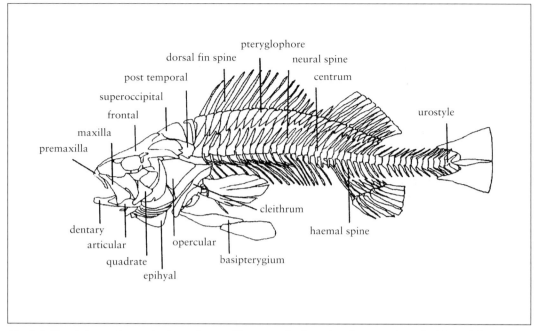

Fig. 2.4. The skeleton of a perch, shown here to illustrate only the major elements of a typical bony fish.

articulations for the adjoining vertebrae, bears the muscles which run along the backbone, and encloses the neural canal. In the neural canal in life is the spinal cord, which distributes impulses from the brain to the outlying parts of the limbs and entrails. In fish the ventral aspect of the more posterior vertebrae (Fig. 2.4) carries another arch, the *haemal arch*. In different classes of vertebrates, the vertebrae may also bear enlarged attachments for tendons and ligaments, notably the neural spine at the apex of the neural arch, and the transverse processes on either side. Because vertebrae lie along the mid-line of the body, they are bilaterally symmetrical.

The vertebral column is conventionally divided into sections. The first few vertebrae (normally seven in mammals) counting back from the skull are the *cervical vertebrae*, which constitute the skeleton of the neck. The first cervical vertebra (*atlas*) is modified to provide a point of attachment and articulation for the skull. The second cervical vertebra (*axis* or *epistropheus*) provides a 'peg' for axial rotation of the skull and atlas. The vertebrae of the chest, or *thoracic vertebrae*, have points of articulation for the ribs: mammals generally have twelve to fifteen thoracic vertebrae. Continuing down the backbone, we come to the *lumbar vertebrae* of the lower back. These have no rib articulations, but often have prominent transverse processes. The hind limb-girdle is fixed to the backbone by way of a block of fused and modified vertebrae called the *sacrum* in mammals, and *synsacrum* or *lumbro-sacrale* in birds. Beyond this lie the *caudal vertebrae* of the tail, a highly variable number of vertebrae often reduced to a simple short rod of bone.

In bony fish the vertebrae are not so obviously differentiated into groups, though there is some variation in form all along the length of the vertebral column. Some authorities (e.g. Wheeler & Jones 1989, 105–6) recognize three groups of vertebrae in fish: the *anterior abdominal vertebrae*, which lack rib attachments; the *abdominal vertebrae*, which have rib attachments; and the *caudal vertebrae*, in which the haemal canal along the ventral side of the vertebrae is closed, forming a haemal spine. In other texts, the terms *thoracic*, *precaudal* and *caudal* vertebrae are also used. Fish have more vertebrae than birds and mammals: typically fifty to sixty in members of the salmon family, for example. In reptiles and amphibians vertebrae are highly variable in number, and usually are not clearly differentiated. Frogs, for example, lack ribs and typically have only nine vertebrae, the ninth of which fulfils the function of the mammalian sacrum.

The chest of a bird or mammal is enclosed by the *ribs*, which curve away from the thoracic vertebrae to meet along the front of the chest. The ribs have an articulation at their vertebral ends which allows movement, to expand and contract the chest during breathing. At the front of the chest, or ventrally, the ribs of most mammals and birds meet the *breast-bone* or *sternum*. In mammals this is usually an elongated plate or rod, often of two or more distinct sections. In birds the sternum is a large, flat plate from the mid-line of which a 'keel' projects forwards to anchor the hugely developed pectoral muscles with which birds flap their wings (Fig. 2.3).

The *skull* consists of many different bones, the details varying from one class of vertebrates to another. Basically, the skull can be divided into the *neurocranium*, plates of bone that surround and protect the brain, and the *viscerocranium*, which carries the sensory organs and the mouth. In the higher vertebrates, the major bones of the neurocranium are the *frontal*, *parietal*, *occipital*, *temporal*, *sphenoid* and *ethmoid* bones. The viscerocranium provides a mounting for the eyes (with parts of the neurocranium), the nose and olfactory organs, and the upper and lower jaws. The major bones of the viscerocranium are the *zygomatic*, *maxilla*, *premaxilla*, *nasal* and *lachrymal* bones. The maxilla and premaxilla bear the upper set of teeth. The lower teeth are borne on the *mandible* in higher vertebrates. In fish, reptiles and amphibians the lower jaw is a more complicated structure comprising the *dentary* (which bears the teeth), *angular* and *articular* bones (Fig. 2.4). In mammals the mandible articulates with the temporal bone near the *auditory meatus*, or ear-hole. In birds, fish and other lower orders the articular bone articulates with the *quadrate*, an element of neurocranium which we mammals manage without. The elongated quadrate bone of some snakes allows them to open their mouths in a dramatically wide gape.

The bony fish have remarkably complex head bones, which take their own nomenclature (Harder 1975). The jaws consist of a tooth-bearing *dentary* bone in the lower jaw and a tooth-bearing *premaxilla* in the upper jaw. In some fish the *maxilla* is also toothed, and some carry teeth on the *palatine* and *prevomer* bones in the roof of the mouth. As if that were not enough, some fish have yet more teeth located on the upper and lower *pharyngeal bones*, located in the throat. The fish neurocranium is founded on the *basioccipital*, *basisphenoid* and *parasphenoid* bones, which form the base of the neurocranium, and the *frontal* and *supraoccipital* bones which form the 'crown' of the neurocranium. To either side of the posterior part of the neurocranium lie the bones of the gill covers, and of the *branchial skeleton*, which supports the gills. Immediately posterior to the head lies the pectoral girdle, which includes a major element not present in other vertebrates: the *cleithrum*. This articulates with the *coracoid*, which in turn articulates with the *scapula* and the *radial bones*, to which the pectoral fin is attached. The closest approximation which fish have to a pelvic girdle is the *basipterygium*, which in some families is located close to the pectoral girdle, while in others it is towards the posterior end of the abdomen. A more detailed overview of the fish skeleton is given by Wheeler & Jones (1989, 87–125), and Cannon (1987) gives useful illustrations of the disarticulated bones of four representative species.

TEETH

This is too big a subject to be considered in great detail here, and a useful general source is Hillson (1986). Fig. 2.5 shows the dental layout and terminology for a typical mammal.

Mammals, fish, reptiles and some amphibians have teeth, of which mammal teeth are the most complex. Most mammals are *heterodont*; that is, their mouths contain different forms of tooth, adapted for cutting, grinding and crushing. All teeth can be divided into a *crown*, which in life is above the gum, and the *root(s)* which anchor the tooth into the mandibular bone. Where the crown runs into the roots, there may be a clearly defined *neck* or cervical zone. Most of a mammal tooth is made of *dentine*, which is a specialized form of bone. The cells that mineralize dentine retreat as the dentine forms, and so are not encapsulated within it as osteocytes are within bone. At the core of the tooth is the *pulp cavity*, containing blood vessels and nerves. The crowns of most teeth in the majority of mammals are covered with *enamel*, which is essentially a form of hydroxy-apatite.

Mammalian adult teeth can be divided into *incisors*, *canines*, *premolars* and *molars*. Mammals normally have the same distribution of teeth in the left and right halves of each jaw, but may not necessarily have the same distribution of upper as of lower teeth. For example, sheep have lower incisors, but no upper incisors. The most teeth a mammal will normally have in any one quarter of the jaws is three incisors, one canine, four premolars and three molars, distributed in that order from the front of the jaw (mesially) to the

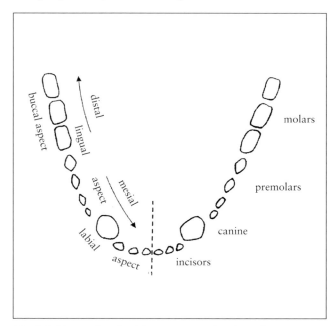

Fig. 2.5. Mammalian dentition summarized to show the application of terms to typical heterodont dentition.

back (distally). Many mammals have far fewer teeth than this: humans have two incisors, one canine, two premolars and three molars per quarter-jaw. Some mammals have two sets of teeth throughout their life: the *deciduous* ('milk') teeth and the *permanent* teeth which replace them in adult life. A species generally has fewer deciduous than adult teeth, and deciduous teeth are usually only differentiated into incisors, canines and premolars. True molars are a feature of permanent dentition, though the deciduous premolars are sometimes confusingly referred to as 'deciduous molars', especially in studies of human bones.

Not all mammals show clear differentiation of their teeth. In shrews, for example, there are obvious incisor teeth, but the remainder are a row of sharply pointed teeth which defy classification. Similarly, in seals the distinction between premolars and molars can not be clearly made in adults: instead, they are generally referred to as *postcanine teeth*.

HIPS AND SHOULDERS, KNEES AND TOES

Vertebrates' limbs are attached to the backbone by way of the *pectoral* and *pelvic* girdles, which also provide a joint within which the leg, wing or fin can move. The limb girdles in fish are close to the skull, and have been outlined above (Fig. 2.4). In other vertebrates the pectoral girdle consists of three bones: the *scapula*, *coracoid* and *clavicle*. In simple amphibians the three bones extend roughly in a 'Y' shape, with the articulation for the front leg at the centre of the 'Y'. The scapula extends along the back, roughly parallel to the backbone; the coracoid extends down the sides of the body and slightly backwards; and the clavicle extends across the front of the upper part of the 'chest'. The articulation for the front leg is a socket made up of part of the scapula and part of the coracoid. In birds the scapula is a slender, cutlass-shaped bone which lies to one side of the backbone, while the coracoid is a big triangular structure which links the pectoral girdle to the *sternum* (breast-bone) and provides a rigid strut to brace the chest against the pull of the pectoral muscles which flap the wings. The two slender clavicles are fused to produce a structure called the *furcula* (wish-bone). In mammals the scapula is the major bone of the pectoral girdle, and is a flat, triangular or D-shaped structure, with an articulation for the front leg. The coracoid is reduced to a small lump beside this articulation, and the shoulder blade in many mammals, ourselves included, should properly be described as the *scapulo-coracoid* bone. Only the most primitive mammals, such as the duck-billed platypus *Ornithorhynchus*, retain a substantial, separate coracoid. The clavicles are struts which connect the pectoral girdle to the sternum, such as the human collar bone. In some mammals, such as sheep and pigs, the clavicle has faded away altogether.

The pelvic girdle is also based on three bones, but is more firmly attached to the backbone by way of the *sacrum*. Each half of the pelvic girdle is referred to as the *os innominatum*. (This means 'un-named bone', which seems a contradiction in terms.) The major orders of vertebrates have diverse modifications of the pelvis, and this is only the most basic of summaries. In amphibians the os innominatum comprises a long, slightly curved, rod (*ilium*), which is expanded at one end where it fuses with the 'straight' side of a D-shaped plate (*ischium*). An articulation for the back leg (*acetabulum*) is located where

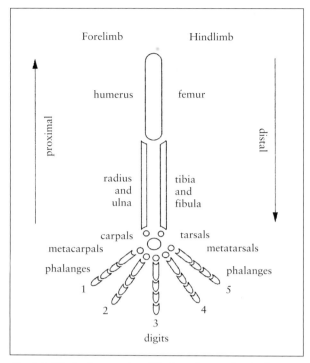

Forelimb   Hindlimb

proximal   distal

humerus   femur

radius   tibia
and   and
ulna   fibula

carpals   tarsals
metacarpals   metatarsals

phalanges   phalanges

1   5

2   4

3

digits

Fig. 2.6. The basic pentadactyl limb, and terms for the fore and hind limb. Note that the number of digits, and the number of phalanges, varies considerably from the pattern shown here. Horses have only one digit on each foot, while we primates have only two phalanges in our first digits.

the ilium and ischium fuse, roughly half of it on each bone. In birds the pelvis is somewhat different. The ilium is a flattened plate of bone which extends along either side of the lower part of the bird's back and is fused to the backbone. The ischium extends posteriorly, and is also broad and flattened. A third bone, the *pubis*, extends from roughly where the ilium and ischium meet, and is a blade-like bone that passes downwards and backwards across the sides of the abdomen. The acetabulum is a neat hemispherical cup located where all three bones meet. (*Acetabulum* is a Latin term meaning 'vinegar cup'.) In mammals the os innominatum is relatively simple. The ilium is generally quite flattened and has a large area of fusion with the sacrum, and the flattened ischium passes posteriorly to a substantial tuberosity (which you're sitting on). The pubis extends across the front of the abdomen to fuse with the opposite pubis, and posteriorly to fuse with the ischium. The acetabulum consists of parts of the ilium, ischium and pubis, which fuse at a Y-shaped junction or suture.

The vertebrate leg can be considered in very simple, general terms. All vertebrates are *pentadactylous*; that is, they have a maximum of five fingers or toes per limb (Fig. 2.6). Not all vertebrates have retained all five toes on the fore and hind feet. As natural selection has driven adaptation and bodily diversity, some animals have achieved greater 'fitness' by losing toes, leaving horses with only one toe per limb, sheep with two, rhinoceros with three, pigs with four, and ourselves and aardvarks with five. Loss of toes has generally been an adaptation to faster, more energy-efficient running, at the expense of the ability to grip and to climb.

The leg can be divided into three zones. By reference to human limbs, these are the *stylopodium*, the first segment from shoulder to elbow or hip to knee; the *zygopodium*, the second part from elbow to wrist or knee to ankle; and the *autopodium*, encompassing the wrist, hands and fingers or ankle, feet and toes. The stylopodium has one bone, with a ball-shaped articulation at the upper (proximal) end and a more complex articulation at the lower (distal) end. In the front leg, this bone is the *humerus*. In mammals the humerus is a tube of roughly circular to oval cross-section, the proximal articulation typically being a flattened hemisphere, and the distal articulation an elongated pulley-shaped articulation (*trochlea*), which forms part of a complex hinge-joint (the elbow). In birds the humerus is similar, but the proximal end is expanded and somewhat flattened. The stylopodium element in the back leg is the *femur*. This resembles the humerus in having a roughly circular cross-section, with a prominent ball-shaped proximal articulation. The distal articulation consists of two strongly convex knobs (*condyles*), with a saddle-shaped surface on the front of the distal end to carry the knee-cap (*patella*). The femur in birds is much as in mammals and it fulfils the same function.

The zygopodium consists of two parallel bones that may be wholly or partially fused along their length. In the front leg, these are the *radius* and *ulna*. The radius has a simple concave proximal articulation, to articulate with the trochlea of the humerus, and a series of concave facets at the distal end to articulate with the bones of the wrist. The proximal part of the ulna is extended by the *olecranon process*: the knob of bone at the tip of your elbow is your olecranon process. This forms a lever with the humerus so as to allow the elbow joint to be straightened. In amphibians the radius and ulna are fused along their length into a composite bone. In birds they are separate, and the ulna is generally much the more robust of the two. In mammals the radius is usually the more robust element, and in some mammals (such as horses, cows, deer and camels) the shaft of the ulna has been reduced to a sliver of bone fused to the posterior surface of the radius, though the proximal end remains as a substantial bone.

In the back leg, the two zygopodium bones are the *tibia* and *fibula*. The proximal end of the tibia bears two, often conjoined, slightly concave articulations for the condyles of the femur, and the distal articulation is also concave. In amphibians the tibia and fibula are fused along their length. In birds the fibula is much reduced, to a roughly triangular proximal end, one corner of which is drawn out into a tapering, slender shaft. The tibia in birds is a robust bone of roughly oval cross-section, the proximal part being elaborated by a prominent crest of bone on the front (anterior) surface. In birds the proximal group of tarsals are fused with the distal part of the tibia, so the bone is more correctly called the *tibiotarsus*, and the distal articulation is distinctly convex. In mammals the fibula is often reduced, sometimes to nothing more than the distal articulation, and is never as robust as the tibia. The tibia typically has a roughly rectangular cross-section in the more distal part of the shaft, and a distinctive triangular form towards the proximal end.

Finally the autopodium. First come the bones of the wrist and ankle, the *carpals* and *tarsals* respectively, which do several jobs (Fig. 2.7). They provide the necessary flexibility for the front and back feet, act as shock absorbers and provide a means of attaching up to five digits to a zygopodium of only two bones. The nomenclature of carpals is complicated, and in species in which the number of toes is reduced, or in which the fore foot is particularly specialized, some carpals may be absent or fused with one another. The tarsals are similarly variable. The tibia articulates with the *astragalus*, attached to which is the *calcaneum*. The calcaneum has a process which extends towards the back of the heel to provide an attachment for the Achilles' Tendon. The astragalus and calcaneum (*talus* in some texts) articulate with a row of smaller tarsals,

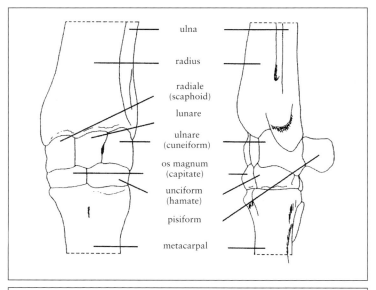

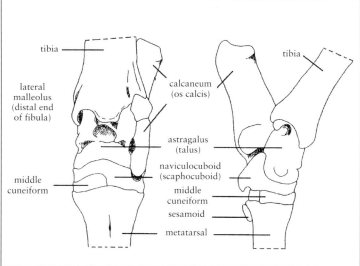

Fig. 2.7. Carpals (above) and tarsals (below) of a typical bovid, illustrated and named.

the largest of which is usually the descriptively named *cuboid*. In hoofed mammals such as cattle and sheep, this is fused to another, smaller tarsal to form a substantial bone called the *naviculo-cuboid*.

Articulating with the carpals and tarsals are the *metapodials*, which form the palm of the hand and arch of the foot. These are simple tubular bones, with a flat or concave proximal articulation and a convex distal articulation, and are termed *metacarpals* in the front limb, and *metatarsals* in the hind limb. In birds the metacarpals are reduced to a fused pair of bones which bear an uncanny resemblance to a safety-pin, and which form the lower portion of the wing. The three metatarsals in birds are fused together along their length, with the distal group of tarsals fused to their proximal ends. The whole unit is termed the *tarsometatarsus*, of which the fused tarsal bones comprise the *hypotarsus*. Mammals with a reduced number of toes obviously have fewer metapodials. Horses have only one toe: it is the third digit, so they retain only the third metapodial. In the two toes of cattle, sheep, and other cloven-hooved animals the third and fourth metapodials are fused together along their length to produce what appears to be one bone, with an obviously doubled articulation at the distal end for the separate third and fourth toes.

The last outpost of the vertebrate leg are the *phalanges*, the bones of the fingers and toes. The first digit (the thumb or great toe in humans) has only two phalanges, while digits two to five have three each. Phalanges are rather stubby, tubular bones, with a concave proximal articulation and a convex distal articulation, except for the last (terminal) phalanges, which may show all sorts of modifications, depending on the form of the foot of the animal. In carnivorous mammals and in most birds the terminal phalanges are sharply curved, to provide a gripping claw. In the hoofed mammals the shape of the terminal phalanges reflects the shape of the hoof. It is crescent-shaped in cloven-hoofed species such as cattle and deer, but flattened and nearly circular in outline in horses.

The scales of fish are an additional category of vertebrate remains which may be found in archaeological deposits. In anatomically primitive fishes such as sturgeon or the garpike (*Lepidosteus*) of North America, *ganoid scales* are formed. These are typically diamond-shaped, and have a coating of a material not unlike dental enamel, termed *ganoine*. Most bony fishes have a covering of scales, and the scales of some species may be sufficiently robust to survive in favourable burial conditions. Identification of scales is often possible to family level, and sometimes to species. Most scales grow during life by the addition of increments (*circuli*), the thickness of which reflects the rate of growth of the fish. The approximate age and seasonality of growth of fishes can thus be read from the scales, and this information can survive on archaeological specimens. Scales are reviewed in greater detail by Wheeler & Jones (1989, 116–20).

Most fish also develop *otoliths*, mineralized structures carried in the neurocranium as a means of sensing and controlling bodily orientation. Otoliths consist largely of calcium carbonate, and so may differ in their survival during burial from bones in the same deposit. The form of the otoliths varies between species, often enabling identification to be made to genus or species level. Otoliths, like scales, grow incrementally, and their analysis allows investigation of the age and seasonal growth patterns of fishes (see Chapter 12).

SUMMARY

It may not seem so to a reader new to the subject, but that is a brief and fairly straightforward review of the vertebrate skeleton and its major elements. If you skipped the detail or just looked at the pictures, the important point to grasp is that birds and mammals, and to a degree reptiles and amphibians, have much the same bones, variously adapted to fit them to their way of life. It is this homology, derived from the single evolutionary origin of the internal bony skeleton, that makes possible the identification of fragmented, disarticulated archaeological material. A femur is a femur, whether it comes from an eagle or a deer. It is relatively easy to see and understand this homology when confronted with articulated modern skeletons. However, archaeological material has usually been broken and dispersed by humans and scavengers, then buried in more or less destructive geochemical conditions, then handled by archaeologists during excavation and study. The physical attributes which typify a particular skeletal element will have been broken up and modified, and physical traces of butchering and gnawing will have been added. The next chapter reviews the process of post-mortem modification. For now, I would stress the importance of familiarity with the vertebrate skeleton in all its diverse forms as an essential start to being able to identify and describe the gnarled old fragments which excavation produces. One may never personally encounter archaeological specimens of ostrich or wallaby, but familiarity with their skeletons is a useful contribution to an understanding of the vertebrate skeleton as a whole.

THREE

TAPHONOMY: FROM LIFE TO DEATH AND BEYOND

'The chief problem of this branch of science is the study of the transition (in all its details) of animal remains from the biosphere to the lithosphere, i.e. the study of a process in the upshot of which the organisms pass out of the different parts of the biosphere and, being fossilized, become part of the lithosphere.'

J.A. Efremov (1940, 85).

DEFINITION

Since the 1960s a burgeoning area of research in archaeological bones has been attempts to understand and model the processes which generate, modify and destroy bone assemblages: the filters which lie between the original living populations of vertebrates and the dead bones on the researcher's bench, and between those bones and the published account of them. This is the domain of taphonomy, described above by Efremov (1940), and expediently extended here to include the subsequent transition of information from specimens to published interpretation. It is fairly obvious that as a bone passes from being a part of a living animal to part of the diet, then part of the refuse of a human population and then part of a sediment, and so on, information about the original animal is lost. Similarly, as an assemblage passes from distinctively patterned human refuse to a fraction of that refuse incorporated in a deposit, and thence to a fraction of the incorporated refuse retrieved as an archaeological sample, so the information which may be obtained about the human activities which led to the formation of the original assemblage is both reduced in quantity and modified in content. A number of authors have reviewed this process, often as a flow-diagram (Davis 1987, 22, based on Meadow 1980; Noe-Nygaard 1979, 112; Reitz & Wing 1999, 111).

A more formalized categorization of the whole taphonomic process has been developed by Clark & Kietzke (1967), and applied to archaeological bones by Hesse & Wapnish (1985, 18–30). This system identifies seven different processes which act upon a bone assemblage at different points in the taphonomic trajectory. Each of these processes will reduce and distort the information content of the assemblage, and some will be more amenable to control by the archaeologist than will others. The processes are summarized in Table 3.1.

Table 3.1. *Subdivisions of the taphonomic processes between life and publication.*

Biotic processes are those characteristics of the natural environment and of the human cultural milieu which influence the presence and numbers of animals at a site at a particular time. This includes the prevailing climate and other attributes of the regional biome and human activities such as the introduction of domesticated livestock. Biotic processes are thus all of the pre-death processes which result in a particular assemblage of living animals being together at a particular time and place, and include much of the human activity that is the subject of archaeology.

Thanatic processes are those which bring about the death and deposition of the remains of animals. In an archaeological setting the killing of animals by people tends to be the dominant thanatic process, but other predators may be involved, and animals will also die of disease and old age. There is some human decision-making reflected, therefore, in the thanatic processes, and possibly decision-making on the part of other predators as well.

Perthotaxic processes are those which result in the movement and destruction of bones before they are finally incorporated into a forming deposit. These processes may include fluvial action, sub-aerial weathering, the effects of scavengers, human garbage disposal and the consequences of local topography.

Taphic processes are the complex suite of physical and chemical agents which act upon bones after burial, and thus include much of what is commonly intended by narrow use of the term 'taphonomy' or by terms such as 'diagenesis'. Taphic processes bring about physical and chemical changes which may result in a bone being well- or poorly preserved.

Anataxic processes are recycling processes by which buried bones are re-exposed to fluvial action, sub-aerial weathering, trampling and other attritional processes. Anataxic processes may accelerate, redirect or even halt the physical and chemical changes initiated by taphic processes. The effects will not be the same as those of the perthotaxic processes which may have acted upon the same assemblage of bones, because by this point the chemical and physical condition of the bones is no longer as it was immediately following death.

Sullegic processes are those archaeological activities that result in further inadvertent or deliberate selective recovery or non-recovery of bones, such as sampling decisions.

Trephic processes are the curatorial and research decisions related to sorting, recording and publication. It is important to recognise this stage, as there may be much selection for and against potential information at this point.

This series of processes may seem over-formalized. Some merge with others, and the taphonomic history of a given assemblage may not lend itself to such simple subdivision. However, the structure gives a useful framework against which to consider how well we understand animal bone taphonomy, and how well we apply what we do know to the interpretation of our samples. The terms defined in Table 3.1 are used elsewhere in this book, and Fig. 3.1 illustrates their use in tracking the fate of an imaginary, but not wholly implausible, moose.

A fundamental aim of archaeological bone studies is the explanation of bone assemblages in terms of biotic and thanatic processes. Whatever our interest in the biology of past bison or mouse populations, it is ultimately the interactions of humans with those bison or mice which brings the animals into the sphere of archaeology. In order to infer past human behaviour from bone assemblages, it is necessary to understand, or at least to observe, different modern patterns of human/vertebrate interaction, and the forms of bone deposition which result.

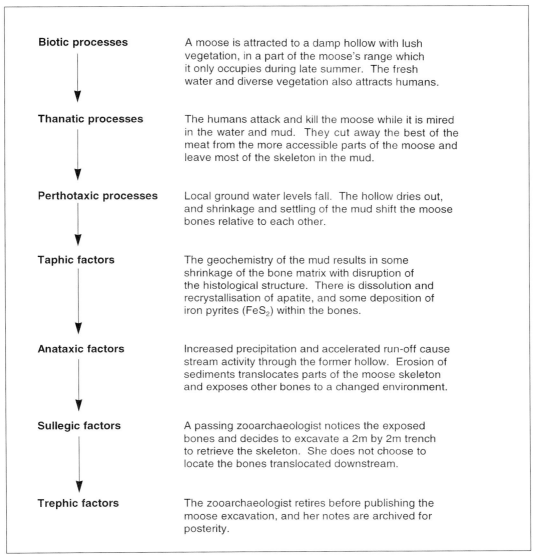

Biotic processes — A moose is attracted to a damp hollow with lush vegetation, in a part of the moose's range which it only occupies during late summer. The fresh water and diverse vegetation also attracts humans.

Thanatic processes — The humans attack and kill the moose while it is mired in the water and mud. They cut away the best of the meat from the more accessible parts of the moose and leave most of the skeleton in the mud.

Perthotaxic processes — Local ground water levels fall. The hollow dries out, and shrinkage and settling of the mud shift the moose bones relative to each other.

Taphic factors — The geochemistry of the mud results in some shrinkage of the bone matrix with disruption of the histological structure. There is dissolution and recrystallisation of apatite, and some deposition of iron pyrites (FeS_2) within the bones.

Anataxic factors — Increased precipitation and accelerated run-off cause stream activity through the former hollow. Erosion of sediments translocates parts of the moose skeleton and exposes other bones to a changed environment.

Sullegic factors — A passing zooarchaeologist notices the exposed bones and decides to excavate a 2m by 2m trench to retrieve the skeleton. She does not choose to locate the bones translocated downstream.

Trephic factors — The zooarchaeologist retires before publishing the moose excavation, and her notes are archived for posterity.

Fig. 3.1. The fate of a moose, used as an example of the categorisation of taphonomic processes.

OBSERVATION AND EXPERIMENT

A full review of the literature pertaining to bone assemblage formation would occupy an entire book. Here we review a few examples of the ways in which the observation of present-day situations and experimentation have provided information that is helpful in the interpretation of archaeological assemblages. For further reading on this topic, Lyman (1994) gives a substantial review, Behrensmeyer & Hill (1980) provide a valuable compilation of detailed studies, and the work of Lewis Binford (1978; 1983) relates ethnographic observation of contemporary people to archaeological interpretation.

The bone debris from archaeological sites will mostly comprise the remains of animals that people have killed and brought to the site. This is quite obvious when, for example, the bones are those of domestic animals that bear clear marks of butchering (Chapter 5), and have been deposited in refuse pits close to house structures. However, in early prehistoric times people shared living space with other predators, and the refuse of human occupation may have become mixed with that of wolves, leopards, bears or porcupines. One important area of observation has been to record the predation and bone transport activities of a range of predators in order to recognize characteristic patterns that may be apparent in ambiguous archaeological material. This is a particular issue in Africa, where bone-accumulating predators are common. The work of C.K. Brain (1981) did much to show that leopards, hyenas and lions show distinctive patterns of bone accumulation and destruction, and Lam (1992) has chronicled the variability seen in bone assemblages from hyena dens. For the New World, Haynes (1982; 1983) has provided criteria for recognizing wolf and coyote prey, and Hoffman & Hays (1987) report the habits of eastern wood rats (*Neotoma floridana*). In this case a series of bones from mammals, fish and reptiles were placed within an occupied wood rat den, and were recovered six months later in order to record the pattern of bone movement and destruction. Wood rats have 'compulsive acquisitive tendencies' (i.e. they collect things), and will both accumulate bone assemblages at their dens, and deplete nearby bone accumulations that have formed by other means, including human refuse. As wood rats are selective in the bones that they accumulate, both their assemblages, and those that they deplete, acquire distinctive patterning.

The recognition of gnawing damage is also important in the identification of assemblages which have undergone reworking and alteration before burial. Brain (1967; 1969) undertook some early research, observing the attrition of goat bones deposited around a South African village where dog scavenging and trampling were both involved. Although much quoted, this study comprised opportunistic observation rather than experiment, and the consequences of trampling and scavenging cannot readily be separated. More rigorously, Payne & Munson (1985) fed a quantity of squirrels to a cooperative dog called Ruby, who was kept in a situation which allowed virtually total recovery of bone fragments which were not totally digested by the dog. The resulting data showed what proportion of ingested bone a dog might be expected to destroy totally, and provided good examples of the patterns of damage and erosion produced by the teeth and gastric environment of a dog (at any rate, of that particular dog). Similar results have been reported by Stallibrass (1990) and Mondini (1995), who have examined the characteristic patterns of gnawing damage and bone redeposition produced by foxes, and Moran & O'Connor (1992) have shown that cats can produce a distinctive pattern of damage on ungulate bones. Examples of characteristic gnawing patterns are illustrated in Chapter 5.

Apart from the obvious predators, familiar species such as pigs and rats have been shown to be capable of destroying bones as they scavenge human refuse, and where archaeological deposits represent dense human settlement, the deposition of fish bones in the faeces of humans and other animals may be common. Fish that are eaten when quite small have bones that can easily be chewed and swallowed with the rest of the fish, and Jones (1986) has demonstrated that humans can eat and pass the bones of a medium-size herring (*Clupea harengus*) with no difficulty. Fish bones passed in faeces sometimes show evidence of the fact, in the form of crushing damage to vertebral centra and other surface modifications.

It is particularly important to understand the taphonomic processes acting upon fish bone assemblages, as processes other than human food procurement may produce death assemblages of fish corpses which become deposits of bones. In semi-arid climates, pools and cut-off meanders of rivers may dry out, producing catastrophic death assemblages which can be difficult to distinguish from, for example, river-edge accumulations of bones deposited by people fishing. In one recent study in Senegal, examination of lake-shore deposits of fish bones known to have been left by people fishing the lake showed them to have many of the characteristics of catastrophic mortality (van Neer & Morales Muñiz 1992). A wide range of species was present, each showing a considerable size range, and many of the fish were represented by articulated, almost complete, skeletons. There was little about the deposits to show that they had been accumulated by human activity. In fact, the deposits represented the sorting of catches by people fishing the lake with nets. Very diverse catches were made and brought ashore, then the undesirable fish were sorted from the desired catch, and simply dumped on the lake shore. Comparing those middens with deposits known to represent catastrophic fish mortality, van Neer & Morales Muñiz suggest that catastrophic mortalities through drought will generally show a lower species diversity than will the garbage deposited from fishing activity. Fishers generally exploit a relatively large area, especially when boats are used, and so will sample the fish faunas of a number of different habitats. Where a body of water has gradually dried up, we might expect a gradual elimination of species, as water depth and oxygenation decrease, and perhaps salinity increases. By the time the final drying-up occurs, only the most tolerant species will be left to comprise the death assemblages. In this example, modern-day observation did not provide directly applicable data, but prompted a reconsideration of assumptions about death assemblage formation that might otherwise have gone unquestioned.

Having considered thanatic and perthotaxic effects on the content and characteristics of archaeological bone assemblages, the next problem is the taphic processes. Following deposition, a range of physical, chemical and biological processes act to reduce the bone tissue still further. These processes may begin before the bones are incorporated in a sediment. Sub-aerial weathering, and in particular sunlight, may begin the process of physical degradation, as splits and cracks develop along lines of weakness in the bone (Tappen & Peske 1970) (Fig 3.2). Once buried, a different range of processes are set in train, and the taphonomic trajectory may be disrupted and redirected many times over before the bone fragments are eventually excavated or totally destroyed.

Bone is a composite of organic and inorganic substances and we have to consider the decay pathways both of the protein collagen and of the crystalline hydroxyapatite (Weiner & Traub 1989). It is often said that collagen is most vulnerable in well-oxygenated, moist, slightly alkaline burial environments, and bones from chalk or limestone

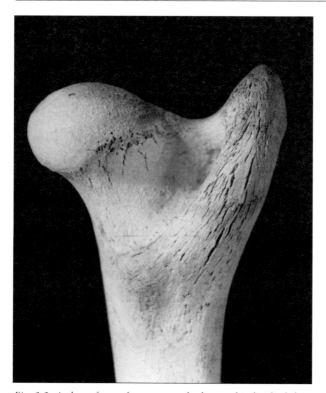

Fig. 3.2. A sheep femur from a recently deceased individual that remained unburied after death to show the cracking patterns typical of sub-aerial weathering.

soils commonly show good survival of the mineral phase, but poor preservation of collagen (Gordon & Buikstra 1981; Grupe 1995). However, this ignores the biotic causes of degradation. Fungal involvement in bone decay has been suspected for many years (e.g. Ascenzi 1969), and latterly attention has turned to bacteria and related microorganisms as factors in collagen degradation (Davis 1997). Some bacteria, especially the genus *Clostridium*, are known to produce collagenases (collagen-destroying enzymes), but in the species most abundant in soils, collagenase production is only active at high temperatures unlikely to be encountered in temperate soils. Other taxa have been shown to degrade bone in the laboratory, though their significance in the decay of buried bone is less convincing (Child 1995a; 1995b). Price *et al.* (1992) and Collins *et al.* (1995) give useful reviews of what we know of the degradation of collagen. A further complication is the the microstructure of the bone itself, which will influence the porosity of the bone, and in turn will affect the surface area available for reaction (Hedges *et al.* 1995).

Because calcium hydroxyapatite can be shown in the laboratory to be soluble in an acidic aqueous environment, it is taken as read that bones are poorly preserved or destroyed in acidic burial conditions (White & Hannus 1983; Weiner & Bar-Yosef 1990). This may well be true as a sweeping generalization, but the details of the processes involved are surprisingly poorly understood. The solubility of bone mineral will depend upon the amounts of other ions already in solution. Sediments with a high content of occupation debris may already have abundant phosphate ions in solution, and this will directly affect the solubility of hydroxyapatite. Bone may also serve as a site for the recrystallization of material from solution, and even before bone is buried there may be physical changes to the hydroxyapatite crystals which compromise the integrity of the bone fragments. None the less, refined analytical methods are showing consistent patterns of bone mineral diagenesis (Farquarson *et al.* 1997; Pate & Hutton 1988; Johnsson 1997).

Understanding bone decay can be essential to the interpretation of bone assemblages. For example, herrings and eels were common in the diet of northern Europe in the medieval period. When Lepiksaar & Heinrich (1977) found some sites with few herring and eel bones, they explained the low abundance in terms of decay. Eels and herrings are rather oily fish, and they proposed that degradation of the fatty tissues accelerated the decay of the bones, leading to the differential decay of oily species, compared with less oily fish such as species of the cod family (Gadidae). However, this differential decay has not been demonstrated under controlled experimental conditions (Nicholson 1992; 1996), and it is now clear that the near-absence of eels from some sites is a reflection of exploitation (Prummel 1986). Minor local differences in water conditions may have been enough to render eel-fishing productive in one place but not in another.

In short, the decay of buried bone is complex, and still not well understood. Some generalizations are helpful. The poor preservation of bone in well-drained, acidic environments can probably largely be attributed to 'leaching' (dissolution) of the mineral component, though the details of this process are poorly understood. The importance of the sediment biota is becoming more clearly recognized, particularly with respect to collagen decay. Experimental attempts to mimic sediment systems so as to allow one factor at a time to be isolated still fail to address the environment as experienced by a bone fragment, namely a diverse range of interacting chemical, physical and biological factors. Observations such as those reported by Nicholson (1996) are more realistic, but cannot separate the agents acting on the bones, so as to record their separate effects. We have a body of theory which allows some useful predictions about preservation to be made, but the theory is based on a poor understanding of the complex processes which go on in sediments, and we will therefore continue to be surprised by unexpectedly good or bad preservation of bones in different deposits (Fig. 3.3).

APPLICATION: BONES UNDERFOOT

Some of the most detailed and meticulous studies of bone taphonomy have been carried out in the context of early hominid sites in Africa, in an attempt to understand whether the bones of animals in the same deposits as hominid remains were prey of the hominids or were scavenged by them from kills by other predators. Shipman (1981; 1983) gives a useful review of this field. Taphonomic studies at archaeological sites of more recent date have often focused on the differential movement of large and small bone fragments by the passage of people's feet. Apparently trivial, such movement can materially affect the distribution of the bones of different species, giving a distinct bias for or against larger-boned species, for example, on different parts of a site, which could be misinterpreted as a deliberate human activity.

A good example comes from the excavation of a house structure dated to a little before 4,000 BP at the Real Alto site in south-western Ecuador (Stahl & Zeidler 1990). The structure was roughly oval, about 11.5m by 8.5m, and with a floor deposit about 20cm thick, within which bone fragments and artefacts were stratified. The distribution of artefacts indicated a hearth and food-preparation area near the centre of the house. Around the hearth area there were high concentrations of bone fragments, and these fragments were predominantly large, flat and of low density (including much cancellous bone). In contrast, deposits around the periphery of the house interior had much lower

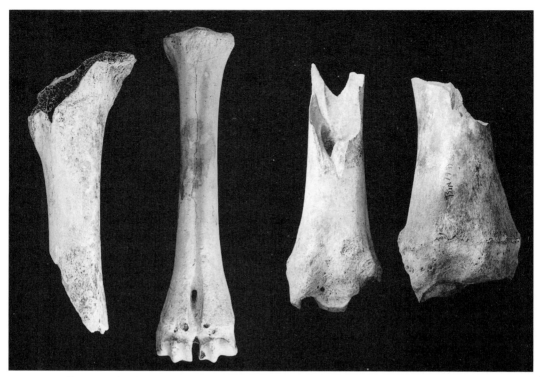

Fig. 3.3. Well-preserved and poorly preserved archaeological specimens of cattle bones. The well-preserved distal radius on the far right conveys more information about the animal, and perhaps about its death and butchery, while the poorly preserved femur shaft on the far left conveys more information about the burial environment and deposit formation. The photograph also illustrates the problem of defining 'well preserved'. The metatarsal (centre left) is complete, but shows some cracking and surface abrasion. The distal tibia (centre right) is incomplete, but the bone itself is probably less degraded than that in the metatarsal.

concentrations of bone fragments, and these were mostly small, slender and of dense bone. These distributions of bone fragments were closely matched by samples taken from currently occupied and recently abandoned structures in the same region. In particular, it was noted that the deposits accumulating around the hearth in the modern structures contained much ash, and so tended to be softer than the earth floor of the remainder of the house interior. This meant that bones dropped around the hearth were more likely to be trodden into the soft ashy earth, and this area was more difficult to sweep clean than the harder areas. In the harder, more trampled areas, only small dense fragments survived in the floor deposits, as these were more likely to be trampled into the earth. Around the hearth, larger and less dense fragments survived because they were more likely to be incorporated into the softer deposits, and less likely to be swept away.

That is only the gist of quite a complex study, but the use of the ethnographic observation to explain the archaeological data is clear. We have to keep in mind that conclusions drawn from any one ethnographic study must be re-examined, as the particular house floor or group of people might have been atypical in some way. Similarly, the people represented in the archaeological record might have been engaging in some activity unrepresented in the ethnographic record. Ethnographic studies and experimentation can only show us some possibilities, and cannot give comprehensive, definitive answers (Evans & O'Connor 1999, 181–8). However, bone taphonomy is sufficiently complex that it is helpful to shed light on even a few possibilities.

SUMMARY

Our efforts to understand the effects of different taphonomic processes should be driven by more than just a desire to be able to predict 'good' or 'bad' preservation of bones in different deposits. Archaeological bones also carry information about the perthotaxic through anataxic processes which have modified them, individually and *en masse*, since the animals in question died. We can choose to recognize that information, be it tooth marks or mineral encrustation, in order to exclude it from the archaeological interpretation of the bones. Alternatively, we can choose to 'read' that information, in order to understand what has happened to the bones and the deposit. This is one of the useful attributes of Clark & Kietzke's classification of taphonomic processes. It provides a framework against which to categorize the various items of data which can be recovered from a bone, a framework which then links those data either with sediment geochemistry, or with pre-deposition modification or with the human activity which caused the animals to die in the first place.

The last two stages of the taphonomic process are the sullegic and trephic factors associated with excavation and recording. Although strictly a continuation of the modifications which began at death, these factors are considered separately in the next chapter because this is the province of archaeological decision-making. We can barely understand, let alone control, the taphic and anataxic factors, whereas the sullegic and trephic factors are at least partly within our control.

FOUR

EXCAVATION AND RECOVERY

The study of 'finds' from archaeological sites, whether bones, pots or gold coins, is often presented as if it begins when the excavation ends. However, excavation and sampling decisions, and the means by which bone fragments are retrieved from sediments, can have a marked effect on the quality and quantity of the sample. The bones that survive to become the archaeological record are already only a tiny proportion of the original, reduced and modified by taphonomic processes beyond our control. Excavation and recovery add further stages of reduction and modification, but we can at least impose some degree of control. Our study of the bones thus has to begin when the excavation is planned, not when it finishes.

CHOOSING THE SAMPLE

The survival of archaeological deposits, and the opportunity to excavate them, may be influenced by the past human activity that created the deposits. For example, the survival of substantial Roman ruins at Caerleon (Chapter 1) affected the location of subsequent settlement, which in turn has affected where excavation can and cannot be undertaken today.

Once the decision to undertake an excavation has been made, further sampling decisions are taken by placing excavation trenches in particular positions. The excavated area may well constitute only 10 per cent or so of the 'site', and is commonly determined either by presumptions about the underlying archaeology, or by the location of areas of expected subsequent destruction, or a combination of the two. Even on sites where a study of the vertebrate remains is seen as an important part of the research, it is rare for the excavation trenches to be positioned by considering expected bone distributions. Thus, the first level of on-site sampling decisions which will influence bone recovery are based on quite other considerations. There are exceptions, of course, and Zeder (1991, 76–9) gives a good example of a bone sample selection strategy, and (*Ibid.*, 98–100) a good review of the sample taphonomy. Some preliminary sampling of a site might be undertaken by excavating small test-pits, and these can give some indication of the distribution and concentration of bone-bearing sediments. However, a test-pit will sample only a small part of a particular deposit. The context of that deposit, and the archaeological potential of any bone assemblage recovered from it, will be unclear.

Having decided which deposits are to be excavated, sampling may proceed in order to reduce the quantity of bones recovered from a particularly extensive or productive

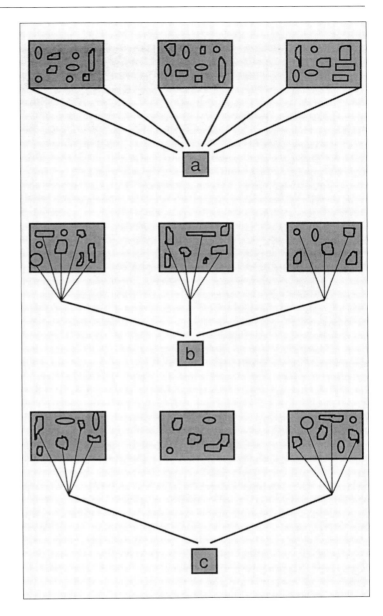

Fig. 4.1. Diagrammatic representation of sampling strategies. Strategy a – all-from-all – is rarely practicable, and most excavations implement a some-from-all (b), or some-from-some (c) strategy. The key decisions then become the selection criteria for the bones and the contexts.

excavation (e.g. Levitan 1983; Turner 1984), or in order to enhance the quality of information to be obtained. If the bone specialist can influence sampling strategies on site, there are several options. First, it would theoretically be possible to attempt to retrieve all bone fragments from the entirety of each excavated context (all from all). Second, sampling could aim to recover some bones selectively from the whole of each context, applying the same selection criteria to each (some from all). Third, sampling could seek to retrieve every bone fragment from each of a selected subset of excavated contexts, or

Fig. 4.2. A particularly bone-rich deposit on an eighth/ninth-century site at Flixborough, UK. An obvious candidate for judgemental sampling, but if a random sampling strategy had excluded this deposit, would not the bones have been collected regardless? (Photo: author)

apply the same retrieval criteria to each of a subset of contexts (all from some, or some from some) (Fig. 4.1). All-from-all tends to be impracticable. At what point does a bone fragment become part of the mineral matrix of the sediment? Some minimum fragment size would have to be imposed, thereby turning an all-from-all procedure into a some-from-all method, and this second strategy is close to that applied on most excavations. The third strategy generally becomes some-from-some on practical grounds, or perhaps seeks to retrieve all that is potentially identifiable from a chosen subset of contexts. (The question of what we mean by 'identifiable' is discussed in the next chapter.) Realistically, we recover what bones we perceive to be necessary for the research questions in hand, and accept that total recovery is an illusion: 'Le ramassage exhaustif des ossements est illusoire' (Chaix & Méniel 1996, 44).

Selecting the deposits to be sampled is another area of decision-making. Judgemental, or purposive, selection is perhaps the most commonly implemented method. We decide which deposits will be the most productive in terms of information yield, or simply sample the deposits which most obviously contain a lot of bones (Fig. 4.2). At its worst, judgemental selection is arbitrary and highly subjective, and may lead to a great deal of information being lost. We have to be confident that the deposits selected for bone recovery will potentially yield information which bears directly upon one or more of the explicit research questions which have been posed.

An alternative to judgemental selection is 'random' sampling of one form or another. Here the subjective element is removed by selecting deposits on a basis such as randomly selected metre-squares, every fifth bucket of spoil, every third context in a number sequence, or something of that kind (e.g. Levitan 1982a; 1983). Despite the general air of scientific rigour and detachment, these random strategies tend to be founded on the premise that any *a priori* statements as to which deposits need to be sampled are probably wrong or certainly inadequate, and in practice are difficult to implement. A site director is unlikely to choose not to sample a blatantly bone-rich deposit such as that in Fig. 4.2 just because it has a non-prime context number or falls into the wrong grid square.

RECOVERING THE BONES

Once we have decided which deposits to sample for bones, the means of excavation of those bones imposes another layer of sampling, ranging from large-scale mechanical excavation to painstakingly slow excavation by hand using very small tools. The circumstances of the excavation, and perhaps the nature of the sediments themselves, will determine the means of excavation. Some methods will cause additional fragmentation of bones (bulldozers, pickaxes), and some may excavate sediments in such large lumps that bones contained within those lumps will not be seen (mattocks, pick and spade). The method and rate of excavation substantially affects the probability of a bone fragment being recovered and recorded, and these factors are often heavily influenced by considerations of time and cost.

Excavations sometimes rely on bones being noticed during excavation and picked up (*hand-collection, trench-collection*), and numerous studies have shown that hand-collection results in the recovery of a very size-biased sample (Casteel 1972; Payne 1975; Clason & Prummel 1977). Large bones, and therefore large-boned species, tend to be seriously over-represented at the expense of small bones. Hand-collection will retrieve most cattle bones, but will miss most fish. The procedure is also poorly controlled. The same excavators, working on different days or in slightly different light conditions during the same day, will vary considerably in their ability to notice and pick up a particular specimen. A large deposit under excavation by several different people at the same time will be sampled differently by each of those excavators, and the assemblage recovered by each of them will differ from that of the others (Levitan 1982a).

Because of these problems, many excavations use *sieving* (in the USA *screening*) techniques. *Sieving* can both increase the recovery of small specimens and standardize the recovery process. Samples of the excavated sediment are passed through a sieve, with a mesh fine enough to retain the smallest specimens which we wish to collect. However, if the mesh is very fine, a high proportion of the sediment will be retained, necessitating prolonged sorting. The optimum mesh size retains the smaller identifiable (or desired) bones, but allows through as much as possible of the sediment. Fine, dry

Fig. 4.3. A typical wet-sieving tank in action. (Photo courtesy of James Barrett)

sediments, such as sand in an arid climate, may simply be shovelled on to the sieve (*dry sieving*), but most other sediments will require some form of *disaggregation* to break up lumps and so to release all contained bone fragments (and pottery, coins, lithics, etc.) (Beatty & Bonnichsen 1994). If the sediment is not thoroughly disaggregated, bones retained by the sieve will be missed during sorting as they will be incorporated in, and indistinguishable from, lumps of sediment. The most common disaggregation procedure is to use water, either by soaking the sample in water so that it breaks up into a slurry which can then be poured through a sieve, or by placing the sample on to the sieve mesh and washing it through with the aid of a jet of water (*wet sieving, water sieving*). Even disaggregation attracts a lot of experimentation: Clason & Brinkhuizen (1978) report the use of a cement-mixer to reduce bone-bearing sediments to slurry. Experiments with cement mixers on sites in York during the 1980s showed that damage to bones and ceramics could be caused by the mechanical churning of the sample, but only if it was prolonged and only if insufficient water was added with the sediment.

Small samples can be wet sieved by disaggregating the sample in a bucket of water and pouring the slurry through a conventional soil-sieve. However, given the sort of concentration at which bone fragments occur in most sorts of archaeological deposit, samples may need to be of the order of 20kg to 50kg, or even more. Numerous devices have been developed, most of them based on oil drums or water tanks, to allow the rapid wet sieving of large volumes of sediment (Williams 1973; Kenward *et al.* 1980; Jones 1983; Ward 1984) (Fig. 4.3). The mesh size used depends upon the purpose of the sieving. If the aim is to recover all potentially identifiable bone fragments, then a mesh aperture of 1mm or even less would be required (Stahl 1996). This will retain anything larger than 1mm in the sample, requiring the bones to be sorted out from coarse-grained sand, small stones and fragments of tile, pottery, slag, whatever. Sometimes it may be helpful to sieve a relatively small sample of a deposit to 1mm to confirm the small species present in that deposit, then to sieve a much larger quantity through a much coarser mesh (4mm, even 10mm is sometimes used) to obtain a substantial sample of the larger species. Sieving through a 10mm mesh may seem to be hardly better than hand-collection. In fact it is much better, not least because the recovery is consistent from one sample to the next (Wing & Quitmyer 1985; Gordon 1993; Saffer & Sanchez 1994). Given consistent recovery and recording of the volume of sediment sieved, it becomes possible to compare the concentration of bone in different sampling units, data which may reflect patterns of human activity.

CASE STUDY: MEDIEVAL FISHERGATE

The sieving strategy employed at the 46–54 Fishergate site in York makes a useful example of the effectiveness and ease of application of sampling and sieving procedures (O'Connor 1988a). This site produced a considerable quantity of bone fragments from contexts variously dated to the eighth to sixteenth centuries AD (O'Connor 1991a; Kemp 1996). All bone samples were recovered by sieving, either by sieving relatively small samples in a tank on a 1mm aperture mesh, or by placing larger samples on a 12mm mesh, and hosing water over the sample to disaggregate the sediment and wash the residue, as a more consistent alternative to hand-collecting bone during excavation. Sample size was determined by weighing whatever sample had been taken on site, rather than by imposing strict minimum and maximum sizes. As a result, 1mm-sieved samples ranged from 1kg to 280kg (276 samples; mean weight 66.8kg), while 12mm-sieved samples ranged from 5kg to 1,274kg (146 samples; mean weight 231.5kg). Comparison of the results from 1mm- and 12mm-sieved samples from the same deposit showed that the coarser mesh retrieved virtually no fish or amphibian bones. In one particular pit fill, fish bones comprised 70 per cent of identified bones in the 1mm-sieved sample, but only 0.2 per cent in the 12mm-sieved sample, a fairly unambiguous indication of recovery efficiency. On the other hand, differences in the ratio of cattle to sheep bones were only minor, indicating that the 12mm mesh was losing a small amount of potentially identifiable sheep bones, but not enough to make a substantial difference to the results. Table 4.1 compares the range of bird taxa recovered from the same deposits by the two different sieving procedures. The greater range recovered by sieving on a 2mm mesh is obvious. Whether the additional identifications contribute much to the overall interpretation of this phase of settlement is a different question, though the 2mm fraction did yield an unusually early record of pheasant, which is of some biogeographical value.

Table 4.1. *The presence (+) and absence (-) of bird taxa in eighth-century* AD *samples from Fishergate, York.*

Samples sieved on a 12mm mesh and a 2mm mesh (adapted from O'Connor 1991a, Table 71). The greater range of species recovered on the finer mesh is obvious, but the additional species are mostly small commensal birds of little archaeological significance, at least in terms of human activities at this site. The presence of jay and jackdaw only in the 12mm samples makes a point about sampling. The coarser mesh allowed much larger samples to be processed, increasing the probability that uncommon taxa would be represented in the sample.

	12mm	2mm	
Grey-lag goose	+	+	*Anser anser*
Small goose	+	+	*Anser/Branta* sp(p.)
Kite	+	+	*Milvus* c.f. *milvus*
Buzzard	−	+	*Buteo* c.f. *buteo*
Domestic fowl	+	+	*Gallus gallus*
Pheasant	−	+	*Phasianus colchicus*
Wood pigeon	+	+	*Columba palumbus*
Swallow	−	+	*Hirundo rustica*
Wren	−	+	*Troglodytes troglodytes*
Thrush	−	+	*Turdus* sp.
Chaffinch	−	+	*Fringilla coelebs*
House sparrow	−	+	*Passer domesticus*
Starling	−	+	*Sturnus vulgaris*
Jay	+	−	*Garrulus glandarius*
Magpie	−	+	*Pica pica*
Jackdaw	+	−	*Corvus monedula*
Rook	+	+	*C. frugilegus*
Crow	−	+	*C. corone*
Raven	+	+	*C. corax*

Some of the larger samples produced very large amounts of residue to sort, and it was recommended that subsequent projects in York should limit 1mm-sieved samples to about 35kg (about four buckets), and 12mm-sieved samples to about 150kg (about two wheelbarrow-loads). Obviously, the same study carried out on a different site would have produced different results, and any strategy has to be pragmatically adjusted to suit local circumstances and research priorities. However, the Fishergate example serves to show the sort of criteria which have to be considered. Selecting a recovery method is a compromise between the desire to recover as much as possible of what is in the deposit, and the need not to build up a logistically impossible backlog of material to sort, identify and record. The essential step is to ask what we are trying to find out, and to gear the recovery method accordingly.

PICKING OUT THE BONES

The sorting of sieved samples can be a logistical nightmare. It is one of the most important stages in the recovery of bones by sieving, yet it is seldom discussed in the literature. Even Stahl's (1996) excellent review paper passes over sorting without comment.

Whatever the deposit and the sieve mesh, the process retains a jumble of mineral clasts, bone fragments and other materials, out of which the bones have to be picked. In theory, the sample will be worked over by a bone specialist who has the knowledge and experience to recognize and collect every fragment of bone. In reality, this sorting of the sieved samples may take longer than identifying and recording the bones. There is an obvious pressure to pass the sorting job to non-specialist personnel, freeing up the specialist to do what they are best at. On many archaeological projects, sieved samples are sorted by non-specialist, often volunteer, personnel, albeit closely supervised. For example, this appears to have been the strategy adopted in Payne's pioneering sieving experiments at Sitagroi, Greece (Payne 1975, 7 footnote). This may be no bad thing in itself, but there is an obvious risk that unusual (unexpected?) elements or even whole taxa may be overlooked. A 'sorter' well acquainted with mammal bones may completely fail to recognize, for example, the tracheal rings of birds, or fish otoliths. That said, the preliminary sorting of sieved residues can often be undertaken by non-specialists with a useful degree of success. My own experience of this procedure is that only one or two per cent of the fish bones in a rich sample will be mis-sorted as mammal or bird bone; more frequent is the mis-sorting of amphibian bones as fish.

Sorting itself presents practical complications. Material retained by a 4mm mesh or coarser can generally be sorted by the unaided eye with little difficulty. At 2mm mesh, lighting needs to be particularly good. Below 2mm, magnification such as low-power microscopy will be necessary, so the sorting of sub-2mm samples is very much slower than for coarser fractions. A sieved sample will generally include material of a range of sizes, and it is often advisable to re-sieve the material to obtain fractions each of a fairly narrow size range. It is much easier to sort quickly and efficiently through material which is, let us say, all from 4mm to 8mm nominal diameter, than to be trying to sort small bones out of a heterogeneous jumble ranging from 4mm to 40mm. In such a jumble, small bones have a curious tendency to hide beneath the larger stones!

CONCLUSIONS

Simple though it may be, it is essential to understand and control the patterns of bias and modification which our recovery techniques add to whatever else has patterned the archaeological sample of bones. It is now well-known that hand-collection during excavation is an unsatisfactory means of bone recovery, but there is a tendency to believe that recovering bones by sieving is a complete, objective solution. It isn't: the effects of sample and mesh sizes have to be understood (e.g. Stahl 1996, Table 1), and require tactical, and often pragmatic, decisions to be taken. The essential point is to see this decision-making as a last step in a series of taphonomic processes which began when biotic processes brought the animals together in the first place. Not least, there may be little point in worrying about very minor biasses in the recovery process, if taphic and anataxic factors have already wrought overwhelming modifications to the sample.

By now, we have retrieved our bone samples and reached the point at which Chapter 1 begins. The next few chapters take the lids off the enticing heap of boxes, and review the identification and study of those bones, and the gradual extraction of the information that they embody.

FIVE

IDENTIFICATION AND DESCRIPTION

'. . . all bones, even the smallest fragments, may be identified given sufficient training
in osteology'.

(Binford & Bertram 1977, 125).

Having recovered a sample of bone fragments, the next step is to identify and record the
specimens. This is the fundamental starting point of data recovery, and a lot can happen if
this stage goes wrong. Much of the published literature on the subject concerns the
identification of mammal or bird bones in general (e.g. Scarlett 1972; Schmid 1972;
Walker 1985; Gehr 1995; Cohen & Serjeantson 1996), or particular groups of species
which present identification problems (e.g. Olsen 1960; Fick 1974; Northcote 1981;
Pieper 1982; Vigne 1995; Lister 1996; Sobolik & Steele 1996). Rather than summarizing
the information in these sources, this chapter looks at the process of identification, and
what we are aiming to do in our recording procedures.

PRINCIPLES

A fragment of bone from an archaeological assemblage could be recorded by a description
such as 'distal epiphysis plus 25 per cent diaphysis left tibia roe deer'. We describe the
fragment using conventional anatomical terminology, and make an identification, if possible,
to species level. This assumes that the most important information to be had about a
particular fragment relates to the anatomy and phylogeny of the animal from which it is
believed to have derived. The description 'tubular element 100mm by 15mm' would also
relate to the same specimen, and would at least describe the *fragment*, not the presumed
source animal. As our concern is generally with the biotic and thanatic processes involved in
assemblage formation, the emphasis on species identification is understandable. Some of the
impetus to put species names to bones also comes from a desire to accumulate lists of species,
to know which species were present at a particular time and place. This tendency has been
termed 'twitching', by analogy with bird-watchers who go to great lengths to see a new species
(Smith 1976; Lyman 1982, 334). However, in studies where the later stages of the taphonomic
process are the main point of study, then fragment description rather than identification may
be more appropriate (e.g. Wolff 1973; Binford & Bertram 1977; Lyman 1984).

The applicability of species labels to bone specimens has been usefully reviewed by Driver
(1992), and deserves brief consideration here. In our example, the tibia fragment was
attributed to roe deer *Capreolus capreolus*, a species widespread in Europe. This implies that

the specimen was, in the analyst's experienced opinion, very closely similar to modern reference specimens of the roe deer bones, and not equally similar to anything else. However, the species *C. capreolus* is defined by a range of characteristics which we cannot infer from the tibia alone, including the form of its antlers and the colour of its coat. Furthermore, all other taxa are rejected. If the specimen is from a site in northern Europe, few other smallish even-toed hoofed mammals are likely to be encountered. The identification of our specimen is thus likely to proceed along the lines, 'Well, it's clearly not sheep or goat, too small for fallow deer, good match for roe deer.' Common sense, that most dangerous of things, means that we will not check the specimen against every known smallish artiodactyl on the grounds that most of them are extremely unlikely to turn up on a northern European site. Such wider comparison would probably only be undertaken if no *plausible* match could be found. In the end, identification depends in part on the characteristics of the specimen, in part on the preconceptions of the bone analyst as to what is likely to 'turn up', and in part on what is available in the reference collection. We can easily see that quite different procedures might be adopted by colleagues working in New Zealand, with its very limited mammal fauna; in Europe, with appreciably more species; or in Sub-Saharan Africa, where the diversity of medium and large mammals presents a serious challenge (Walker 1985).

My second encounter with Roman dormice provides a useful cautionary tale. Roman deposits at the General Accident Extension site in York were extensively sieved for small bones, among which were a number of specimens of mandibles and maxillae of a small rodent not attributable to any currently native British rodent (O'Connor 1986a; 1988b). The dental structure and overall morphology of the mandibles indicated the species to be one of the dormice (Gliridae), though not the hazel dormouse *Muscardinus avellanarius*. At this point, George Boon's words about Romans eating dormice came back to mind (Chapter 1), and I came to suspect that the bones would be from dormice eaten on or near the site, and therefore from the edible dormouse *Glis glis*. No reference collection in York included any non-British dormice, and it would have been very easy at this point to attribute the bones to *Glis glis* for quite the wrong reasons. Fortunately, a visit to the Natural History Museum, London, showed the specimens to be of the garden dormouse *Eliomys quercinus*, a species which 'common sense' would not have led one to expect, as it had not previously been recorded in Britain, dead or alive. The dormouse affair served as a warning that unexpected species may occur in bone assemblages, and that the assumptions underlying the identification of the bones may be wrong.

The identification of small vertebrates such as dormice offers a particular challenge. In many parts of the world there are numerous closely related species within rodent families and genera. For example, among the microtine voles of Eurasia some species can be distinguished only by details of the shape of their teeth, and to some degree by details of the shape of the jaws. Reptilian and amphibian remains are often considered to be a major identification problem, though one suspects that this is as much a matter of their unfamiliarity and lack of comparative collections as it is a characteristic of the bones. 'Atlases', which give explanatory notes and illustrations of the bones of different species, are of some value (e.g. Sobolik & Steele 1996), but even these are lacking for most herpetile groups for most parts of the world. A valuable exception is Böhme's (1977) description and illustration of major skeletal elements of European frogs and toads and a similar guide, based largely on photographs, is available

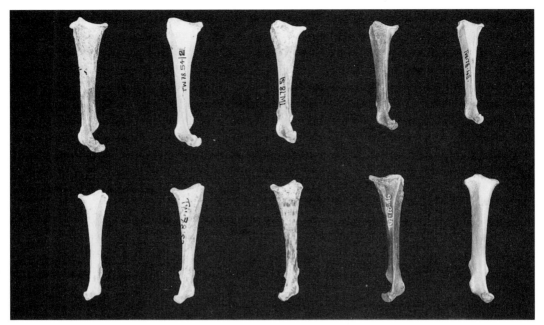

Fig. 5.1. An illustration of the challenge which the identification of bird bones can present. These are coracoid bones of domestic fowl Gallus gallus, *except for one, which is from guinea fowl* Numida meleagris. *Which one? Read the chapter.*

for British material (Gleed-Owen 1998). Even for the more familiar orders of vertebrates, such illustrations can only be of a 'typical' specimen of each element of each species. A useful means of giving some indication of the variation within a species can be to include metrical data from modern specimens. Thus Vigne (1995) gives guidelines for the identification of major limb elements in five taxa of western European rodent, and includes a table of measurements, outline illustrations, a text description of the main features on which identification can be made, and a key based on those features.

Precise and confident identification may be essential to the interpretation of the samples. For example, a study of mouse remains from Iron Age sites in Central Spain required confident attribution of *Mus* specimens to the native *M. spretus* or to the introduced, commensal *M. musculus*, as this would make a major contribution to our understanding of the spread of commensal house mouse in western Europe (Morales Muñiz *et al.* 1995). To make that identification with confidence required detailed examination and measurement of the shape of the zygomatic arch of the skull, and microscopic examination of the pattern of cusps on the upper molar teeth. To the authors' great credit, the features which they used are illustrated and described at length.

Identification of bird bones can be particularly difficult. In most parts of the world birds are speciated into more species per family than mammals. For example, Walters (1980) lists 221 species in the family Accipitridae (hawks, kites, eagles, buzzards, Old World vultures), including 48 species of hawk in the genus *Accipiter* alone. Skeletal differences between bird families are usually clear enough, but there may be close skeletal similarities between genera within families, and even more between species within a genus (Fig. 5.1).

It may be quite straightforward to decide that a bone is from a wading bird of the family Scolopacidae, but impossible even to identify the genus within that family. With birds almost more than any other group, we resort to 'most probable' identifications. A very good example of this is given by Gotfredson: 'No bones of razorbill (*Alca torda*) and common guillemot (*Uria aalge*) . . . were present in the bone materials of the 16 localities. Therefore all alcid bones that could not be determined to the minor alcids black guillemot (*Cepphus grylle*) or little auk (*Alle alle*) or great auk (*Pinguinus impennis*) were considered to be Brünnich's guillemot (*Uria lomvia*)' (Gotfredson 1997, 273). On paper, this may look to be a questionable procedure, though faced with the reality of the material, it is probably the most sensible approach that could have been adopted.

Good reference material is essential, and comprehensive reference collections are few and far between, so bird bones are particularly subject to the danger of identifying archaeological specimens as the species which one happens to have in the collection. None the less, bird bones can be identified with an acceptable degree of confidence, given a comparative collection, sufficient experience to engender caution and a familiarity with the published sources. Stewart & Carrasquilla (1997) have provided a useful review of the literature pertaining to extant European bird taxa. They list nearly ninety sources, but admit that many gaps remain, not least for the economically important Charadriiformes (gulls, auks, waders). The guinea-fowl in Fig. 5.1 is at the right-hand end of the lower row.

Much of what has been said regarding rodents and birds applies to fish as well. In some parts of the world certain families pose notoriously difficult problems. Within northern Europe and North America, for example, the carp family (Cyprinidae) includes many of the most abundant and widespread freshwater species, and identification below the level of family is often only possible on a few elements in a sample. In tropical regions freshwater and marine fish of the order Perciformes present similar identification problems, with families such as the wrasses (Labridae) being identified principally on their jaws and pharyngeal bones. Comprehensive comparative collections are unlikely to be available for many parts of the world, other than at a few museums of international standing. Accordingly, it is not unusual for the fish bone specialist to find it necessary to purchase or catch (and eat!) quantities of fish from a particular region in order to assemble the necessary comparative material before the samples can be identified and recorded.

Because of all the difficulties outlined above, it is fair to say that what we record are taxonomic *attributions*; records which convey the meaning 'I attribute this bone to roe deer', rather than 'This bone definitely originated in the body of a *Capreolus capreolus* and categorically not anything else'. The distinction may seem a small one, of little practical value, but it is important, because it means that the taxon 'roe deer' as used by one person may differ slightly from the same taxon as used by another. The clearest example of this is a particular use of the taxon 'sheep' by many analysts (including the present author). In circumstances where assemblages contain much material firmly attributable to sheep, and little or no material attributable to goat, the term 'sheep' may be used to convey 'Any caprine clearly not attributable to goat and not otherwise distinguishable from sheep', which is not quite what Linnaeus meant by *Ovis aries*. One of the functions of Linnaean binomials ('Latin names') is, of course, their translingual applicability, but they are also supposed to be definitive and objective, and not subject to local redefinition by different users. That almost seems to be a case for avoiding the use of Linnaean binomials for archaeological material, on the basis that my taxon *Ovis aries* may be more loosely defined than yours. However, we need comparability between languages, and even within English (is *Prunella modularis* a hedge sparrow or a dunnock?), and should retain the use of binomials for that reason, but clearly understand that they are compromised by the nature of our material and our methods of working.

PRACTICALITIES

Having reviewed something of the theory of bone identification, we turn to the practicalities. To a degree, the best way to proceed will depend upon the material concerned, and the experience of the individual researcher.

The mistake is to start by saying 'What animal does this come from?' The proper starting point is 'What part of the anatomy is this?' Not until the specimen has been located within the general vertebrate skeleton can we begin to envisage the size of animal from which the specimen derives, or to use its obvious adaptations to decide what *sort* of animal it may have come from. Some anatomical clues are obvious. If the specimen has teeth in it, or sockets (*alveoli*) from which teeth have dropped out, then obviously it is a mandible or maxilla. If the specimen is clearly bilaterally symmetrical, then it must come from a point on the mid-line of

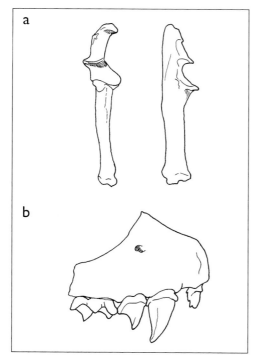

Fig. 5.2. Two hypothetical bone specimens, to illustrate the procedure of identification. Specimen a is a limb bone of some form, lacking obviously convex articular surfaces, so not humerus or femur. One articular surface lies away from the physical end of the bone, at which there is a long process. This identifies the bone as an ulna. It is not fused with the radius, so the animal is not an ungulate, and the rather robust shaft indicates an animal with powerful forelimbs, but poorly adapted to fast running. The specimen is 165mm long, so the animal is somewhat smaller than a sheep but bigger than a cat. Depending on the geographical region, this process of elimination would leave relatively few possibilities. In fact, the ulna is that of an aardvark Octeropus afer. Specimen b is part of a jaw bone with four teeth. The overall shape of the bone is more consistent with maxilla than mandible. The large canine tooth probably indicates a predatory animal, but the multi-cusped form of the first post-canine tooth rules out any of the Carnivora, as does the rather odd incisor. The wide but low crowns and numerous pointed cusps on the post-canine teeth indicate an animal that feeds predominantly on insects. The specimen is barely 4mm long, and the small size and distinctive multi-cusped teeth indicate a small species of bat, in this case mouse-eared bat Myotis myotis.

the body (e.g. vertebrae, sternum, base of the neurocranium). If a limb bone has convex articulations at both proximal and distal ends, then it is a humerus or femur (Fig. 5.2).

Size is a more useful parameter with mammal or bird bones than with fish or amphibians. Mammals and birds attain an adult size beyond which the skeleton does not substantively increase in size, although it may undergo other remodelling. We can therefore describe a specimen as 'sheep sized', knowing that, although sheep vary in size, they are generally larger than cats but smaller than moose. Fish, on the other hand, continue to grow throughout their lives: a big cod is an old cod, and *vice versa*. We can use size in fish as an aid to identification only to a rather limited extent. Conspicuously large fish bones are only likely to be of certain species, as many will not attain that size however long they live. Apart from that generalization, however, approximate size is not a useful criterion with fish, as there is far greater within-species size variation than is the case with mammals or birds.

Archaeological material is usually broken, so we may need to record *which part* of what bone our specimen represents. The descriptive categories used may follow anatomy precisely (distal epiphysis of humerus) or may be categories of convenience (long bone shaft fragment). Two rather different approaches have been applied to the recording of fragments. One is simply to describe the fragment in terms of what proportion or percentage of the whole element is represented. The example used at the beginning of this chapter uses this approach, describing a specimen as the distal epiphysis plus 25 per cent of the diaphysis. An alternative is to subdivide the major elements into zones, defined by distinctive anatomical landmarks and perhaps also by commonly observed patterns of breakage, and to define a fragment in terms of which zones are present (e.g. Dobney & Rielly 1988; Shaffer & Baker 1992, 26–33). Both procedures have their strengths and weaknesses: the 'zones' method in particular tends to be complex in application and inflexible. However, the main requirement is that the fragment descriptions allow both unambiguous recording and the ready retrieval of the data required for quantification of taxa (Chapter 6) or of body parts (Chapter 7).

Having decided which part of the skeleton we have, the next step is to look for characteristics of the bone which indicate something about the size and adaptation of the animal concerned. Teeth are the obvious example. There are big differences between the pointy-gripping-and-rending-flesh teeth of a carnivore, and the millstone-like-grinding-up-grass teeth of a herbivore. A brisk review of the illustrations in Hillson (1986) shows how readily the adaptations of dentition may be recognized, even in unfamiliar groups. Basically, a big herbivore such as an elephant has teeth not unlike those of a tiny herbivore such as a vole (but much bigger). Toe bones are also helpful. Do they appear to belong to an animal which can grip with its fingers and/or toes, such as a primate? Does it look as if the animal stood on tip-toe and had hooves: a typical ungulate? Are the third phalanges curved and pointed to carry claws? Particularly long and slender limb-bones may indicate an animal which either has to be very light (birds and bats?), or which is adapted to fast running, such as deer and gazelles. By looking at the bones in this way, we can quickly narrow down the list of suspects to some broad category (medium-sized ungulate; large wading bird; small carnivore), from which it is relatively easy to move to reference specimens to refine the identification.

The theoretical objections and practical constraints regarding the use of Linnaean binomials have been reviewed above, and it would be wrong to lay down general rules about the limits to which identification should be taken. The most important thing is that the procedures and limitations which have been applied in each study should be made clear in the published report. In some circumstances, the inclusion and exclusion of potential identifications hardly needs to be spelt out. The large bovid bones that dominated the assemblages from Caerleon were attributed to domestic cattle (*Bos* sp.). For some parts of the skeleton, cattle can be hard to distinguish from *Bison* species, or from some large African bovids. However, it would have been pathologically pedantic, or just plain silly, to have listed some Caerleon specimens as 'cattle or gnu'. On the other hand, bones of kite (*Milvus* spp.) found in northern Europe are usually attributed to red kite (*Milvus milvus*), not to the black kite (*M. migrans*), because only the red kite is found in northern Europe today. Yet the bones of the two *Milvus* species are virtually indistinguishable (Morales Muñiz 1993), and black kite is widespread throughout southern Europe. In this case, the published report would need to make clear the limitations of the taxa to which the specimens are attributed.

It is not uncommon for a species to be clearly recognizable by some parts of the skeleton but not others. Sheep and goat bones are notoriously difficult to separate (Boessneck *et al.* 1964; Kratochvil 1969; Payne 1969; 1985a; Prummel & Frisch 1986; Helmer & Rocheteau 1994; Buitenhuis 1995). In a mixed assemblage with both species, the horncores and metapodials may be separated with confidence, the radii and scapulae with less confidence, and other parts of the skeleton not at all. Do we record the bones as three taxa: definite sheep, definite goat, and possibly either? In this case, the number of specimens attributed to each taxon will depend upon the experience and confidence of the individual researcher. For example, I am particularly familiar with the sheep skeleton, and would probably give a confident identification to a higher proportion of sheep/goat specimens than would some colleagues. On the other hand, I would be much less confident with mixed horse/ass material, simply because of experience and familiarity. In the end we are pragmatic. Taxonomic categories may be quite specific (*Panthera leo*), or to a definite genus (*Corvus* sp.), or family (Scolopacidae). Other taxa may offer uncertainty between pairs of species (sheep/goat), or within larger groupings (large ungulate, small *Macropus*). And if the most useful taxa do not happen to coincide with Linnaean taxonomy, that should not be an obstacle to their use. It is more important that we use taxa about which we are confident and consistent than that every specimen should be coaxed into order, family, genus or species.

Some material, perhaps much of it, must be left as 'unidentified'. That is not the same as 'unidentifiable', but states clearly that the analyst in question did not believe there to be enough informative detail surviving on the specimen to allow taxonomic identification. This is a positive decision, not an admission of defeat. The statement that prefaces this chapter was chosen because it is wonderfully optimistic, and utterly wrong.

FRAGMENTATION AND PRESERVATION

There is further information to record about an archaeological bone specimen. The size of the fragment may be of some importance if we wish to investigate the effects of deposition and recovery (Watson 1972). However, with a large sample, it will generally be logistically impracticable to take exact measurements of each specimen. Besides, what do we measure? Bone fragments are seldom conveniently geometrical shapes with an easily defined length or diameter. A useful compromise can be to put each fragment into a size class on the basis of its longest dimension. For ease in working, the size classes can be drawn out on the bench, allowing each specimen to be quickly compared and allocated a size class. The class intervals need not be equal: in fact, a geometric progression (2–4mm, 4–8mm, 8–16mm, 16–32mm and so on) is more useful in practice than an arithmetical progression (5–10mm, 10–15mm, 15–20mm, 20–25mm and so on). In a typical sample, a high proportion of the fragments may be in the same few size classes. In view of this, it may even be useful to allocate a 'modal fragment size' to the whole sample. Thus a modal fragment size of, say, 70–100mm indicates that the great majority of the fragments in the sample fall into that size range. If a 'snapshot' record of the fragments patterns in the sample is all that is required, this procedure, which takes only a few seconds, may be all that is needed. There is, after all, further information on fragment size implicit in the identifications that are made.

The state of preservation of bones in a sample can be a very difficult attribute to record. When we describe a specimen as 'well preserved', we are summing up our more-or-less subjective impressions of the state of the bone tissue itself, and the state of the overall morphology of the specimen. None the less, sweeping statements about the state of preservation of bones in a series of samples can often be helpful, not least in giving a possible explanation for differences in the content of those samples. It is probably most useful to separate the state of preservation of the bone tissue *per se* from the survival of the original morphology. The degree of chemical and histological alteration is likely to be a reflection of taphic processes alone, whereas alterations to the morphology may reflect a wider range of taphonomic processes.

A useful series of stages of bone weathering and preservation are summarized in Table 5.1 (Behrensmeyer 1978). The criteria which this procedure uses to represent 'preservation' are all readily visible, and are obviously related to degradation of the bone and consequent loss of integrity. Behrensmeyer's scale is useful and generally applicable, and may be used to describe individual specimens or as an overall record of the 'typical' state of preservation of a sample. Others may prefer a more intuitive classification – I managed with a 'good, bad, horrid' scale for years – but the defining criteria of cracking and flaking are likely to be much the same. Certain states of preservation may be very distinctive. In high pH, free-draining conditions, bone may show excellent preservation of overall morphology, with minimal flaking and cracking, but with a distinctively brittle, chalky texture.

Taphonomic processes of movement and deposition may have rounded-off formerly sharp edges, and this is an attribute which it can be difficult to record objectively and in detail. There may be circumstances in which the angularity of individual fragments merits record, but more often it is the overall condition of the bone sample which matters. In particular, it is important to note samples in which some fragments show angular breaks and some show marked rounding, as this indicates that the sample mixes specimens with quite different taphonomic histories. Such mixing may be a consequence of sampling, or may reflect an earlier stage in deposit formation. Angularity may also reflect human activity. White (1992, 120–4) records an unusual pattern of rounding and bevelling of edges of bone fragments from an Anasazi site in the American South-west. A connection is inferred with the use of corrugated and rather rough-tempered ceramic cooking pots, and White experimentally replicated the rounding patterns to support his hypothesis.

Table 5.1. *A summary of the weathering stages defined by Behrensmeyer (1978) to allow objective recording of the 'state of preservation' of bone specimens.*

Stage	Diagnostic criteria
0	The bone surface shows no cracking or flaking
1	The bone surface shows cracking, usually parallel to the orientation of collagen fibres. Articular surfaces may show cracking in a mosaic pattern.
2	Bone surfaces show flaking, usually along the edges of cracks. Crack edges are angular, with no rounding.
3	Bone surfaces show roughened patches resulting from the flaking of surface bone, but only to a depth of 1.0–1.5mm. Crack edges are typically rounded.
4	Bone surfaces are rough, with loose splinters. Cracks are wide, with rounded or actively splintering edges.
5	The bone is disintegrating into splinters, and the original shape may no longer be apparent.

Another attribute which may vary within a sample, reflecting a mixing of material, is the colour of the fragments. Fresh bone is just off-white while bones from archaeological deposits range through shades of orange and brown through to black. This change in colour is largely a consequence of the deposition in the superficial layers of the bone of a range of minerals derived from the surrounding sediment, in particular oxides and sesquioxides of iron. This predominance of iron oxides gives conspicuous brown (i.e. rust) colours. Recording the colour of specimens gives a record of the degree of superficial mineral uptake, and may show up contrasts between samples or variation within samples.

The importance of colour was demonstrated to me while recording material from Anglo-Scandinavian deposits at 16–22 Coppergate, York (O'Connor 1989). The great majority of the bones from these highly organic deposits had been stained almost black, presumably by deposition of organically bonded iron (humins). However, a minority of fragments in some samples were orange-brown, often with blue specks of vivianite (hydrated iron phosphate $Fe_3(PO_4)_2.8H_2O$). The colour of these specimens closely matched those from the almost inorganic, underlying Roman deposits, and the orange-brown specimens were particularly noted in Anglo-Scandinavian deposits which were stratigraphically close to, or cut into, Roman deposits. My conclusion was that anataxic processes had redeposited some Roman material into Anglo-Scandinavian deposits, but only after the Roman specimens had superficially acquired hydrated iron oxides, giving the orange-brown colour and preventing subsequent staining of the bones by black humins. Instead, the phosphate-rich environment of the Anglo-Scandinavian deposits had resulted in vivianite formation, but only on the Roman specimens where some chemical alteration of the bones had already occurred.

Recording colour is apparently simple: Munsell soil colour charts provide a series of standards against which a specimen can be compared, and the colour recorded to a high degree of precision (Munsell 1946). The weakness of using Munsell charts to record bone colour is that bone specimens are almost invariably mottled, and matching a mottled bone with the absolutely homogeneous colour of a chart colour chip is remarkably difficult. Furthermore, the Munsell charts give a very high degree of precision, and the colour variation shown within one bone specimen may range across several colour chips. It may be more practical, therefore, to adopt a less precise scale, perhaps using intuitive terms such as 'light brown, dark brown, black', and giving Munsell codes to define the limits of those terms. As with fragment size, all that may sometimes be needed is a summary description of the colour typical of a sample, with particular note taken of any variations: hence 'mostly dark brown; about 10 per cent ginger'.

BURNING AND BUTCHERING

Some human activities, including deliberate garbage disposal, may have exposed bones to fire, causing a range of changes in appearance which we may summarize under the term charring. Exactly what happens when a bone is charred is imperfectly understood. An early stage involves the carbonization of at least some of the organic content, but higher temperatures and sustained heating substantially alter the collagen and hydroxyapatite components. Empirically, three distinct stages can generally be seen: black charring with no distortion; grey discoloration with minor distortion and cracking; white discoloration (calcining) with distortion and shrinkage, giving the bone a porcelain-like texture (Shipman *et al.* 1984; Nicholson 1993; Stiner *et al.* 1995). These three stages can be approximately correlated with the temperature to which the bone was heated. Other inferences may be drawn from charring. A detailed study of the distribution of charring patterns on bones of the extinct lagomorph *Prolagus sardus* at a prehistoric rock-shelter site in Corsica showed that the animals had been spit-roasted (Vigne & Marinval-Vigne 1983). The routine recording of charring can range from the minimal, such as noting the approximate percentage of charred fragments in a sample, to allocating individual fragments to a series of classes of charring. The nature of the sample and the research questions under investigation will determine the level of detail required. An important point is that charred bone will behave differently to uncharred bone on exposure to taphic, anataxic and sullegic processes. Where a sample contains a mixture of uncharred, lightly charred and thoroughly calcined bones, interpretation will require a complex modelling of differential survival.

Another aspect of human behaviour which may be apparent on a bone specimen is the dismemberment of the animal. A prey animal may have been killed, skinned, jointed and eaten with the aid of various tools, including hand-axe, lithic blade, iron or copper-alloy knife, or steel cleaver. Each of these tools can leave distinctive traces on the bones, which constitute one form of evidence for past butchery practices, the other being the distribution of different body parts, discussed in Chapter 7. Recording butchery marks focuses on two main attributes: the type of mark and its location.

At its simplest, we can divide butchery marks into two categories: cut-marks, resulting from the cutting of overlying tissues by a knife-like implement; and chop-marks, resulting from chopping of muscle and bone by something like an axe or cleaver (Fig. 5.3). Although

Fig. 5.3. A chop-mark produced by a metal blade on the distal end of a cattle metatarsal.

this is a simplistic categorization, it differentiates between butchery marks, which largely result from attempts to cut meat away from the bone, and marks which largely result from attempts to subdivide the carcass. More subtle recording might, for example, separately record marks resulting from bone surfaces being scraped clean of soft tissue.

The different forms taken by cut-marks and diagnostic criteria for their identification are reviewed in detail by a number of authors, notably Fisher (1995, 12–25). The use of stone tools tends to produce short, multiple, often roughly parallel marks, with a V-shaped cross-section. Within the cut, there will often be fine striations parallel with the cut, reflecting a sawing motion on cutting. Chop-marks made by a metal tool, on the other hand, often show striae nearly at right angles to the mark. These are produced by irregularities in the cutting edge of the tool. Where a sharp metal knife has been used in de-fleshing, the cut-marks may be very narrow and deep, with little associated cracking of the bone.

One reason for recording butchery marks may be in order to distinguish a sample of bones which has accumulated through human activity from bones accumulated and characteristically modified by some other species or some abiotic process (e.g. see Brain 1981; Shipman 1981). When people are clearly the agent of accumulation, the questions asked of butchery marks tend to be more specific, and butchery practices can be distinctive cultural phenomena. Reviewing the use of tools in dismantling carcasses at a medieval Cluniac monastery in France, Audoin-Rouzeau (1987) draws attention to the 'cut and crack' technique of using a cleaver, by which the tool is used to cut a notch in the bone, and further force cracks the bone along that line, rather than cutting it. This raises an important point for recording. If a bone has split open along, perhaps, a longitudinal plane, the broken surface may be indistinguishable from breakage from other causes, apart from a smooth, straight cut surface located at one end of the break. The practice of splitting carcasses into 'sides' of meat became general at La Charite-sur-Loire during the fourteenth century, having previously been occasional: observations like this can lead us to question what else had happened which might have caused or facilitated such a change.

Some butchery marks are evidence of very particular practices, for example in a single deposit of twenty pig mandibles from a pit under the floor of a late eighth-century AD house at Kootwijk, Netherlands (Van Wijngaarden-Bakker 1987). All of the pigs were adult at death, and all showed a chopping mark along the horizontal ramus of the mandible, from the angle of the jaw towards the mesial part, apparently to open the cavity which runs underneath the molar teeth. Experiments were conducted with modern pigs' heads, and the results suggested that this chopping had nothing to do with the recovery of meat from the head, but was intended to allow the recovery of fat and marrow when the jaws were boiled for stock. Other sites of this date in the Netherlands (e.g. Medemblik, Dorestad) show opening of the mandibular cavity by transverse, not longitudinal, cuts, making smaller pieces that may have been more suitable for the pottery vessels of that time. Van Wijngaarden-Bakker observes that Kootwijk yielded rather more large pots than these other sites, and she further suggests that the deposit of twenty mandibles might represent one butchery event carried out by a travelling butcher. The jaws would represent about one pig from each of the farmsteads thought to have been occupied at Kootwijk at that time.

Some butchery marks can be baffling. Sheep metapodials with holes roughly cut in the proximal articular surface and the distal part of the shaft are not uncommon in medieval material from the North Atlantic region, and have been a source of puzzlement to some of us for quite some time. Were they toys, or crude tools of some kind? Arge (1995) reports examples from the Faroe Islands dated to AD 1100–1200 at Leirvík, and 1600–1700 from Tórshavn, and gives a delightful account from a present-day Faroe Islander which shows that the purpose was to blow nutritious bone marrow out of the marrow cavity, preferably straight into a child's mouth. More prosaically, Müller (1989) details marks on the axis vertebrae of Migration Period horses from 'ritual' burials in Slovakia and Germany. There were fine knife cuts on the dorsal aspects of some vertebrae, and the ventral aspects of others. In the latter case, the horse must have been dead, or at least thoroughly stunned, before the cutting could be carried out. Taking a knife to the throat of a conscious and frightened horse does not sound like a plausible means of slaughter, though the knife cuts could well show that the horses were first stunned, then bled to death.

The reason for detailing these examples is in order to show what sort of information might be recovered from butchery marks on bones, and therefore what information might be noted. Recording individual knife or cleaver marks on a bone is one thing: making a record which will allow an overview of butchery procedure across a large sample is another. One recording technique which has been used with some success is to use outline drawings of the main skeletal elements of the more abundant taxa, and to draw on the location and direction of any cuts or obvious cut-and-crack lines. Fig. 5.4 reproduces one such drawing, made as part of the recording of the Caerleon cattle bones. Despite having been made 'at the bench' by a zooarchaeologist of negligible drawing ability, it gives a useful record of where, and in what direction, the majority of the butchering took place.

GNAWING

Other species impose surface damage to bones, and the effects of various scavengers as taphonomic agents have already been discussed in Chapter 3. During the recording of a bone sample, we may come across tooth-marks and other damage caused by gnawing, and this should be recorded as a matter of course. It is a part of the taphonomic record for that

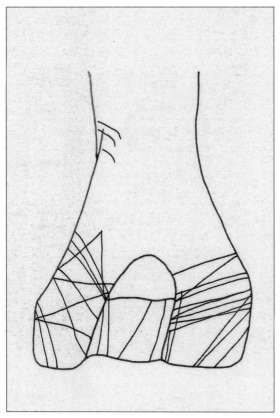

Fig. 5.4. An example of using a bone outline diagram to map cut- and chop-marks.

bone, and it may also be related to any evident deletion of particular elements from the sample (discussed further in Chapter 7, see Tables 7.1, 7.2). Species such as dogs and cats do not select bones for gnawing at random. Some elements are very clearly favoured, notably any with a high proportion of cancellous bone, especially if major muscle attachments mean that there is some attached soft tissue. In bovids the proximal end of the humerus fulfils these criteria, and is a common site of gnawing, as is the *tuber calcis* of the calcaneum, where the Achilles' tendon attaches. The pattern of gnawing damage caused by different species can be distinctive (Haynes 1983). Dogs tend to crunch and chew repeatedly at a bone, producing areas of overlapping tooth-marks. Individually, the tooth-marks tend to be relatively shallow and rather wide – craters rather than punctures – and may be associated with broad grooves, where teeth have dragged across the surface of the bone (Fig. 5.5). In contrast, cats are less inclined, or physically equipped, to chew bones, but leave tooth-marks where the bone has been picked up and moved around. Typically, the tooth-marks are narrow and deep, and only a few are found in any one place (Fig. 5.6).

Rodents cause damage to bones, and rats especially can leave very distinctive tooth-marks (Fig. 5.7). A rat will typically work its way along the edges of a bone in a very systematic manner, leaving rows of tooth-marks which, on close examination, clearly reflect the paired, chisel-like front teeth typical of a rodent. In the example shown in Fig. 5.7, measurement of the tooth-marks shows the size of the teeth to be consistent with the black rat *Rattus rattus*. Other tooth-marks may occur, and the perpetrators may not be so obvious. Ungulates occasionally chew bones, especially females suffering calcium depletion during pregnancy or lactation. This has been recorded in deer (Sutcliffe 1973; Kierdorf 1994) while Brothwell (1976) has noted bone-chewing by sheep in a feral population. My own observations of the same sheep population indicate that this bone-chewing is not uncommon. Fig. 5.8 shows the characteristic damage which results as the high-crowned, prismatic teeth of the sheep slide across the bone surface.

Gnawing damage may mimic human modification of bones. For example, d'Erico *et al.* (1998) have reassessed an alleged bone flute from Middle Palaeolithic levels in a cave in

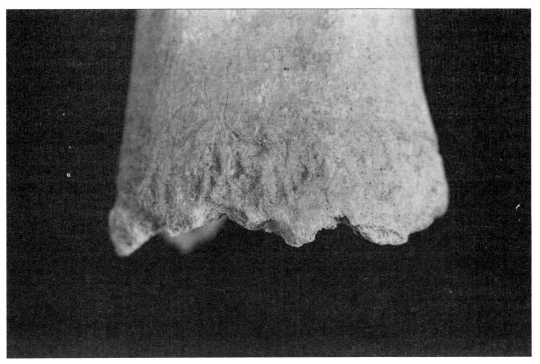

Fig. 5.5. *Typical canid gnawing on the distal end of the shaft of a cattle tibia.*

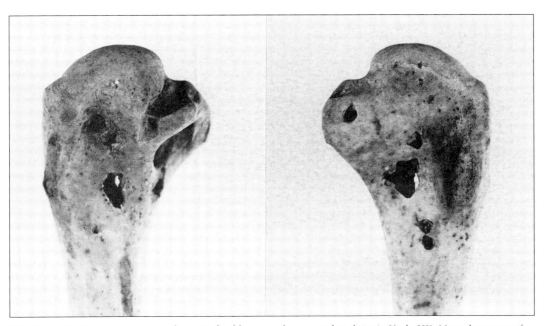

Fig. 5.6. *Typical cat gnawing on a domestic fowl humerus from a medieval site in York, UK. Note that some of the tooth-marks occur in closely spaced pairs, matching the two cusps of the cat's carnassial teeth.*

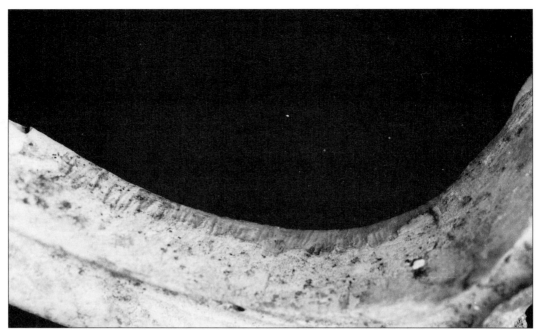

Fig. 5.7. A good example of rat gnawing damage on a cattle rib bone from a post-medieval site in York.

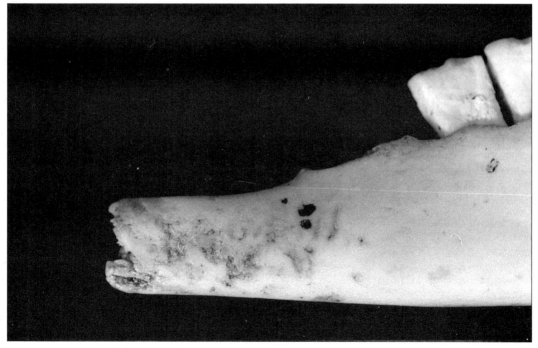

Fig. 5.8. An example of damage produced by sheep gnawing a sheep bone, in this case a modern sheep mandible from Orkney.

Slovenia. The bone in question is an immature cave bear femur shaft with two prominent perforations. Microscopic examination of the perforations shows them to be more like cave bear tooth-marks than holes cut with stone tools. Furthermore, similarly perforated bones can be found in bone accumulations from cave bear lairs at which there is no unambiguous evidence for the presence of humans. This example may lead one to think that there is a high degree of inter-observer variability in recognizing different forms of surface modification. However, well-controlled blind tests show that a high degree of agreement between observers can be obtained using only hand-lens and low-power microscopy (Blumenschine *et al.* 1996).

Other surface modifications may merit recording. The trampling of bones on a surface may produce a distinctive pattern of fine striations, generally variable in width and criss-crossing at various orientations (Fisher 1995). Surface striations of a different form can also be produced by the roots of plants, apparently through etching of the bone by acids produced by the roots. Root-etching is usually quite obvious, as the lines produced are irregular and sinuous, sometimes branching, and generally U-shaped in cross-section. This is commonly seen on bones from shallow, superficially buried deposits, and remnants of root may even be found in the etched features.

Medium and Message

There remains the vexed question of the recording methods and medium, an important topic which has generated a certain amount of literature. At one end of the range of techniques, Grigson (1978) offers a perceptive, if brief, review of what ought to be in a report, and advocates the use of *pro forma* recording as a means of summarizing the essential data of how many of which bones of which taxa were in the sample. In sharp contrast, Aaris-Sørensen (1983) presents a computer-based system which allows the recording of great detail about each fragment. A similar specimen-based approach is used by Klein & Cruz-Uribe (1984), and by Shaffer & Baker (1992). As desk-top computers have become generally available, other bone analysts have developed ever more ingenious 'front-ends' for commercial software, adapting them to the recording of animal bones. The widespread availability of computers has facilitated the generation and handling of databases in which each record details an individual specimen, and this is by far the most common procedure.

To illustrate the contrasting approaches, Fig. 5.9 reproduces part of one of the paper *pro forma* records for a sample from Caerleon, and shows how the identity of individual specimens is lost in gaining an overall summary of the sample. In this procedure, data such as dental eruption, measurements, knife cuts and gnawing marks are recorded separately (often on the back of the *pro forma*). Fig. 5.10 shows a few records from a system in which specimens are individually recorded. There is more detail here, though a further level of analysis would be needed in order to gain an overview of the sample.

Neither is the 'better' approach. The circumstances of the research, its aims and objectives, will determine the more appropriate recording procedure. The underlying issue is that of the primary archive. Bone-by-bone recording implicitly sets out to create an archive for subsequent re-analysis, making no presumptions about how data will be grouped or interrogated: posterity can re-analyse the data. That assumes, however, that

SITE: CFB79	PHASE: Bath infill	CONTEXT: 10	SPECIES: Cattle	
BONE	LEFT	UNSIDED	RIGHT	
Humerus	16d 2p 3s	16 frags	26d 3p	Dist. 36f 2u Prox. 1f 1u
Radius	16d 14p	42 frags	13d 8p	
Ulna	10	18 frags	8	
Carpals		22 various		
Metacarpals	11p 9d	40 frags	11p 9d	Dist. 10f 6u
Phalanges I		41 + 3 frags		

Fig. 5.9. Part of a paper pro forma record for a bone sample from Caerleon.

CFB79

10	hum	l	d+s	bos	f	1	Bd 65.3	gnawed (Photo 121/4)
10	hum	l	d	bos	f	1		
10	hum	r	d+s	bos	f	1		charred
10	hum	r	d	bos	u	1		
10	hum	u	s ff	bos		10		
10	hum	r	p+s	ovis	f	1	BFp 31.0	
10	mc3	l	p+s	sus	du	2		
10	fem	u	s ff	sus		8		
10	mand	l		ovis		1	p4 f, m1 h, m2 g, m3 e	

Fig. 5.10. Part of a bone-by-bone record, typical of most zooarchaeological recording.

the initial recording correctly predicted what posterity would want to have recorded, and whether posterity would trust the original record. My own experience suggests that subsequent re-analysis of bone samples is better, and more often, undertaken by going back to the bones themselves. It is, after all, regarded as good practice generally in the natural sciences to collect one's own data for a specific study, not to re-mix and re-heat someone else's. When the proper curation and storage of the bones can be reasonably assured, they constitute the primary archive, not an electronic database of what some previous researcher recorded. In those circumstances, then, it may be quite appropriate for the purposes of a particular study to direct the recording at the level of the sample, not of the individual fragments. Should some colleague wish to reinterpret the bones summarized in Fig. 5.9, they are curated for posterity, and form a far better archive than any paper or electronic record.

Such is the matter of recording. This chapter has deliberately subsumed several different things, notably taxonomic identification and the recording of butchery marks, because they are all a part of the process of describing the bones on the bench. We describe specimens in part to categorize them for subsequent analysis, and in part to retrieve the different forms of data inherent in them, each of which conveys information about the original animal, its life and death, its interface with people, and the complex events and processes which have led to its survival as an archaeological specimen. In the next five chapters we proceed to the next stage of analysis, taking different categories of these data and manipulating and investigating them.

SIX

COUNTING BONES AND QUANTIFYING TAXA

'I really can't be expected to drop everything and start counting sheep at my time of life. I hate sheep.'

Dorothy Parker, *The Little Hours.*

Tables of numeric data and their manipulation seem to arouse strong feelings, usually of fear and loathing. However, in studying our bone assemblages, we want to know not only what taxa can be identified, but which of them are particularly abundant, and whether that pattern of abundance persists throughout an extensive or deeply stratified site. If our assessment of abundance is to be objective, we have to convert the piles of identified bones into numbers, and to understand those numbers. As a result, this is a technically detailed, rather solid, chapter. However, quantification is an important part of the analysis of animal bone samples, and must be mastered in some detail if the quality and limitations of published data are to be understood. So don't skip this chapter – it matters.

The deceptively simple process of establishing 'how much' there is of different identifiable taxa in a series of samples can obviously be undertaken in a number of different ways. There have been almost as many different quantification methods applied to bone assemblages as there have been specialists analysing them, and as fast as new methods come into the literature, other papers show up their shortcomings and recommend their rejection. This chapter sets out to consider the more commonly used procedures: those based on raw counts of identified specimens (NISP, TNF); those based on the weight of identified fragments; those based on estimation of the minimum number of individuals in the identified assemblage (MNI); and those which seek to estimate the 'killed population' which has contributed to the assemblage. An important concept to keep in mind from the outset is the distinction between the *reliability* of a technique (i.e. the extent to which a procedure yields the same result on repeated trials), and its *validity* (i.e. the extent to which the procedure measures what it purports to measure) (Carmines & Zeller 1979; Lyman 1982, 343). Our concern here is whether widely used quantification methods are either reliable or valid.

COUNTING IDENTIFIED FRAGMENTS

The simplest way of quantifying an animal bone assemblage would seem to be to count up the number of specimens attributed to each taxon. This procedure is often described as either the Number of Identified Specimens (NISP, which abbreviation is used in this chapter) or Total Number of Fragments (TNF) method. The former term begs the question whether a 'specimen' must be a single bone or a fragment of one, or whether a group of fragments obviously derived from the same bone could comprise one specimen. Similarly, the total is generally of all fragments attributed to that taxon by that analyst, rather than the total number of fragments which could have been attributed to that taxon, given more time or a different attitude to species attribution. In short, the procedure can be used in different ways by different analysts, and the detail of the working method needs to be defined for each analysis if NISP data are to be regarded as reliable.

It can be argued that NISP methods are only valid if they are limited to describing the sample on the bench, rather than the death assemblage from which it was derived, or the original living community. The interpretation of NISP data often steps across the line between the recovered sample and the death assemblage from which it is derived. The different taphonomic histories of different samples will mean that the relationship between the sample and the death assemblage will differ from sample to sample, meaning that we can only rather approximately state what the NISP data are measuring in this respect. Beyond the immediate sample, then, NISP methods lack validity. Another important issue

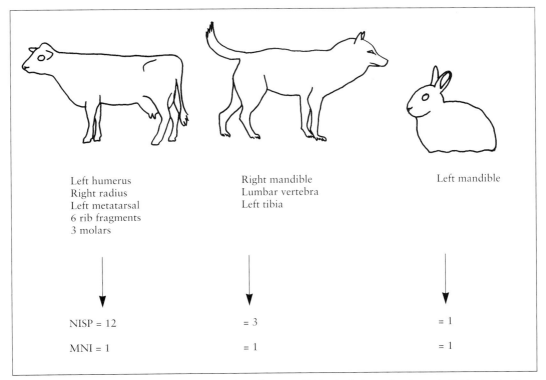

Fig. 6.1. *An illustration of the problem of interdependence in NISP calculation, whereby an individual animal which contributes more than one identifiable bone to the archaeological assemblage will be 'counted' several times over, over-representing that taxon in the NISP data. Because MNI counts are based on non-reproducible elements, an individual cannot be counted twice. But see Fig. 6.2!*

is that of *interdependence* (Grayson 1979, 201–2; 1984, 20–3). NISP methods implicitly treat each recorded specimen as a separate individual. However, some of the bones in a sample may all have derived from the same animal: some individual animals may each be counted many times over in a set of NISP data (Fig. 6.1). Again, this does not matter if the data describe only the sample, but it becomes important if the NISP data are taken as a proxy measure of the original biotic community.

The degree of fragmentation of the sample may complicate comparison between samples where the degree and pattern of fragmentation differ (Chase & Hagaman 1987; Ringrose 1993, 132–3; Noe-Nygaard 1979). As an interesting variant, Watson (1979) describes an alternative to NISP for circumstances where highly fragmented material is recovered. His recommended procedure has been imitated by some subsequent work, but has not been generally adopted, perhaps because the point of the quantification is moved away from animal taxa towards abstract fragment categories.

NISP methods are also inherently biased if some of the taxa involved have more identifiable bones per individual than others (Gilbert *et al.* 1982). For example, a systematic over-estimation of pig remains relative to bovids may result from using raw NISP data, pigs having more toes and teeth than bovids. This effect is obviously more pronounced when NISP data are compared across widely differing taxonomic groupings, as when comparing mammals with birds, and either with fish. Identification protocols become significant, as some taxa may be identifiable on a greater number of elements of the skeleton than others, thus producing a bias which is not simply a consequence of differences in anatomy. Goats, for example, may (or may not) be confidently identifiable on a limited number of skeletal elements which is considerably fewer than the total number of elements in the goat skeleton (Table 6.1).

Table 6.1.   *A dummy set of NISP data, to illustrate some of the problems inherent in this procedure.*

Sheep and goat were only consistently distinguished on a few elements of the skeleton, so the NISP value for goat is depressed. There was evidence for the working of red deer antler on the site, and the NISP for that species is inflated by the inclusion of antler fragments. The NISP for dog is inflated by the inclusion of sixty bones from one skeleton. The 'unidentified large ungulate' bones are probably mostly cattle bones, and 'unidentified small ungulate' are probably mostly sheep (or goat?), but pig bone fragments not positively identifiable as pig could have gone into either taxon or both.

Taxon	NISP
Horse	25
Cattle	375
Sheep	250
Goat	51
Red deer	75
Pig	120
Dog	102
Cat	30
Unidentified large ungulate	150
Unidentified small ungulate	85

Among European freshwater fish the common eel *Anguilla anguilla* may be identifiable by every one of its numerous head bones and scores of vertebrae, while a cyprinid such as the roach *Rutilus rutilus* may only be identifiable to species by its pharyngeal teeth. In this case, raw NISP data may over-represent the abundance of eels relative to roach by a factor of twenty or thirty. The obvious compromise is to compare taxa only by a limited set of elements by which all of them may be confidently identified. In reality, it would be quite difficult to nominate such a set for bovids alone, never mind a more taxonomically diverse sample, and the consequence would be that the great majority of the sample would be discounted for the purposes of quantification.

Gilbert & Singer (1982, 31) amusingly described NISP procedures as 'ideal for ideal samples only', and NISP has fallen out of general use in palaeontology (Holzman 1979, 79–80). On the brighter side, Gautier (1984) has suggested that interdependence may be less of a problem than we think, because taphonomic attrition is so high in many samples, so reducing the probability of any one individual contributing more than one fragment to the recovered assemblage. Gautier also expresses an irrational point of view with which many of us might privately agree: 'My own experience . . . also suggests, at least to me, that fragment counts work.' (Gautier 1984, 245). One's assessment of whether something works depends upon one's objectives in using the procedure in the first place. And we return to the question of validity: if NISP procedures work, then for what purpose? It is particularly significant that two of the most thorough published reviews of quantification methods reject NISP methods (Grayson 1984; Ringrose 1993), although Winder (1991, 116) allows that NISP may at least serve to show the rank order of taxa. If that is the only valid use of NISP methods, one might legitimately ask, then why bother with precise quantification at all? The answer is that, although rank order of taxa may be adequate for some purposes, there is a big difference between a sample in which the first-ranking taxon comprises 90 per cent of identified specimens, and one in which the first rank comprises only 35 per cent of identified specimens. Quite what that difference *means* in terms of past animals and people, is another, more complex, question.

WEIGHING IDENTIFIED FRAGMENTS

An alternative to counting all of the fragments attributed to each taxon is to weigh them instead. Large-bodied taxa will clearly be seriously over-represented if quantified by weighing: the skeleton of one horse will be many times the weight of the skeleton of one rabbit. However, the relationship between the weight of the skeleton and the weight of the whole live animal is much the same in the cow, the horse, the cat and the rabbit, and herein lies the attraction of quantification by weighing. The procedure was first explained in print by Kubasiewicz (1956), using an example in which the aim of the study was to assess the relative contribution to the diet of each of a number of mammalian prey species. This context is important, as it shows that quantification by weight was developed with regard to hunted wild animals, in order to quantify relative meat contribution. Kubasiewicz argued that as a predictable and sufficiently constant proportion of the weight of a mammal is its skeleton, and another predictable and sufficiently constant proportion is potentially edible muscle, then comparing the relative abundance of taxa by weight of bone fragments would give an estimate of their potential dietary contribution in the form of meat.

The objections to quantification by weight are many and varied. Chaplin (1971) and Casteel (1978) set about rejecting the method with commendable clarity. The differential destruction and transport of bone fragments of different densities may cause an assemblage to contain a disproportionate amount of dense fragments, thus skewing the meat:bone weight comparison. For example, an assemblage in which loose cattle molars, which are particularly dense, comprised a high proportion of the identifiable fragments would misleadingly indicate a very marked predominance of beef in the diet. There is also the obvious problem of weighing bone fragments, rather than bones plus soil. Some bone fragments can be washed clean with comparative ease, but large volumes of cancellous tissue, such as long bone epiphyses or vertebral centra, may contain quite substantial amounts of sediment which resists removal, even in bones which have been recovered by wet-sieving. There is also a difference between potential meat yield and actual meat usage. In late twentieth-century Britain, for example, it is unusual for the internal organs of fish to be eaten: I will happily eat the roe (i.e. gonads) of most fish species, but draw the line at the liver and swim-bladder, which in other cultures might be considered a delicacy. Differing cultural practices will result in more or less of the carcass of an animal being used, and so quantification by weight can only, at best, quantify potential yield.

There is a more subtle problem, too, with the original assumption that bone weight comprises a constant proportion of the total body weight of an animal (Casteel 1978; Jackson 1989; Barrett 1993). Bigger animals require proportionally bigger bones to support their weight. Barrett (1993, 5) demonstrates that bones comprise about 6 per cent of the body weight of a young lamb, but about 10 per cent of the body weight of an adult cow. Although this allometric scaling effect is quite minor within a narrow range of body weight, it becomes very marked in comparisons of taxa which differ substantially in body size. In short, the relationship between bone weight and body weight is a power relationship of the form $Y = aX^b$ (Alexander *et al.* 1979; Prange *et al.* 1979). Although the value of the exponent *b* may only be quite small, this power relationship none the less precludes comparing the meat yield of, say, cattle, sheep and chickens by direct comparison of the weight of fragments identified to those three taxa.

In an heroic attempt to salvage quantification by weight, Barrett (1993; 1994) has devised an ingenious use of the method which takes account of allometric scaling with respect to fish. The body size of fish can be predicted from measurements of their bones with a high degree of accuracy, and conversion of bone measurements to weight at least gives an approximation to the potential meat yield. Barrett has also experimented with the relationship between bone weight and meat yield in fish. Apart from the objections already raised against taxonomic quantification by bone weight, there is the additional problem with fish that identifications are often not possible to species level. However, Barrett has demonstrated general equations linking bone weight to body weight which can be applied across the cod family (Gadidae), so maximizing the amount of data which can be used in the calculation. The problems of taphonomic effects and of cultural variation in utilization still remain, however, and quantification by weight must be seen as applicable only in the special circumstances in which Barrett and a few others have managed to apply it.

ESTIMATING MINIMUM NUMBERS

Precisely because of the problems and distortions inherent in NISP and weight methods, many analysts (though not this one) prefer to estimate minimum numbers of individuals (MNI) (Table 6.2). If all the papers which have been written on this topic were to be laid end to end, they would cover a very great distance, without reaching a conclusion. The introduction of MNI methods to archaeology is generally credited to White (1953a), with subsequent refinements by Chaplin (1971) and Bökönyi (1970). Despite their venerable age, these early papers give a useful insight to the origins of this controversial technique.

Table 6.2. *A worked example to show the estimation of MNI with and without allowance for apparent pairs.*

Suppose that the cat bones in a sample comprise the following:

4 left, 3 right mandibles
2 left scapulae
3 left, 3 right humeri
1 left, 2 right radii
1 right os innominatum
4 left, 5 right femora
3 left, 2 right tibiae
1 left calcaneum

A cat has only one right femur, so there must be a minimum of five cats, assuming that each of the other bones comes from one of the five cats represented by the right femora.

But suppose that we decide that three of the right femora make pairs with three of the left femora. Then we have:

Three cats each represented by a pair of femora
One cat represented by an unpaired left femur
Two cats each represented by an unpaired right femur

Allowing for the three pairs, that gives an MNI of six cats.

The procedure is relatively straightforward, at least on paper. For each taxon in the sample, the specimens of the most abundant skeletal element are sorted into left- and right-side specimens (if appropriate – obviously not if the most abundant element is an unpaired bone such as the atlas). As originally proposed by White, the higher of the left- and right-side counts is then taken as the smallest number of individual animals which could account for the sample: the minimum number of individuals. Other authors have pointed out that this assumes each left-side specimen must pair with a right-side one: if there were no such pairs, then the MNI would equal the sum of left-side plus right-side. White was clearly aware of this point, but wisely dismissed the reconstruction of pairs as 'a great deal of effort with small return' (White 1953a, 397). None the less, most MNI calculations attempt to take account of pairs, requiring efforts to match left- and right-side specimens until the analyst is satisfied that only specimens which derived from the same individual have been paired up, and no others. Unfortunately, in most mammals, the degree of left–right asymmetry within one individual is small, but not non-existent, and in some species is on almost the same scale as the degree of size variation between adult individuals. Thus apparent pairs will arise by chance from bones from different individuals, and pairs from somewhat asymmetrical individuals will not be recognized. My own attempts to match pairs in samples of modern bones in which the true pairs are known have been abysmally unsuccessful, prompting a swift retreat from MNI estimation. Others have more confidence in the procedure, however, and it continues in use.

From the start, there has been a lack of clarity about, and therefore serious misuse of, the raw numbers produced in MNI estimation. A few authors (e.g. Clason 1972, 141) have been careful to stress that MNI is only an estimate, as calculation of the real number of individuals represented in the recovered assemblage is not possible. Donald Grayson (1981; 1984, 28–49) has been especially critical of MNI calculation, stressing our uncertainties over what it measures and hence its validity, and showing that MNI may be closely correlated with sample size (Grayson 1981), and thus with NISP. If, argues Grayson (1984, 62–3), MNI values can normally be tightly predicted from NISP counts, then whatever information resides in MNI data resides in NISP data as well, so why take the extra step of calculating MNI? Another fundamental problem with MNI methods is that rare taxa are always over-estimated. A single specimen attributed to a rare taxon will give an MNI of one, while other taxa with the same MNI might be represented by ten or twenty bones each. Thus MNI estimates for rare taxa are over-estimated relative to NISP counts. This does not mean that either figure is 'right'. In one sense, NISP estimates the *maximum* numbers of individuals, which might be just as valid a descriptor as the minimum.

Aggregation of sedimentary units complicates MNI estimation, as the total MNI obtained for one taxon by totalling estimates based on sub-samples from a fossil assemblage is nearly always much greater than if the fossil assemblage were to be analysed as one sample (Grayson 1979; Watson 1979, 137; Ringrose 1993, 126–8). For example, if one phase of a site is represented by six refuse pits, the MNI estimate for sheep could be calculated by pooling all of the bones from the six pits and examining them as one sample, or by examining the sample from each pit in turn and then summing the six sheep MNI estimates. The latter procedure will almost invariably produce a much higher MNI estimate than the former (Fig. 6.2).

It can be argued that this inflation of numbers is informative, in showing that some individual animals have contributed to the catchment of more than one sedimentary unit, as one might expect if different sedimentary catchments have sampled different (but possibly overlapping) parts of the life-space of an animal (Winder 1991, 113; but see Gilinsky & Bennington 1994). However, this does not overcome the analyst's problem of deciding how to subdivide material prior to making MNI estimates, or how to aggregate the data afterwards, apart from aggregating all the bones from major phases of occupation and re-estimating a MNI value with which to compare estimates from individual samples.

Any further numerical analysis based on MNI estimates should be avoided, as MNI values are not finite numbers, but minimum estimates (Plug & Plug 1990). As 'more than twenty' cannot be added to 'more than ten' in any sensible way, it follows that MNI values derived from any one assemblage cannot be combined with those from any other. The

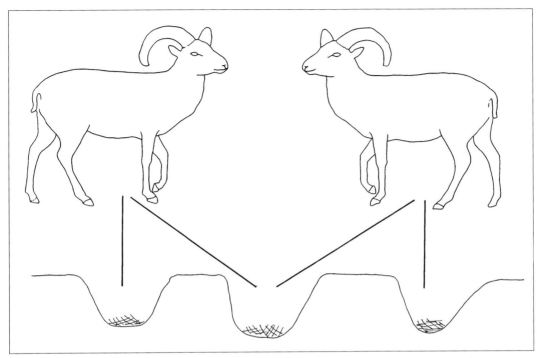

Fig. 6.2. A greatly simplified illustration of the problem of aggregation with MNI estimation. Two sheep are butchered and eaten, and their bones are disposed of with other refuse into three refuse pits. If MNI for sheep is estimated separately for each pit, then the estimates are added together, the aggregated MNI will be 1 + 2 + 1 = 4. However, if all the sheep bones from the three pits were physically aggregated and treated as one sample, the estimated MNI should be only 2.

problem of aggregation is thus simply resolved: the data cannot be arithmetically aggregated, so any aggregation of sedimentary units requires physical aggregation of the bone samples and complete re-analysis. Furthermore, conversion of MNI estimates within a sample to percentage data, to facilitate comparison with another sample, is a mathematical nonsense as it involves the summation of a series of minima. Plug & Plug's concise paper deserves wider attention, as it effectively sinks MNI estimates, showing them to be neither valid nor reliable. None the less, MNI estimates are strikingly robust in at least one sense: despite two decades of criticism and refutation, they are still trotted out by bone analysts as if all of the above had never been written.

ESTIMATING KILLED POPULATIONS

The other group of quantification procedures which merit attention are those which seek to estimate not only the individuals present in the recovered sample, but those which have been lost altogether, in order to estimate numbers in the original death assemblage. It may well be thought that if we have such difficulty agreeing a procedure for calculating the numbers of animals *present* in a recovered sample, then estimating the numbers which have gone missing between death and analysis would be a hopeless task. However, the point of 'killed population' estimates is that what matters for archaeological interpretation is what *was*, rather than what *is*. Just as the interpretation of an occupation site will seek to put posts which no longer exist into extant post-holes, so killed population procedures seek to elucidate the past through quantified inference from extant data.

These procedures are largely based on using any observed disparity in the abundance of paired elements as an estimator for the missing individuals. It is assumed that equal numbers of left- and right-side elements will have entered the death assemblage, and that taphonomic attrition is equally unlikely to destroy left-side as right-side elements. The larger the observed disparity, therefore, the larger the number of pairs of bones which must have entered the death assemblage in order for the disparity to have arisen by chance elimination of left- or right-side elements. In fact, the first premise may sometimes be wrong. If animals are utilized as joints, not as whole carcasses (Chapter 7), then human selection will be involved in the separate deposition of left- and right-side elements. There is no certainty that this deposition will always be random with respect to body side.

Table 6.3. *Calculation of estimated killed-population size using three different published algorithms.*

For a sample of bones of one taxon, let
L = the number of left side specimens
R = the number of right-side specimens
P = the number of apparent pairs
N = the estimated killed population

To calculate N, Krantz (1968) proposes: $N = (R^2 + L^2)/2P$

Using population ecologists' Lincoln (or Petersen) Index, Fieller & Turner (1982) recommend: $N = (RL)/P$

For small samples, Wild & Nichol (1983) prefer: $N = \{((R + 1)(L + 1))/(P + 1)\} - 1$

To compare these algorithms, let L = 20, R = 12.

If P = 2, then Krantz gives N = 133.5, Lincoln Index gives N = 120, and Wild & Nichol give N = 90.

If another observer decides that there are more pairs in the sample, and lets P = 8, Krantz gives N = 34, Lincoln Index gives N = 30, and Wild & Nichol give N = 29.3.

One killed-population procedure was proposed by Krantz (1968), based on counts of left- and right-side elements and apparent pairs – the basic data of MNI estimation. An alternative has been suggested by Fieller & Turner (1982; Turner 1983), based on the logic of biologists' mark-and-recapture methods for population estimation (the Lincoln or Petersen Index). These procedures are summarized in Table 6.3. Poplin (1981) has also proposed the same index, and is enthusiastic about its wide applicability, despite his evident, and rather charming, concern for the distorting effects of anatomically abnormal individuals – 'Attention aux unijambistes, aux moutons à cinq pattes . . .' (Poplin 1981, 161).

However, to ensure validity, the context of each assemblage has to be considered separately in order to decide what killed population the recovered sample represents. This requires at least informal modelling of the depositional processes which brought the bones together in the first place. One outcome of that modelling may be the realization that different taxa arrived through quite different depositional processes, and thus that comparison of killed population estimates within one sample may be invalid. If a large sample gives killed population estimates of 125 white-tailed deer and 37 pronghorn antelope, then what? The data will only be useful if those numbers can be related to a particular human population and a particular period of time, allowing, for example, estimation of numbers of prey per person per year. Such precise attribution of estimated killed populations will be rare, but the figures are otherwise estimates devoid of context.

More mundanely, killed population estimates require the construction of pairs of elements out of a pool of left- and right-side elements. This procedure is fraught with subjectivity and guesswork, and at best produces only a count of enantiomorphic (i.e. appearing to match) pairs, which is taken as an estimate of the number of actual pairs. Unfortunately, both the Krantz and Fieller & Turner algorithms are sensitive to quite small variations in the number of pairs, so the inaccuracy inherent in reconstructing pairs becomes multiplied to give considerable inaccuracy to the killed population estimates (Table 6.3). Killed population methods are thus unreliable, in that repetition of the procedure is unlikely to produce consistent results, and invalid, in that the parameter which is being estimated is poorly defined.

CASE STUDY: TWO BATHS, SOME DOGS AND LOTS OF CATTLE

To illustrate both the application and the weaknesses of some quantification methods, two samples of mammal bones from Roman deposits at Caerleon are summarized in Table 6.4. Sample A is from the back-filling of the large rectangular *natatio*, and is dated by coin evidence to the beginning of the fourth century AD. Sample B is from the fills of a nearby apsidal pool, and is dated to the later years of the fourth century.

Looking first at the NISP data, cattle bones clearly predominate in both samples. In sample A, cattle bones are nearly six times as abundant as the next most abundant taxon (dog), and over four times as abundant as dog in sample B. Compare this with the MNI data. In sample A, the disparity between cattle and dog is of a similar order as in the NISP data (nearly five times as many cattle) but not in sample B (less than twice as many). Can we infer from this anything about the two death assemblages involved?

First, we might note that each of the cattle 'individuals' estimated for B is represented by nearly 100 fragments (i.e. 2534/26) compared with about 29 fragments (657/23) in A. Reviewing the original data, fragments of long bone shaft comprise over one-fifth of cattle NISP in B, but only about one-tenth in A. Perhaps these fragments, which make no contribution to MNI estimation, have skewed the NISP figures? Clearly they have, but not enough: removing long bone fragments from cattle NISP counts reduces 'fragments per individual' to 26 in A and 77 in B, still a big difference. Perhaps MNI in A has been boosted by the deposition of a number of heads or feet, or some other body part that has contributed numerous individuals in just a few fragments? This is a more plausible explanation. MNI for cattle in A is based on 23 right scapulae. There are 21 left scapulae, but counts of limb elements are all 10 or less. In B, the MNI estimate derives from 26 right humeri, with 24 right scapulae, 20 left calcanea, and so on in a more equitable distribution of numbers. The differences between these two samples in the relationship between cattle NISP and MNI appear to have arisen because of differential deposition of body parts, and we return to these data in the next chapter.

Table 6.4.   *Mammal bones from two deposits at Caerleon fortress baths, Gwent. Sample A is dated to the beginning of the fourth century* AD; *sample B to the late fourth century.*

NISP

	Sample A	Sample B
Horse	25	13
Cattle	657	2534
Sheep	51	193
Goat	1	–
Red deer	15	8
Roe deer	3	–
Pig	100	257
Dog	118	604
Cat	15	9
Human	7	3

MNI

	Sample A	Sample B
Horse	2	2
Cattle	23	26
Sheep	4	9
Goat	1	–
Red deer	4	2
Roe deer	2	–
Pig	5	14
Dog	5	18
Cat	2	2
Human	1	1

At the other end of the abundance scale, we can also see the inflation of MNI relative to NISP in rare taxa. In sample A, two roe deer are represented by just 3 bones, while the two horses are represented by 25 bones. In fact, a strict MNI estimate for these horses would give only one individual, an immature individual represented by unfused limb bones and deciduous teeth. However, the sample also contains an upper first molar too far worn to have come from an immature animal. Thus we have one horse represented by 24 specimens, and one represented by a solitary tooth. Similarly, the MNI estimate for pigs in sample B is based on the most abundant element: fourteen left mandibles. An analysis of the state of tooth eruption and wear in all 25 of the left and right mandible specimens indicates the presence of nineteen individuals. Which MNI estimate is 'right'? Neither of them, of course, but the lower figure was arrived at by a procedure more analogous to that used when the most abundant element is part of the post-cranial skeleton. Fourteen it is then, but the pig mandibles show how unreliable such estimates can be.

This analysis has pulled just a few details out of the Caerleon data in order to illustrate the importance of not taking NISP or MNI figures at face value. Neither is 'right', and a useful archaeological interpretation will often only arise from a careful dissection of the published figures.

OTHER MEANS TO SIMILAR ENDS

Research into animal bone quantification has largely succeeded in making it more problematic, and impenetrable to the non-specialist. Clearly there is some information resident in the different numbers of fragments identifiable to different taxa, and equally clearly whatever quantification method is used will introduce its own distinctive 'noise' to mask that signal. Some analysts will take NISP data at face value, but will only regard as significant quite large variations and differences in those values. Thus an increase in sheep between phases from 25 per cent to 40 per cent NISP would be regarded as worthy of comment, while an increase from 32 per cent to 37 per cent NISP might not be trusted as a 'real' difference.

Table 6.5. *Two imaginary samples compared in terms of the number of identified specimens modified to percentages (NISP%), and those percentages re-expressed as their natural logarithms ($\log_e$NISP%). The log-transformed data enhance the inter-sample differences in the less abundant taxa, making clearer the marked difference in relative abundance of cat, goose and hare.*

| | NISP% | | $\log_e$NISP% | |
	Sample 1	Sample 2	Sample 1	Sample 2
Cattle	37	38	3.61	3.63
Sheep	28	24	3.33	3.18
Pig	18	15	2.89	2.71
Horse	5	2	1.61	0.69
Cat	5	8	1.61	2.08
Goose	3	6	1.10	1.79
Hare	4	7	1.39	1.95

There are two problems (at least) with this approach. The first, and most obvious, is that in the example given above, a 15 per cent difference is regarded as 'real', while a 5 per cent difference is not. What about 10 per cent? The answer to that question is wholly subjective. The second problem is one of scale. If we only trust numerically large differences in NISP, or MNI, or whatever, then our interpretation of groups of assemblages may tend to be over-focused on the numerically abundant taxa. It is unlikely, for example, that an increase in crocodile bones between phases from 2.5 per cent to 4 per cent NISP would be regarded as important, yet it is an increase of the same proportion as the 'significant' increase in sheep cited above. One way around this problem may be to depress the higher values through log-transformation of the data, and Table 6.5 gives an example of such a procedure.

An alternative is to experiment with semi-quantitative forms of quantification. People who study plant remains from archaeological deposits only rarely concern themselves with counting every last chaff fragment or fig seed. Semi-quantitative categories are used instead, whether vernacular (few, some, many) or locally defined, such as integer values of abundance on a four-point scale (see, for example, Kenward & Hall 1995). Semi-quantitative scaling has certain advantages. One is that it removes the need to make detailed decisions about, for example, small diaphysis fragments, or the need to count every last fragment of rib. Once the fragments have been sorted by taxon, the fragments attributed to each taxon can be placed in a semi-quantitative category without exact counting. This may seem arbitrary, but the boundaries between categories on, for example, a four-point scale can be simply defined. It may even be appropriate to consider defining categories on different criteria for different taxa. Taxa which are only confidently identifiable on a few elements of the skeleton may be recorded as 'abundant' on the basis of fewer identified specimens than another taxon in the same assemblage. In some cultural contexts, an assemblage in which cattle bones comprise 40 per cent of identified fragments would be unremarkable, whereas cat bones comprising 40 per cent of fragments would catch the attention. At 40 per cent NISP, cats are very abundant indeed, while cattle are not. The ecology of different species will also affect our perceptions of abundance. Herbivores should always be more abundant than carnivores of similar body size, on simple grounds of energy attenuation through successive trophic levels. Table 6.6 shows a means of tabulating both the relative abundance and relative frequency of taxa on semi-quantitative scales.

Table 6.6. *Taxa represented in fifty-three sieved samples from eighth/ninth-century* AD *deposits at 46–54 Fishergate, York (O'Connor 1991a, 254–67), tabulated according to their frequency and abundance.*

Common = present in more than two-thirds of samples examined
Frequent = present in less than two-thirds but more than one-third of samples
Occasional = present in less than one-third of samples
Usually numerically abundant = comprising at least 25 per cent of NISP in at least two-thirds of samples
Occasionally numerically abundant = comprising at least 25 per cent of NISP in at least some, but less than two-thirds, of samples.
Never numerically abundant = never comprising 25 per cent of NISP in any samples.

The table gives more information than a simple list of NISP, showing, for example, that house mouse bones were distributed around the site in quite a different pattern from those of cat, and goose bones differently from those of hens.

	COMMON	FREQUENT	OCCASIONAL
USUALLY NUMERICALLY ABUNDANT	cattle, fish, sheep	–	–
OCCASIONALLY NUMERICALLY ABUNDANT	frog, red deer	–	house mouse
NEVER NUMERICALLY ABUNDANT	pig, hen	cat, goose	dog, goat, fox, horse, human, shrews, snakes

There is still a great deal of room for imaginative thinking in animal bone quantification, though the first necessity may be to shed much of the methodological baggage which currently encumbers the topic. NISP counts have their place, but it is as a description of the sample rather than as an estimator of any population parameters. MNI values have little to recommend them, and killed population estimates raise more questions than they resolve.

As this chapter has already pointed out, taxonomic quantification is only a first stage in enumerating the sample, and may not be the most informative. In cultural settings where a few taxa of domestic animals provided the great majority of the utilized meat, there may be far more information in studying which elements of those few taxa entered which deposits than in trying to estimate how many sheep or pigs a particular sample represents, and the next chapter turns to the matter of body-part representation.

Seven

Out on a Limb:
Body-Part Quantification

We saw in the previous chapter that in order to understand the data quantifying the 'amount' of each different taxon in the assemblage, we also need to quantify how much we have of each different skeletal element of each taxon. This chapter considers how these data can be obtained, and what the limitations are to this form of analysis.

When humans farm or hunt animals, the utilization of that resource involves killing and (usually) dismembering the animal, and often involves the selective removal of some parts to a location other than the kill-site. In undertaking these activities, humans are acting as thanatic and perthotaxic agents (Chapter 3), and we may infer information about the killing and butchering of the animals from the distribution of different body parts. To take a simple theoretical example, a hunter-gatherer group will hardly fail to note that mammals carry far more useful meat and fat on some parts of the carcass than others. As it is likely that animals will be hunted and killed at some distance from the home-base of the group, decisions will have to be made about which parts of the carcass it is worth taking back home. With a large ungulate, it might be smart to remove the head and feet at the kill-site and to leave them behind. These parts of the carcass carry relatively little useful meat or fat, compared with the shoulders or haunches. In this simplistic example, we would expect a kill-site to have large numbers of head and foot bones, and few bones from the meatier parts of the carcass. Conversely, the home-base site would have an abundance of limb and girdle bones, and a dearth of head and foot bones.

This is very simple, and makes all sorts of assumptions about what constitutes a more or less useful part of the carcass. However, a number of archaeological examples show just such a simple division of body parts. A particularly clear example is given by Theodore White (1953b; 1954), in the series of reports in which he developed what was to become the basis of MNI calculation (Chapter 6). In his investigation of two village sites near Pierre, South Dakota, White questioned how the size of bison might affect their butchery, as a half-tonne bison 'must necessarily be butchered where it is killed' (White 1953b, 160). White tabulated the numbers of various elements of the bison skeleton found in the two sites in a manner similar to that widely used today; for example, counting limb bones as separate proximal and distal ends, counting only the prominent proximal end of the ulna. The most abundant element (distal end of the tibia) was taken to indicate the minimum number of butchered animals, and other elements were considered in terms of how far they deviated from the count for the distal end of the tibia.

White's analysis would be familiar to anyone who has made a similar study of large bovid bones: abundant mandibles and distal tibiae; scarce proximal tibiae and proximal humeri. Much of this White explains in terms of butchery and utilization of the carcass. The dearth of proximal ends of humeri is explained by the re-use of this element as a tool, and by the smashing of this part of the skeleton in the preparation of bone grease. Thoracic vertebrae (listed as *dorsal vertebrae*) are scarce, and White speculates that these were left at the butchering site, and not brought to the village. Similarly, numbers of distal radii and proximal metacarpals are roughly the same, but much below the counts for more abundant elements, leading White to suppose that the front foot was detached by cutting through the carpus or through the distal part of the radius, with the heavy and relatively inedible foot then left at the butchering place.

In his 1953 paper White showed how an analysis of body-part representation could lead to inferences about human utilization of the carcass. In a later paper White (1954) went on to compare the different body-part distributions seen in large- and small-bodied prey, relating these differences to the greater need to avoid transporting low-utility parts of a large animal: the feet of a bison constitute a serious load, whereas those of an antelope weigh little. It may seem a little eccentric to illustrate the principles of body-part analysis with examples from the 1950s. However, White's work on Native American sites in the Plains gave this area of animal bone studies a particularly clear and well-argued starting point, and the influence of his work can be traced through many later studies. For example, at the Olsen-Chubbuck site, Wheat (1972) identified stacks of articulated limbs and part-carcasses distributed around the immediate location of the kill, and was even able to show that the less accessible carcasses towards the bottom of the mass kill were subject to minimal, or even no, butchering, presumably as the amount of meat already recovered reached the maximum which the hunters could immediately utilize or store. We return to the Olsen-Chubbuck site in Chapter 12.

WAYS OF PROCEEDING

As with the quantification of taxa, there cannot be said to be a recommended procedure for the quantification of body parts, more a series of guidelines which are open to interpretation according to the material in hand and the research questions to be addressed. The obvious first step is to define the subdivisions of the mammal or bird body which will be used for the analysis. This subdivision may be quite coarse (fore limb, hind limb, vertebrae and ribs), or based on whole skeletal elements (humerus, femur, scapula), or based on the fragment classes in which disarticulated archaeological material is more usually recovered (distal humerus, proximal femur, ilium+acetabulum). Fig. 7.1 shows a range of degrees of fragmentation of one skeletal element.

Although this last approach has the obvious advantage of subdividing the material in the same way that bones tend to fragment, it generates a large number of categories, with relatively few specimens in each, producing a dataset which it is difficult to grasp and digest. One way around this is to use anatomically narrow categories, but only a limited number of them, so excluding from the analysis much of the recovered sample. This procedure may be advantageous in some circumstances, and we return to it below.

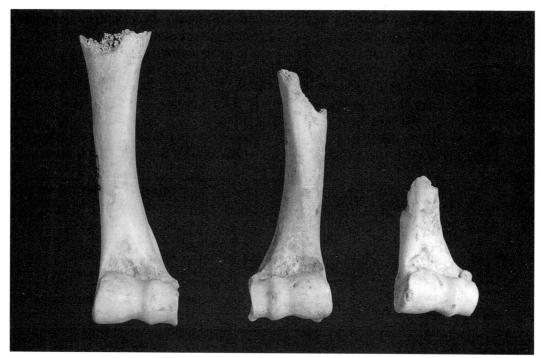

Fig. 7.1. A series of specimens of sheep humerus in varying degrees of fragmentation, to show the flexibility required in recording procedures. The specimen on the left lacks only the proximal epiphysis; that in the centre lacks some of the shaft as well. Would these two be recorded as different fragment categories? The specimen on the right includes only a little of the shaft: would that be enough to count as more than just the distal epiphysis?

Subdividing by whole elements is only really useful in those unusual circumstances where whole bones comprise a substantial proportion of the sample. This may sometimes be the case with samples of bird and fish bones, but is rarely so with mammal bones. Subdividing by still larger anatomical units may be useful for some analyses of butchering procedure, but tends to necessitate quantification by finer anatomical units first, before conflating several smaller units to obtain a total for, say, the fore-limb.

In all cases, there are problems inherent in the counting procedure. If we are attempting to quantify, for example, all cattle humerus specimens, do we include shaft fragments? These may be confidently identifiable as cattle humerus, but the possibility of counting one humerus several times over may necessitate taking some decision as to the 'minimum number of shafts' represented by the shaft fragments. This immediately gets us into the same arithmetical problems as are inherent in MNI estimates (Chapter 6), and still leaves open the question of whether a distal end with 25 per cent of the shaft counts only as one distal humerus, or as one distal humerus and one shaft fragment. Loose teeth similarly require expedient decisions to be made: to count each molar separately, or group them into upper and lower molars, or just pool all loose molars? The answer to such questions will depend in part on the quality and quantity of the material, and on the purpose of the analysis.

In the end there is much to be said for defining a limited number of unambiguous, anatomically explicit categories. After all, if we are looking for evidence that body parts have been differentially moved and deposited, it is only necessary that the analysis includes sufficient elements to represent the major zones of the body. This approach has been proposed, and used with some success, by Davis (1987, 35–6; 1992). Similarly, if our concern is to look for possible effects of taphic and anataxic factors, we may only need to ensure that a range of large and small, robust and fragile elements is included in the analysis. It is seldom necessary to accommodate all identifiable specimens in a body-part analysis, and such a 'book-keeping' approach will usually only result in an over-complex dataset in which the useful information is hard to spot. There is a counter-argument that by selecting a limited list of elements to count we are limiting the information which we can infer. In theory this is so, but in practice many parts of the skeleton are so problematical in terms of definition and counting that their inclusion is unlikely to add anything to the analysis other than some ambiguous and questionable numbers.

Eventually, we arrive at a dataset which consists of a simple list of numbers of specimens for each of a limited list of anatomical elements. This list will then need modification, to allow for the fact that some elements occur more often in the skeleton of one individual than some others. For example, we cannot directly compare counts of 'cattle distal humerus' with 'cattle first phalanx', because one individual will have only two distal humeri (one left and one right), but eight first phalanges (one per toe; two toes per foot; four feet). The simplest modification is to divide the raw count for a skeletal element by the number of times that element occurs in the skeleton of one individual; hence one for cattle axis vertebra, two for distal humerus, eight for first phalanges. The modified counts can then be directly compared. (From here on, the term *modified count* refers to body-part counts that have been modified as described here to account for the number in one individual.)

Table 7.1 gives an example of this procedure. Modification of the data will be necessary when making comparisons across species. For example, a body-part analysis for roe deer would take the total number of distal metacarpals, and divide that total by two (two metacarpals per deer). In order to compare those figures with wild boar in the same assemblage, we would need to make allowance for the more complex anatomy of the boar foot. Pigs have four metacarpals per foot, two of which (the third and fourth) are very much larger than the others (the second and fifth). In order to obtain data which are directly comparable with those for roe deer, we might count all boar metacarpals and divide by eight. Alternatively, we might decide only to count the large third and fourth metacarpals, and to divide the total by four. Either option would give modified counts directly comparable with those for the roe deer.

Data such as those given in Table 7.1 can be read and understood fairly readily, though it is a subjective decision as to which elements are regarded as 'over abundant' and which as 'under represented'. White's (1953b) original approach to this was to regard all counts as under represented compared with the most abundant element in the sample, but this assumes that the deposited assemblage comprised anatomically complete animals, from which some elements have been preferentially deleted by taphonomic processes. It is quite possible that human activities at the thanatic and perthotaxic stages could result in a deposited assemblage which is supplemented with respect to certain particular elements (O'Connor 1993b, 64–5), and for this over-abundance of certain elements still to be detectable in the recovered sample. What we need, then, is an analytical procedure which establishes a norm for the sample against which both over- and under-abundance of elements can be assessed. And that requires some arithmetic.

Table 7.1.   *Part of an imaginary body-part analysis for cattle bones.*

The raw counts per element are modified to allow for the different numbers per individual. This sample has fewer proximal humerus specimens than we might expect. That does not indicate that the whole shoulder area is under represented, because we have a reasonable number of scapulae. What is particular about the proximal humerus? It is a big piece of spongy bone. So is the distal end of the radius, and that is rather under represented too. Maybe something has happened to this sample that has preferentially damaged spongy bone elements, rather than dense, robust elements such as the distal end of the humerus. That could be an anataxic process, such as redeposition of bones, or a perthotaxic process such as the gnawing of bone refuse by dogs. Perhaps we should look for tooth-marks on the surviving specimens?

Element	Number in sample	Number per individual	Modified count
Cattle axis	4	1	4
Cattle scapula articulation	10	2	5
Cattle proximal humerus	3	2	1.5
Cattle distal humerus	18	2	9
Cattle proximal radius	12	2	6
Cattle distal radius	7	2	3.5
Cattle first phalanges	56	8	7
Cattle proximal femur	13	2	6.5
Cattle distal tibia	16	2	8

One means of establishing a figure against which to assess the modified counts is to total the modified counts for all of the elements in the dataset, then divide that total by the number of elements to obtain the mean modified count per element. If our concern is to examine the degree of disparity in the numbers in the sample, then this mean value can be taken as the 'expected' number (E), if all elements were equally represented. Then, if the modified count (O) for each element is divided by this mean number, we obtain an 'observed/expected' value (O/E ratio). An element for which the O/E ratio exceeds 1 is over-represented in the sample, and an element for which the O/E ratio is less than 1 is under-represented. Obviously, minor deviations of this ratio from 1 tell us very little. In any sample, the O/E ratio will have a mean of 1, and a range of values dispersed around that mean. A simple way of filtering the data, then, is to calculate the standard deviation of the O/E ratio for that sample, and to focus attention on those elements for which the O/E ratio lies more than one standard deviation above or below the mean. This will normally be one-third of the elements in the analysis, and they may or may not be symmetrically distributed above and below the mean. Table 7.2 gives a worked example of this procedure, which is actually simpler to undertake than it is to describe.

Table 7.2.   *Cattle bones from a medieval sample from York, used to illustrate the analysis of body-part representation. Data from Bond & O'Connor (1999).*

Column O gives counts for each of twenty elements, modified where appropriate for the number of times that element occurs in one individual. The total for the sample (705) is divided by the number of elements in the list (20) to give an expected value E, if specimens in the sample were evenly distributed across all of the elements. The ratio O/E (i.e. O/35.25) is calculated for each element, then the standard deviation of O/E is calculated. This is used to identify which elements lie more than one standard deviation above the mean (in **bold** type) or one standard deviation below the mean (italics).

The contrast between the proximal and distal ends of the humerus is particularly clear, as are the low values for the distal end of the radius, and the more friable skull elements (horncore and maxilla). Much of the patterning in these data thus seems to be related to the density or otherwise of the elements, and so may mostly have arisen as a consequence of preferential destruction of elements by scavengers.

Element	O	O/E
Horncore	*12*	*0.34*
Maxilla	*18*	*0.51*
Mandible	34	0.96
Scapula	42	1.19
Humerus, proximal	*20*	*0.57*
Humerus, distal	**54**	**1.53**
Radius, proximal	43	1.22
Radius, distal	*19*	*0.54*
Ulna	36	1.02
Metacarpal, proximal	34	0.96
Metacarpal, distal	29	0.82
Pelvis, acetabulum	**55**	**1.56**
Femur, proximal	47	1.33
Femur, distal	31	0.88
Tibia, proximal	31	0.88
Tibia, distal	**58**	**1.65**
Astragalus	45	1.28
Calcaneum	37	1.05
Metatarsal, proximal	32	0.91
Metatarsal, distal	28	0.79
Total	705	
E(=Total/20)	35.25	
Standard deviation of O/E		0.36
±1σ range		0.64-1.36

Tabulation of the data, as used in Tables 7.1 and 7.2, gives a fully quantified overview of the data. A useful form of graphical presentation is to arrange the elements in rank order. This allows rapid recognition of the most over- and under-abundant elements, and gives a visual impression of the fall-off of abundance with rank (Fig. 7.2). This fall-off may be of some importance. There is, for example, an obvious difference between a sample in which five or six elements comprise the overwhelming majority of the sample, with the remaining elements each represented by only one or two specimens, and one in which the fall-off from most to least abundant element is very gradual. We might suspect in the former case that the deposited assemblage was heavily supplemented by the abundant elements, with the relatively scarce elements representing a 'background' component of bones acquired during deposition, anataxic reworking, or during excavation and sampling.

A graph such as Fig. 7.2 obviously lends itself to numerical analysis, and we might be tempted into quantifying the gradient of the fall-off of abundance with rank. Though not wishing to discourage objective numerical analysis of animal bone data, I have never undertaken such a step, in part because it places unrealistic requirements on the quality of the original data, but largely because it is the changes of gradient in fall-off, the breaks in the curve, from which the most useful information may be inferred. In the instance described above, the group of abundant elements which represent the activity that brought about deposition in the first place may be separable from the 'background' component by noting either a distinct change of gradient or a sharp break in the fall-off (Fig. 7.3).

Whether we present our data in tables or graphs, one essential step is to attempt to separate the consequences of excavation and recovery from those of earlier stages in the taphonomic history of the sample. To a large extent, we proceed by inspection and inference. If the elements at the 'scarce' end of the distribution are mostly small but have little else in common, then some sullegic effects must be suspected, biassing the sample against smaller specimens. On the other hand, if our scarce elements are predominantly those which consist largely of cancellous bone (e.g. proximal humerus, distal radius, proximal tibia), we might more reasonably suspect that scavengers before burial and taphic processes afterwards have inequitably affected soft, porous elements (e.g. see Table 7.1).

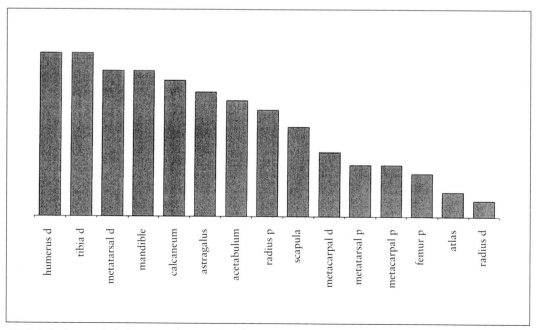

Fig. 7.2. Body part analysis presented as a rank-order curve.

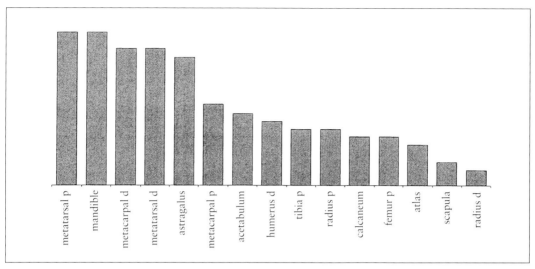

Fig. 7.3. Body-part analysis as rank order curve, showing the interpretation of a sample with a clear break in the curve.

There is an obvious danger of circular argument – of finding an explanation for the observed pattern in the data – and this part of the analysis is better conducted by deciding *a priori* what effect on the data a range of plausible processes may have had, and then to examine the data for some approximation to those predicted effects. Although some general principles may be laid down (scavengers targeting certain sorts of element, excavation failing to recover other sorts), the consequences for the dataset will depend upon the circumstances of that particular sample, not least the taxa which are represented in it.

CASE STUDY: BACK TO THE BATHS

The examination of NISP and MNI data for two samples from Caerleon raised the possibility of differences in the abundance of cattle body parts (Chapter 6). In order to investigate this further, the cattle bones from samples A and B are set out in Table 7.3, subdivided by skeletal elements. Because we are concerned with the relative abundance of major parts of the carcass, limb bones are not subdivided into proximal and distal ends, but as whichever gives the higher 'minimum' number for that element.

Even without further modification, ranking, or graphical presentation, the difference between the two samples is very clear. In A, the fall-off in numbers from most to least abundant is quite gradual. Among the most abundant elements are robust limb bones, the larger tarsals and mandibles. Elements with a high proportion of spongy bone, notably the vertebrae, are distinctly under-represented. Among the limb bones, the femur, which has particularly 'spongy' epiphyses, is the least abundant. In all, sample A looks to have been modified more by taphonomic processes during burial and recovery than by butchery and deposition.

Table 7.3. *Body-part analysis of two samples of cattle bones from Caerleon fortress baths, showing marked differences in body-part representation.*

For each sample, the table shows the number of specimens recorded (n) and that number divided by the frequency of that element in a single individual (O).

Element	Sample A		Sample B	
	n	*O*	*n*	*O*
Scapula	32	16	44	22
Humerus	42	21	9	4.5
Radius	29	14.5	7	3.5
Ulna	18	9	3	1.5
Metacarpal	22	11	14	7
Pelvis	22	11	11	5.5
Femur	17	8.5	2	1
Tibia	25	12.5	6	3
Astragalus	29	14.5	–	–
Calcaneum	35	17.5	3	1.5
Metatarsal	17	8.5	16	8
Phalanges I	41	5.1	14	1.8
Phalanges II	29	3.6	3	0.4
Phalanges III	21	2.6	2	0.3
Horncore	24	12	14	7
Mandible	22	11	33	16.5
Atlas	5	5	5	5
Axis	8	8	2	2
Other cervical verts	27	5.4	13	2.6
Thoracic vertebrae	21	1.6	21	1.6
Lumbar vertebrae	8	8	2	2

Sample B, on the other hand, shows a very marked over-abundance of just a few elements, notably the scapula and the mandible, and to a lesser extent the metapodials. Apart from the scapulae, this could be seen as a 'heads and feet' deposit, and therefore as debris from primary butchering. The abundance of scapulae could be taken to indicate a butchering procedure in which scapulae were removed as part of the initial 'dressing' of a carcass. However, the scapulae lies deep in the shoulder muscles, and it seems unlikely that this bone would have been removed along with the head and feet. The scapulae might therefore represent a separate component to the deposit: a heap of scapulae added to a deposit which already included heads and feet from primary butchering. In fact, just such deposits of cattle scapulae have been noted at other Roman sites (e.g. York; O'Connor 1988b), and appear to be the debris from some specialized preparation of smoked or salted shoulder of beef (Fig. 7.4). As I was unaware of any published parallels when I originally examined the Caerleon material, my interpretation was accordingly cautious. It is reassuring that subsequent work has shown the Caerleon assemblages to be part of a wider pattern, and not some unique phenomenon. Archaeology has quite enough of those.

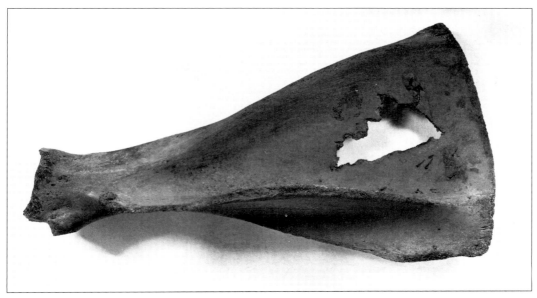

Fig. 7.4. A cattle scapula from Roman deposits in York. The spinus scapuli *has been cut off, and a rough hole has been cut through the blade with the point of a knife, apparently to allow the shoulder to be suspended for some purpose. (Photo courtesy of York Archaeological Trust)*

DISCUSSION

Thus far, we have concentrated on recognizing the butchering of animals for food. However, bone itself can be a valuable raw material, and this may be apparent in body-part analyses. Bird bones are often thin-walled, straight or gently curving tubes, and so make excellent raw material for artefacts such as musical pipes, decorative cylindrical beads, or pointed awls and gouges. For example, Crockford *et al.* (1997) noted a rather high proportion of wing bones of short-tailed albatross (*Diomedea albatrus*) among bones from a pre-European site on Vancouver Island, and suggested that this represented collection of bones for tool-making. Similarly, a difference has been demonstrated between the bird taxa represented among worked and unworked bones at Neolithic sites in the Netherlands, apparently showing that bones for tool-making were deliberately collected from large-bodied species which were not otherwise commonly hunted (van Wijngaarden-Bakker 1997). An exceptional example is Prummel & Knol's (1991) identification of the bones of wading birds among cremated human bones from the early medieval grave field at Oosterbeintum, Netherlands. Specimens of humerus, radius and carpo-metacarpus were variously identified as dunlin (*Calidris alpina*) and stint, either *C. minutus* or *C. temminckii*. It seems that the wings of these waders were cremated with the human body, either as a decorative element in some garment or cover, or as a separate offering placed on the pyre. As the *Calidris* species are all essentially small grey-brown birds, their use in a funerary context indicates some fairly subtle appreciation of the birds by the people concerned.

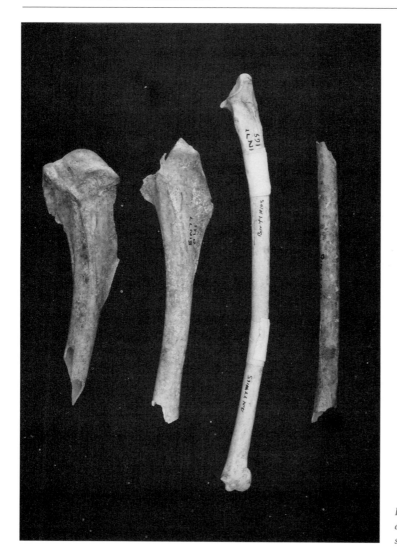

Fig. 7.5. Bones of white-tailed eagle: scavenger, totem or source of feathers?

Within western Europe a series of questions have been raised about the occurrence of bones of white-tailed eagle (*Haliaeetus albicilla*) (Fig. 7.5). This splendid bird was clearly far more widespread within Europe even in the last few centuries, and may have been a familar sight around human settlements into the medieval period (Mulkeen & O'Connor 1997). Reichstein & Pieper (1986) report a number of finds of this eagle from early medieval sites across western and central Europe, and note that some of these sites lie well beyond the recent range of the species. They add that at some sites the records are predominantly of wing bones, and this raises the possibility of eagle wings being traded as a source of feathers, for example for fletching arrows, so taking the bones beyond the range of the species. In a quite different cultural setting, Bökönyi (1978) noted that white-tailed eagle was much the most abundant bird at the Mesolithic settlement at Vlasac, in the Iron Gates gorge of the Danube. Furthermore, a high proportion of the bones were tarsometatarsals and posterior phalanges, and Bökönyi speculates that eagles' feet may have been curated as 'some kind of trophy'.

One final point needs to be made before leaving body-part representation. In the analytical procedures discussed above, and in most of the examples used, we examine our data to see how far they deviate from equal abundance of all elements. How sensible is this? We know that the bones have been buried, decayed and dug up again, and that those processes and more will have affected different elements in different ways, so is there really any sense in using procedures in which the norm is parity of abundance? To some extent, there is none, and our analytical procedures start from a false premise. However, the alternative is to generate theoretical distributions of numbers which express expected abundances of elements in the recovered sample, having made allowance for a range of taphonomic processes and their different effects.

An approach to this form of analysis is seen in the frequent use of a goat bone dataset collected by Brain (1967; 1969) as an 'expected' distribution of numbers against which to compare the observed data. Brain's dataset is from a village where bones were deposited, trampled around and chewed by dogs, so that his data have the effects of trampling and canid scavenging 'built in'. Unfortunately, the pattern of differential destruction noted by Brain was typical of a particular Namib village, given particular ground surfaces, particular population densities of people and dogs, and observing the particular case of what happens to goat skeletons. Given all of that, it is not appropriate to use those data as a comparandum for data from, for example, a Roman well in Yorkshire (Serjeantson 1989, 140), or data from the Maglemosian site at Star Carr, also in Yorkshire (Legge & Rowley-Conwy 1988, 72–3), though in the latter case the authors clearly appreciate this point. Brain's data pertain to one particular set of circumstances, and so too would any other dataset which we attempted to use as a 'standard' against which to compare our archaeological data. In the circumstances, parity of abundance of elements is a naïve basis for our analytical procedures, but at least it is generally applicable and unambiguous.

Lastly, we should note that a number of attempts have been made to approach the analysis of fragmented animal bones from, as it were, a different direction. Notable among these is the procedure reported by Moreno-Garcia *et al.* (1996), which adapts a statistical technique originally developed for the analysis of broken pottery assemblages to a series of intra- and inter-site comparisons of bone samples from sites in London. As the authors point out, the procedure is particularly valuable when used as an heuristic tool, as it allows comparisons to be made between samples on the basis of numerous different combinations of attributes. This is an important general point about body-part analysis: there is no 'right way' to do it, but by applying a wide range of procedures to the same datasets, we can at least see which patterns in the data are inherent to those data, and which are characteristic of a particular analytical technique.

The analysis of the abundance of different body parts is obviously closely related to the quantification of different taxa in the sample, and gives us information about butchering and food distribution practices. In the next chapter, we review a source of information about decision-making at an earlier stage: the selection of prey and the management of domestic herds and flocks.

EIGHT

ESTIMATION OF AGE AT DEATH

At an early stage in the development of archaeological animal bone studies, it was recognized that the age at death of hunted prey and domesticates could yield information about hunting and husbandry strategies. The age distribution of the sample may show a pattern different to that expected of 'natural' attrition of a population of that species (i.e. die-off through old age, disease and misadventure), and that deviation represents selection by the hunters or farmers, and thus human decision-making. The estimation of age at death has generated a great deal of research, principally into better ways of attributing age at death to archaeological specimens.

This chapter consists of a short review of the literature relating to three of the most commonly used techniques for estimating the age at death of mammals, and the archaeological application of those techniques. The three principal techniques reviewed here are the analysis of cementum increments; analysis of the eruption and attrition of the teeth; and analysis of the fusion of the epiphyses of the post-cranial skeleton. Much of what is reviewed in this chapter consists of studies of modern animals. However, our collection and interpretation of archaeological data depends for its reliability and validity on our understanding of the modern analogue data, and it would be irresponsible to review age at death estimation without a careful, critical look at the underlying zoology.

CEMENTUM INCREMENTS

Dental cementum is rather similar to bone in general composition, and serves to hold teeth in their sockets by providing a surface for attachment of the periodontal ligament. It follows, therefore, that the roots of teeth are normally coated with cementum, though in many mammals a coating of cementum extends over parts of the crown as well. As occlusal wear reduces the height of teeth, so cementum is deposited in such a way as to raise the tooth in the jaw, compensating to some extent for the loss of crown height. This is most obvious in such as the apices of the roots, and the base of the crown of multi-rooted teeth, where roots and crown meet. In humans, a clear correlation can be seen between the age of the individual and the thickness of cementum at root apices. This relationship has been used for many years to estimate the age of individuals in forensic studies (Gustafson 1966; Stott *et al.* 1982) though Kvaal & Solheim (1995) cast doubt on this procedure.

In other mammals, use has been made of the fact that incremental structures that appear to have a predictable cycle can be observed in cementum. In humans, ungulates, carnivores and an assortment of other mammals a roughly annual periodicity has been noted. This has an obvious application in archaeology, the only weakness being that the underlying cause of the circum-annual periodicity has yet to be demonstrated with any certainty. A number of successful studies have been made, particularly exploiting the acellular cementum located towards the coronal end of the roots, and Lieberman & Meadow (1992) point out that the number of correlations which have been demonstrated between acellular cementum bands and age in modern populations gives us confidence in their application to archaeological material, even if the underlying biology is imperfectly understood.

Cementum increments are commonly studied in thin-section, using decalcified sections for modern specimens. Archaeological material is often so degraded that decalcification leads to rapid disintegration, and undecalcified sections are generally preferred, usually ground to 30μm thickness (Lieberman & Meadow 1992, 66–70). The examination of polished surfaces of thick sections by reflected light has also been used successfully (Morris 1972; Bourque *et al.* 1978). Stallibrass (1982) reviews the study of archaeological material at some length, and her recommendations concerning practical methods are nicely pragmatic: 'if the section is not clear, try a slightly or radically different method' (1982, 118). In short, any attempt to describe the 'best' practical methods for cementum increment examination would be folly, as much will depend on the species concerned and the state of preservation of the cementum. However, the proliferation of practical methods does raise the question of whether different researchers are seeing and counting the same incremental structures, and a further layer of complexity has been added by the use of image-enhancement techniques (Lieberman *et al.* 1990). Some standardization of terminology and procedures is essential if inter-observer variation is to be minimized (Gordon 1993).

Cementum increments have been routinely used as an age-estimation technique for modern populations of wildlife for a great many years. For example, Novakowski (1965) investigated the correlation between cementum increments on fourth premolar teeth of bison and the age and incisor wear of the same individuals. In bison older than about four or five years, the cementum increments were a good estimator of age. Although satisfactory in its outcome, this study suffered from a problem that recurs in many such studies, namely poor control of the sample. The age of each bison was estimated in roughly half-year classes from the state of eruption of their teeth and the time of year of slaughter. The cementum increments were therefore shown to be a satisfactory means of estimating the age of animals, the age of which was already an estimate. In order to monitor the population ecology of red deer on Rhum, Scotland, Mitchell (1967) examined the correlation between cementum increments and age in known-age deer. The results confirmed the utility of the method, although Mitchell notes that increments were easier to see in some individuals than in others, and that some stags developed narrow, winter-like layers during the rutting season. On roe deer, Aitken (1975) found a good correlation between cementum increments and known age, but had a sample of just nine known-age deer. Disruptions to regular cementum increments may also be introduced by trauma and other factors which induce resorption of tissues (Rice 1980; Quéré & Pascal 1983). A comparison of cementum increments with four other age-estimation techniques on a good sample of fifty fallow deer (*Dama dama*), all from one population, showed that cementum increment counting was less accurate than other procedures, and that the accuracy differed between male and female deer (Moore *et al.* 1995).

A more generalized survey of modern applications was made by Spinage (1973), who is one of the few authors to voice doubts about the 'annual' nature of cementum increments, observing that they may be a rhythmical calcification, which need not be annual (*Ibid*, 178). More recently, Lieberman & Meadow (1992, 65) have questioned whether the optically observed increments are to be correlated with bands of differing degrees of calcification. Looking at the modern literature, there seems to be an uneasy consensus emerging that cementum increment counts are an acceptable estimator of age in some species for certain age ranges. For example, the method works well for California ground squirrels (*Spermophilus beecheyi*) through their first four years of life, but not afterwards, when the annuli seem to deteriorate (Adams & Watkins 1967). Cementum increment counts tend to underestimate the known true age of black bears (*Ursus americanus*) over six years old, and there is minor inter-observer variation in counting the increments (Keay 1996). Roberts (1978) has noted that the apparent age of coyotes studied by this method may depend upon which tooth is sectioned.

Clearly, there are some problems with the general application of cementum increment counting to archaeological material. The procedure is destructive, which may not always be acceptable, and is relatively slow in giving a result from each specimen. The state of preservation of the material may not be conducive to the preparation of sections. In an early archaeological application, Bourque *et al.* (1978) noted that 'Simple sectioning of teeth by grinding or sawing tended to damage the fragile cementum layer . . .' (*Ibid*, 530), and this led them to setting the specimens in a block of epoxy resin, a practice normally followed today. The procedure has acceptable reliability, in that the few published accounts of inter-observer error indicate that repeated measurements give acceptably consistent results, though validity must be called into question given that there are still uncertainties about the physiological basis for the deposition of the forms of cementum which comprise the light and dark (or translucent/opaque) bands. We cannot be quite sure whether what we are measuring (cementum banding) measures what we believe it to measure (regular age increments).

None the less, the analysis of cementum has led to some valuable conclusions regarding the seasonality of occupation of sites. Thin-section examination of gazelle (*Gazella gazella*) teeth from occupation deposits in Hayonim Cave, Israel, showed that Natufian occupation in the cave was either permanent or occurred at least twice per year, in contrast with the preceding Kebaran period occupation (Lieberman & Meadow 1992, 71–4). In terms of the relationship between human sedentism and the emergence of agriculture, this is an important conclusion. Burke & Castanet (1995) examined cementum increments in a known-age series of horse teeth, and used the resulting data to interpret results from Upper Palaeolithic horses from south-western France. They concluded that seasonality of use of sites could be demonstrated in this way, in preference to other sources of data.

The analysis of cementum increments remains a technique which may be valuable in particular circumstances, such as the example quoted above, but unsuitable for routine application to archaeological samples. Until the physiological basis of the increments is fully understood for all of the species to which the technique is applied, there will be questions about its validity. There may be an undue tendency to accept cementum increment counting as objective and valid because it is a technical, laboratory-based procedure: the processes of sectioning, impregnating, polishing and microscopic examination of sections contrast somewhat with the low-tech procedures reviewed below. However, gadgets are no guarantee of validity, and in applying and evaluating cementum increment studies, we must keep in mind simple questions of accuracy, reproducibility and what it is that is actually being measured.

Dental Eruption and Attrition

We expect our children to gain and lose teeth at reasonably predictable ages, and it is intuitively simple to grasp that other mammals do much the same. In order to use the state of eruption of the deciduous or permanent teeth of an individual animal as a guide to its age, we need to know the age at which a given tooth typically erupts. Ideally, the overall dentition of one individual can be examined, and an approximate age at death attributed, on the premise that the timing of dental developments in that individual was not abnormal.

Immediately, two difficult matters of definition need to be addressed. First, there is the question of what constitutes eruption of a tooth. In living mammals this is fairly readily defined as the first appearance of the tooth through the gum, but this is not a definition which can be used with archaeological material. We can decide whether the tooth had, at death, erupted through the alveolar bone of the mandible or maxilla, or decide whether it had grown far enough above the alveolar bone to have reached the occlusal plane of the adjacent teeth (Fig. 8.1). The first of these points will precede the gum-eruption seen in

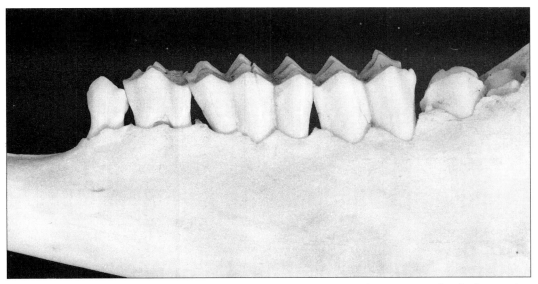

Fig. 8.1. The problem of defining 'erupted'. In this sheep mandible, the second permanent molar (furthest tooth to the right) is in the process of erupting. Although clearly visible above the bone, in a living sheep this tooth would be barely visible above the gum. Thus a state of eruption that is clearly 'erupting' in the dry bone specimen might have been recorded as 'unerupted' in a study of the live animal.

live mammals, while the second will be preceded by it. How long it takes a tooth to go from eruption through the alveolar bone to attaining the occlusal plane will depend upon the species and the tooth concerned. Perhaps the safest definition to use with archaeological material is, in fact, to state when a tooth was in the process of eruption (i.e. between alveolar bone and occlusal plane) at death, and to seek modern data which would allow a probable age range to be put on that process. There are interesting differences between the timing of tooth eruption in cattle as recorded by early nineteenth-century agricultural writers, and that seen in later cattle, and inferred from archaeological specimens (Payne 1984). One plausible explanation for this is to suppose that the early writers were using a different definition of eruption.

The second question to address is to consider what constitutes a normal individual, and so how to define the 'normal' age range for a particular eruption process. Physiological processes within the individual may affect eruption, or the genotypic or environmental circumstances of a population may affect eruption in all individuals in that population. To obtain useful data for archaeological purposes, then, we need to examine the degree of variation in the eruption times for a particular tooth, and to review the factors which may possibly be contributing to that variation. This requirement means that our analogue data need to be of good quality, and a review of the literature shows that this is not always the case.

An important early source is Lesbre (1898). Although principally concerned with the growth and maturation of the post-cranial skeleton, Lesbre's review tabulates typical times of eruption of permanent teeth for humans, horses, cattle, sheep, goats, pigs and dogs. His sources are in part documentary, and these are listed in the paper, and in part the extensive collections of the Veterinary School in Lyon, France, where Lesbre was Professor of Anatomy. There is an ambiguity in Lesbre's tabulation of eruption times. When the author gives, for example, forty to fifty months as the eruption time for the third molar in horses, it is not clear whether this indicates that the tooth takes to take ten months to go through the full process of eruption, or whether it indicates that a particular point of eruption (through the gum?) typically occurs between those ages. One tends to assume the latter, not least because Lesbre gives eighteen to thirty years as the eruption time for the human third molar. In that case, we have no information regarding the rate of eruption, and that rate affects the precision with which any particular tooth gives an age estimate for a given species. None the less, Lesbre's work is important. He was particularly concerned to know how far modern (i.e. late nineteenth-century) husbandry practices might affect skeletal development, a question which is far from resolved a century later. As a part of this discussion, Lesbre tabulates times of eruption of cattle and sheep incisors in normal and precocious animals (*animaux ordinaires* and *animaux extrément précoces*), showing differences of over a year, for example, in the eruption of the third incisor in cattle.

Subsequent studies have leaned heavily on the nineteenth-century sources, not always with sufficient regard for their reliability. Two of the most frequently quoted sources are Habermehl (1961), which is quite critical in the use of earlier sources, and Silver (1969), which is not. Some studies of modern data have been particularly thorough. For example Andrews (1973) gives minimum, maximum, median and mean ages for each of nineteen dental development stages in a sample totalling 778 cattle, and adds the standard deviation of the distribution for each stage, as a measure of the tendency for eruption times to vary between individuals. Andrews' last data table compares his results with previously published data, showing comparatively little difference for most dental stages. The value of his study lies more in its rigour than in overturning prior beliefs, but his concentration on the maxillary dentition reduces the value of his study for archaeology, which tends to concentrate on the usually more complete mandibles.

Dental development in sheep has been studied by a number of authors, and Moran & O'Connor (1994) give a review and add some further modern data. They note the general consistency in times of eruption given by different sources, but note from their own survey a group of individuals all of the skeletally primitive Soay breed in which eruption of the third molar seems to have been delayed by as much as a year. Franklin (1950) reports feeding experiments in which dental development was delayed and disrupted in sheep fed on a deficient diet during early stages of growth, though skeletal development was generally stunted as well, which was not the case with these anomalous Soay sheep. Other sources show that tooth eruption in wild sheep occurs around the same ages as in domestic sheep (Hemming 1969).

Data for dental development and eruption in domestic pigs is given by Wenham & Fowler (1973) and by Ripke (1964). Bull & Payne (1982) give a useful dataset from a population of Turkish wild pigs, and cast doubt on the eruption times given in much of the veterinary literature. Reiland (1978) reviews tooth development in male domestic pigs, including a careful distinction between the time of eruption of a tooth through the alveolar bone, and the time by which the tooth is fully into the occlusal plane, often months later. To widen the range of species, Deniz & Payne (1982) tabulate analogue data from Turkish Angora goats. Similar data have been published for, among others, red deer (Brown & Chapman 1991; Kierdorf & Becher 1997), mule deer (Main & Owens 1995), reindeer (Hufthammer 1995), fallow deer (Brown & Chapman 1990), gazelle (Davis 1980), cats (Berman 1974), otters (Zeiler 1988), buffalo (Frison & Reher 1970), caribou (Miller 1972), Himalayan thar (*Hemitragus jemlahicus*) (Caughley 1965) and collared peccaries (Kirkpatrick & Sowls 1962). This last source is one of the few to mention the physical hazards of examining the teeth of uncooperative live animals: with delightful irony, Ralph Kirkpatrick's address is given as the Arizona Cooperative Wildlife Research Unit!

The state of eruption of the permanent dentition is a useful guide to age at death up to the age at which all permanent teeth are fully erupted. Fig. 8.2 demonstrates the procedure for a sub-adult pig mandible. In most mammals full eruption is attained well before the maximum age attained by that species: in humans, compare full dental eruption by twenty-five years old with the traditional seventy year life-span. After full eruption, age at death attribution uses the fact that teeth are constantly being worn down to estimate age by assessing the degree of dental attrition. The degree of attrition can be assessed in two ways: by direct measurement of the height of the tooth, or by examination of the pattern of dentine exposure produced as the enamel of the occlusal surface is worn away.

Direct measurement of crown height is particularly suitable in herbivorous mammals with high-crowned teeth, as the abrasive, high-volume diet will ensure a considerable rate of loss of tooth crown height, thus giving us something substantive to measure. Crown height measurement has been used as a means of age attribution in red deer, and this study

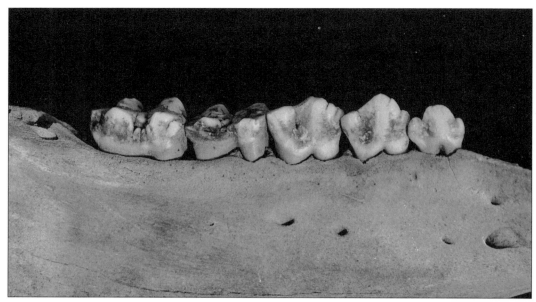

Fig. 8.2. Pig mandible to show the estimation of age at death given the presence or absence of particular teeth. The tooth in the centre of this group is the fourth permanent premolar. It shows very slight traces of attrition, and had clearly just erupted before the animal died. The two teeth to the left of it are the first and second permanent molars, both of which were erupted and in wear. The pig was certainly over 12 months old, and the state of the premolar suggests an age of at least 18 months. At the left-hand end of the tooth row, the third permanent molar is unerupted. As this tooth is normally in wear by about 24 months old, an estimate of 18–24 months would be plausible.

showed that individuals of the same age frequently show appreciable variation in crown height on any particular tooth (Lowe 1967). This rather limits the procedure as a means of attributing age to individual specimens, but might allow individuals to be placed into age categories, and thence to construct an age profile for the population as a whole. The relationship between crown height and age is not linear but exponential, and assuming a linear relationship will over-estimate the age of young individuals, but under-estimate old ones (Spinage 1973, 173–4; Klein *et al.* 1981). Modern data give the best fit when the natural logarithm of crown height is used to predict age. Levine (1982) has published an extensive series of modern data for horses, including graphs of tooth crown height against age with which archaeological specimens can be directly compared to obtain an age at death estimate. Essentially, then, this procedure requires that a sample of specimens of one tooth for the species concerned can be measured with sufficient consistency to give a distribution of crown heights. This can either be calibrated to give estimated age, by means of a regression equation derived from modern data, or used as it is to give an impression of the pattern of mortality.

Recording dental attrition other than by measuring tooth crown heights requires some form of classification of wear stages, and this is usually achieved by noting and utilizing the sequence in which different cusps of each tooth come into wear, and by noting the typical sequence of exposure of dentine as the enamel covering is worn away. Again, this is a form of recording which lends itself quite well to high-crowned ungulates, such as cattle and sheep. Payne (1973; 1987) has devised a method for sheep and goat mandibles, by which dentine exposure is recorded as a series of symbols which give a visual mnemonic for the pattern of dentine exposure on fourth premolars and molars (Fig. 8.3). Different combinations of the attrition states reached by teeth in one mandible then allow that mandible to be put in one of a series of classes, which have approximate age-equivalents based on observations from modern animals.

Grant (1982) has taken a slightly different approach, publishing diagrams of tooth wear stages through which the lower fourth premolars and molars of cattle, sheep and goats, and pigs pass (Fig. 8.3). Whereas Payne's approach is to facilitate the recording of the wear stage observed on the teeth, Grant's procedure requires the specimens to be recorded according to pre-determined categories. That said, the wear stages which Grant illustrates enable the recording of the great majority of teeth in most mandibles of the three most common Old World domestic mammals. My own experience of this procedure, and

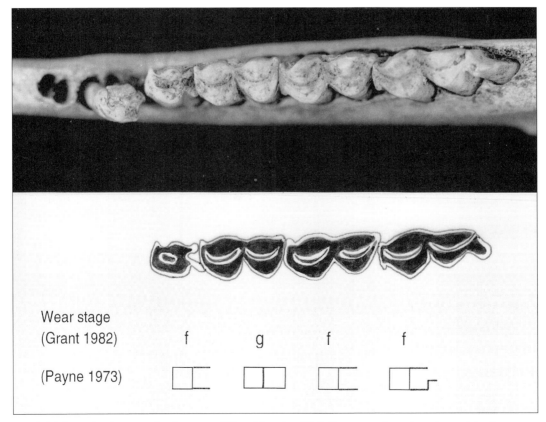

Fig. 8.3. The occlusal aspect of a sheep mandible, with a simplified diagram to show the pattern of dentine (black) and enamel (white) and the corresponding coding of wear stages for the major teeth.

especially of asking several people to record the same sample of mandibles, indicates that the wear stages for cattle and sheep/goats are quite well defined and replicated reliably, while those defined for pig teeth are much less reliably replicated, with quite a high degree of inter-observer variation. This is hardly surprising: the structure of cattle and sheep molars, especially, is well suited to the categorization of wear stages, whereas the intricately wrinkled cusps of pig molars are much more challenging. Ease and consistency of operation are obviously vital to any recording procedure, and Levitan (1982b) details a series of tests on sheep and goat mandibles recorded in different ways, under varying time constraints. Gibson (1993) has succeeded in designing an expert system which allows a computer to allocate sheep mandibles to Grant's wear stages with the same facility as a human observer: one doubts that the same could have been done for pig mandibles.

Though Grant's system is useful as a recording procedure, the subsequent analytical steps are open to criticism on several grounds. Each permanent molar in each mandible in the sample is allocated a tooth wear stage (TWS) according to its resemblance to the published illustrations. Each TWS has a numerical equivalent, including numerical equivalents for stages of tooth formation and eruption. The numerical equivalents for each of the permanent molars in a mandible are added together to give an overall mandible wear stage (MWS). The MWS values can then be used to place the mandibles in the sample into a rank order, which is presumed to be analogous to their order of increasing age. The overall distribution of the MWS values for a sample are taken to be analogous to the overall age distribution. There is clearly a problem when the sample includes numbers of mandibles from which permanent molars are missing. These might have to be excluded from the analysis, thus reducing the sample size and possibly biassing the results if, say, teeth are more likely to have dropped out of the mandibles of elderly sheep than of young sheep. In an attempt to circumvent this problem, Grant has published tables which list the many combinations of TWS values which she has observed on, it must be said, a considerable number of archaeological specimens. The idea is that a specimen which has, let us say, the first and third molars present and recordable can be allocated an approximate, or 'most likely', TWS for the missing second molar, thus allowing the MWS value to be calculated. This introduces an element of approximation to a procedure which is otherwise systematic and apparently objective.

The other objection which can be raised is that a difference of one TWS adds the integer 1 to the MWS total, regardless of what tooth wear stages are involved. It is now quite clear that some tooth wear stages in some species last very much longer than others – Moran & O'Connor (1994) detail these 'standstill stages' for sheep – yet a long-lasting stage contributes the same to the MWS as does an early stage in the eruption process, which may only last for a couple of weeks in the live animal. Because the standstill stages add a particular TWS value to the MWS total, certain MWS totals are more likely to be obtained than are others, imposing inherent patterning on the dataset. One can see why Grant has tried to quantify the complex business of dental attrition, and her wear stage illustrations are widely used, but the remainder of the analytical procedure is less satisfactory.

Whether one uses a procedure such as Payne's, or one more akin to Grant's, or some simple attribution of mandibles to attrition categories according to rather coarse, simple criteria, at some point the attrition stages have to be equated with approximate age categories. This is not an objective process: a Grant MWS total of 32 for a sheep mandible does not automatically convert to a age of x months or years, nor is a mandible of MWS 35 necessarily a certain number of months older than one of MWS 25. Much depends upon the rate of dental attrition experienced by the population from which the sample is derived, and it is obviously important for us to understand how far that rate can vary between populations. For sheep, Healy & Ludwig (1965; Cutress & Healy 1965; Ludwig *et al.* 1966; Healy *et al.* 1967) exhaustively explored the influences on dental attrition in flocks in the Wairarapa and Te Awa districts of New Zealand. In brief, their conclusions were that ingested soil was largely responsible for the excessive wear rates observed at some farms; that the chemical composition of the plants being eaten had no effect; and that the great majority of the attrition occurred in late winter and spring, and could be alleviated by supplementary feeding. More subtle studies of tooth wear in sheep have used the microscopic pitting and scratching of the occlusal surface to characterize the plant materials in the diet, testing, for example, whether a flock has mostly grazed fresh grass or has been fed dried hay (Mainland 1995a; 1995b).

The implications for archaeological studies are that different management practices applied to sheep within one region could produce differences in attrition rates, leading to apparently different distributions of age at death if data from two sites were analysed to a high degree of precision. Something of this sort has been reported by Bond & O'Connor (1999), in a study which shows samples of sheep mandibles from two roughly contemporaneous medieval sites within York to show different rates of dental attrition. The problem lies in deciding which is unusually rapid, or which unusually slow: there is no external evidence to calibrate the two datasets, and we can only say that they are different. A similar problem has been reported in studies of dental attrition in modern reindeer (Sokolov *et al.* 1996). Four different populations in the northern Eurasian tundra appear to show different rates of dental attrition, but the rate is measured against age, which has been estimated from cementum increments. Although Sokolov *et al.* prefer to accept the cementum age estimates and so question the rates of attrition, it is also possible that the rates of wear are the same in all four populations, but there is a consistent difference between them in the deposition of cementum. Or both.

Difficulties aside, age at death distributions derived from dental eruption and attrition are widely used in the interpretation of hunting practices and animal husbandry, and a number of examples are discussed in context in Chapters 12, 13 and 14. An important point is that the archaeological data are often compared with postulated 'expected' age distributions, derived either from observation of extant populations of the species concerned, or from *a priori* arguments based on the potential productivity of a species and an assumption that this will be optimized. In a celebrated example, Payne (1973) postulated models for mixed populations of domestic sheep and goats which maximized production of meat, wool and milk, then compared archaeological age distributions derived from eruption and attrition data with those postulated models to see whether any conclusions could be drawn about the economic aims of the pastoralists concerned. A similar procedure has been widely applied since then by many different researchers, in many different cultural and geographical contexts. Certain assumptions in such a model are probably quite robust, such as that a herd or flock kept primarily for milking will generate a surplus of young males which are neither needed for breeding nor useful for milking. Alternatively, if a flock is kept principally to supply meat, animals will be slaughtered as they approach maturity, as their rate of growth begins to slow down.

Other archaeological applications require other assumptions. Lauwerier (1983) set out to determine the season of death of piglets found in fourth-century Roman graves at Nijmegen, Netherlands. To do so required determining the age at death to a high degree of precision, and making confident assumptions about the month in which the piglets would have been born. For example, if pigs are only born in April, then in October of any year there can only be pigs aged 6 months, 18 months, 30 months, 42 months and so on. As the Nijmegen pigs were very young at death, and so died during a period of rapid skeletal development, Lauwerier could estimate their age at death quite precisely, but he goes on to point out that historical sources show that the modern practice of breeding pigs at least twice a year is of considerable antiquity. There is no reason to think that Roman farmers in the Netherlands were unaware of this potential yield, and so no reason to assume annual, seasonal breeding.

A more positive example of the use of eruption and attrition data is given by Rolett & Chiu (1994), in their delightful study of pig remains from a site in the Marquesas Islands. Grant's procedure for recording eruption and attrition states is adapted to record individual teeth, on the grounds that the samples involved included few mandibles but many loose teeth. By distributing the numbers of teeth recovered along an axis of progressive molar development, Rolett and Chiu show that the sample reflects selective culling of sub-adult pigs, mostly just under or around a year old. This, they conclude, shows that the pigs were systematically harvested as they reached an age at which their growth rate would have slowed down, and any further gain in meat would have been disproportionately small in relation to the amount of food consumed by the pigs. Despite the rather fragmentary nature of the material, a conclusion is reached which has a direct bearing on the economy of the settlement and the decision-making of the population.

CASE STUDY: LAMBS IN ROMAN YORK

Roman sites in England have a reputation for producing bone assemblages dominated by adult cattle, and that seldom makes for interesting age at death analyses. However, the 24–30 Tanner Row site in York produced an assemblage of sheep mandibles from late second- to early third-century AD deposits which serve as an informative example. A published analysis of the bones from Roman deposits at this site is given in O'Connor (1988b), and the overlying medieval material in Bond & O'Connor (1999).

From late second- to early third-century deposits (structural periods 3 to 7), sixty-four sheep mandibles were recorded, on which at least two molars or fourth premolars were either in wear or erupting. Of these, only twenty-four had all three molars and the fourth permanent or deciduous premolar. An analysis based on mandible wear scores (MWS) would have used less than half of the sample (twenty-seven specimens), or would have required estimated values for teeth in over half of the specimens.

An examination of the data showed that many of the specimens fall into one of two categories: those in which the deciduous fourth premolar (DP$_4$) shows just the early stages of wear on the mesial part of the tooth (Grant stages a to d), and those in which all three molars are in wear, with dentine exposure conjoining across all cusps of the first molar (LM_1 at Grant stage g). The second group usefully illustrate how difficult it could be to predict stages for absent teeth. Fourteen specimens have LM_1 at stage g, and the stages of LM_3 in these specimens range from just beginning to erupt through the alveolar bone to stage e, at which there is appreciable dentine exposure on the mesial cusps.

How old are these two groups of sheep? The older group seems to span the time of eruption and early wear of LM_3. Modern data would lead us to expect this tooth to erupt at or soon after two years of age (Moran & O'Connor 1994), so these sheep could be grouped as two to three years old. Specimens with LM_1 at stage h and beyond mostly show stages f or g on LM_3, so could be safely presumed to be older than three years. The oldest mandible in the sample has LM_1 at stage j and LM_3 at stage g, with an overall MWS of 40, and this is not particularly advanced wear. The adult sheep, then, seem to include a group of two- to three-year-olds, and a few somewhat older individuals.

The young sheep died when their deciduous teeth were only just in wear, and before LM_1 began to erupt. Modern data show LM_1 erupting at three to four months old, and DP_4 will begin to wear as soon as the lambs begin to graze. As DP_4 is much the largest of the deciduous teeth, it takes most of the attrition in young lambs, and so wears relatively rapidly, at least until LM_1 erupts and increases the total crown area. These lambs are therefore probably about two months old: old enough to have been grazing for sufficient time to have begun to wear DP_4, but too young for LM_1 to have erupted. Assuming a spring lambing period, they died in about May or June of their first year.

Were their deaths accidental or deliberate? While disease or accident cannot be wholly ruled out, death at birth is far more likely than a couple of months later. Early summer is a time of rapid grass growth and ample food, and the lambs are too young to have acquired a fatal burden of parasites such as liver fluke. Furthermore, the bones are from a city, not from a farm, where one might expect to find the corpses of diseased or misadventurous lambs.

So why kill such young lambs? If the aim were to keep sheep for milking, the lambs could have been surplus males. Dairy farmers want adult female animals, yet births tend to be equally male and female. It is expedient, if ruthless, to keep just a few fortunate males as breeding stock and to slaughter the rest. That is why dairy cattle and veal production are so inextricably linked in modern Europe. As we cannot discern the sex of lamb mandibles, we cannot categorically refute this interpretation. However, sheep remain useful dairy animals to quite an advanced age, so we might expect the other age group in the death assemblage to be of rather old animals, whereas these are adult but not particularly elderly. To kill dairy ewes at two to three years old would be foolish.

When I originally published this material, I proposed that these Roman mandibles were the kill-off from dairy flocks (O'Connor 1988b). In retrospect, that conclusion is difficult to support in view of the likely age of the adult sheep. Instead, we have to consider the possibility that there was a specific demand for young lambs in Roman York. This might have been for the skins, either with the wool attached or as a particularly fine leather, or simply because religious observance required the slaughter of lambs around May or June. Either of these interpretations is alien to a modern mind attuned to notions of economic productivity, and further investigation of either would require data that goes beyond consideration of age at death.

EPIPHYSIAL FUSION

The limb bones of mammals develop from several centres of ossification (Chapter 2). In an immature animal, a typical limb bone has three parts: the shaft or diaphysis, and the proximal and distal epiphyses, which are attached to the diaphysis by an intervening layer of cartilage (the epiphysial cartilage). New bone formation on either side of this cartilage allows the bone to grow in length. If a mammal dies while immature, the epiphysial cartilage will generally decay more rapidly than the bone, resulting in separation of diaphysis and epiphyses (Fig. 8.4). It is thus possible to record for an archaeological sample how many specimens of a particular epiphysis were fused to the diaphysis at death, and how many were unfused. Just as with the eruption of the permanent teeth, the different epiphyses of the immature skeleton undergo fusion with the diaphysis at different, and approximately predictable, times. In order to use the resulting data to reconstruct the age at death of the animals represented by the sample, we need to know the typical times of fusion of the different epiphyses for that species, and we need to be confident that the timing of that fusion is likely to be reasonably consistent from one population to the next.

Data describing the fusion of the epiphyses of the common domestic mammals have been published since the time of Lesbre (1898), who tabulates such information for horses, cattle, sheep and goats, pigs and dogs. For each epiphysis, Lesbre gives a range of age over which fusion typically occurs: for example, 12–15 months for the proximal epiphysis of the cattle radius, and

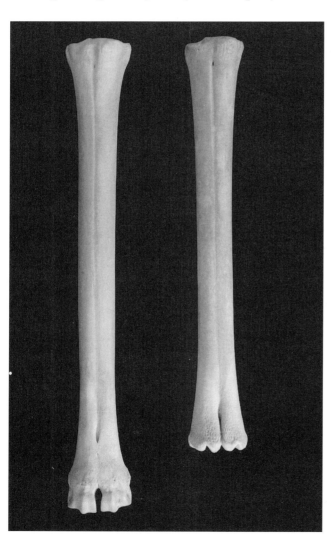

Fig. 8.4. Epiphysial fusion in metacarpals of roe deer. The specimen on the left is fully fused. In the right-hand specimen the distal epiphysis was unfused at time of death. The sharply undulating surface visible at the distal end of the shaft is typical of an unfused epiphysial junction.

the less exact 'vers 3 ans' for the *tuber calcis* of the calcaneum in cattle. This practice of quoting a 'typical' range for each epiphysis has been followed by most later researchers, notably Silver (1969) and Amorosi (1989). As research in this area proceeded, it quickly became apparent that the sequence in which the epiphyses of a particular species fuse is consistent and predictable. Thus Todd & Todd (1938) observe of even-toed ungulates as a whole that 'so far as epiphysial fusion goes, the order is uniform', a sweeping assertion which their data certainly support. The emphasis in subsequent research, therefore, has been on determining the timing of fusion, and circumstances which might cause this to vary.

There are two different means of collecting modern data on epiphysial fusion. The first is to kill the animals at a known age, to dissect out the bones and then to observe the state of fusion, much as one would with archaeological bones. This procedure is wasteful of animals, unless they are being killed for some other reason, in which case the range of age at death might not be optimal for the epiphysial fusion study. It might also be unclear in some circumstances whether a particular epiphysis which retains traces of the epiphysial cartilage would, on decomposition of that cartilage, separate from the diaphysis, or whether sufficient fusion had taken place for the specimen to survive in the archaeological record as 'fused'. Some researchers have attempted to replicate cartilage decomposition by boiling the specimens in water as part of the preparation process (Tchirvinsky 1909; Noddle 1974).

The second procedure, more commonly used with live animals, is to x-ray the limbs at particular points in the animal's life, ideally taking repeated x-rays of one cohort as they mature. This has the advantage of allowing the longitudinal study of one cohort, and of allowing the animals to survive the process. An early example of the use of x-rays for this purpose is Küpfer & Schinz (1923), an exhaustive monograph which sets out the development of the cattle skeleton from foetus to full maturity. The degree of variation between populations in timing of fusion was noted by Emara (1937), who compared data from Egyptian cattle with previously published data from American herds, and noted slightly later fusion in the Egyptian animals. The same issue was tackled for sheep by Dhingra (1976), who compared Indian data with those published by Smith (1956).

Smith's data nicely illustrate one of the problems with the x-ray study of epiphysial fusion, namely being sure that the same radiographic features are noted by different researchers, and that those features actually correspond with the fusion of epiphysis to diaphysis (i.e. the validity of the observations). Dhingra tabulated his own and Smith's data alongside other sources known to that time, and Moran & O'Connor (1994) have repeated this comparison with additional sources to that date. The comparisons show Smith to be at odds with virtually all other sources, giving times of fusion which are younger, often much younger, than other studies. Smith is quite explicit that he was monitoring a radiolucent (i.e. dark) line on the x-rays which was taken to be the epiphysial cartilage. When that dark line was not visible on the x-ray, the epiphysis was regarded as fused. Lewall & Cowan (1963) studied thirty-four skeletons of black-tailed deer (*Odocoileus hemionus*) by dissecting out the bones of the fore and hind limbs, and then x-raying the bones, thus allowing direct correlation of the state of the bone and the x-ray image. On their criteria, the radiolucent line is present in definitely unfused specimens, but confirmation of fusion requires absence of the radiolucent line *and* the presence of a radio-opaque line (white on the x-ray) along the line of the epiphysial cartilage. This line is broad as fusion begins, then thins and disappears when fusion is complete. It is possible, therefore, that Smith was diagnosing full fusion at a time when the process of fusion was only just beginning, an ambiguity not unlike deciding on the point at which a tooth is regarded as having erupted.

I have set out the pitfalls of identifying epiphysial fusion by x-ray only to make the point that the quality of the modern data has to be examined critically. The data are certainly commonly available in the literature. Apart from the sources for cattle and sheep already noted, Curgy (1965) and Silver (1969) give mostly second-hand data for a wide range of species; Reiland (1978), van Wijngaarden-Bakker & Maliepaard (1982), and Bull & Payne (1982) give useful data for pigs and wild boars; Ahnlund (1976) includes brief information on epiphysial fusion in badgers; Smith (1969) describes epiphysial fusion in cats (based on x-rays and dissection); Noddle (1974) and Bullock & Rackham (1982) record fusion in goats, both wild and domestic. Bement & Masmajian (1996) rather cleverly infer epiphysial fusion times in extinct *Bison antiquus*; and no review would be complete without mention of Zuck's (1938) pioneering study of epiphysial fusion in guinea pigs.

Given careful scrutiny of the published data, we are in a position to estimate the age at death of an individual mammal encountered in archaeological deposits. By examining the whole skeleton, noting which epiphyses are fused and which still unfused, the age can be bracketed: older than the earliest likely fusion time for the last fused epiphysis, but younger than the latest likely fusion time for the first unfused epiphysis (Table 8.1).

Table 8.1.   *The process of attributing age at death to an excavated sheep skeleton. The fusion ages quoted here are based on Moran & O'Connor (1994).*

Suppose that we are examining the excavated remains of one individual sheep, and wish to estimate the age at death from the state of fusion of the epiphyses.

Of the bones present, the earliest fusing are the distal humerus and proximal radius. These are fully fused, so the sheep is older than the youngest likely age for full fusion of these epiphyses: *6 months*.

The latest-fusing epiphyses – distal femur, proximal humerus, proximal tibia – are unfused. The sheep is younger than the greatest likely age for fusion of these epiphyses – *42 months*.

The distal end of both tibiae are fully fused, as is one of the metacarpals (the other is missing), but both metatarsals are unfused. This suggests the sheep to be older than the youngest likely age for the fusion of these epiphyses (*about 18 months*) but younger than the greatest likely age for the fusion of the metatarsals (*about 24 months*).

This gives us an estimated age at death of *18–24 months*. As a cross-check, we examine the one surviving calcaneum, which is unfused, and the first phalanges, the proximal epiphyses of which are all fused. That is consistent with the estimated age at death.

Unfortunately, most of the bones which we encounter in archaeological deposits are disarticulated and often broken, and to be able to examine a whole skeleton is a rare luxury. Usually, the simplest procedure is to list the epiphyses recorded for a particular species in their order of fusion, and to tabulate for each how many specimens in the sample were fused and how many unfused (Table 8.2). The proportion of fused specimens for a particular epiphysis can then be taken to reflect the proportion of animals represented in the sample which survived beyond the typical age of fusion of that epiphysis. In fact, for most species it is possible to put the epiphyses into groups which fuse at around the same time, thus simplifying the dataset.

Table 8.2. *Dataset for a sample of disarticulated sheep bones.*

By grouping the epiphyses that fuse at roughly the same age, we see that nearly half of the animals died before fusion of the 1st phalanges, i.e. by a year old, but relatively few died during their second year. Only about one-quarter of the sheep survived their fourth summer, and very few survived to five or more years old. The results lack precision, but they do give an impression of the overall mortality profile.

Epiphysis	Number fused	Number unfused	% fused	Approximate age of fusion
Humerus, distal	12	4		
Radius, proximal	9	3		
Total	21	7	75%	6 months
1st phalanges, prox.	15	12	56%	12 months
Tibia, distal	10	9		
Metacarpal, distal	6	7		
Metatarsal, distal	7	8		
Calcaneum	3	6		
Total	26	30	46%	18–24 months
Femur, distal	3	10		
Tibia, proximal	4	9		
Humerus, proximal	1	5		
Total	8	24	25%	36–42 months
Vertebrae	4	40	10%	42–54 months

All of this assumes that we have sufficient confidence in the times of fusion, and in the consistency of those times. The degree of inter-observer variation noted by Moran & O'Connor (1994), for example, partly reflects differences in the recording criteria, but also reflects differences in the rate of skeletal maturation between the different sheep populations. As long ago as 1909, Tchirvinsky noted that chronic malnourishment and castration of males could delay epiphysial fusion to an unpredictable degree, and Todd & Todd (1938) observed that removal of the thyroid gland from sheep delayed epiphysial fusion, though apparently not the eruption of the permanent teeth. Wallace (1948) noted delayed fusion in under-fed sheep, and Hatting (1983) reported appreciable delay in fusion in castrated sheep, though Clutton-Brock *et al.* (1990) did not. Moran & O'Connor (1994) found some delay in castrates in their study, with the effect more marked in epiphyses which normally fuse around 18–24 months, rather than in earlier or later fusing epiphyses. Even for the well-studied sheep, then, the matter has still to be resolved in detail. Because of uncertainties surrounding epiphysial fusion data, it is common practice to examine those data in parallel with results from dental eruption and attrition, and some of us are frankly much more inclined to believe the teeth.

The archaeological interpretation of epiphysial fusion data presents a number of difficulties, and is in many ways quite unsatisfactory. The difficulties arise from the lack of precision regarding the time of fusion of any one epiphysis, and the fact that we are dealing with disarticulated material from an unknown (or at best roughly estimated) number of individuals. Quite different age at death distributions can be inferred from the same dataset, depending on whether one takes the earliest likely time of fusion, or the latest, or some point between (Watson 1978). We also have to consider that our analysis of the data often takes the form of a longitudinal study – x per cent dead by this age, y per cent by that age – which is a form of analysis better suited to the monitoring of a live population. If we examine an early-fusing epiphysis, the specimens which are fused are taken to represent individuals which survived beyond that age, but those individuals are not necessarily represented in our data for a later-fusing epiphysis from the same sample. Each age grouping of epiphyses which we examine samples a different population, yet we string the data together as if they were replicate samples of the same population.

My own approach to epiphysial fusion data from disarticulated samples is to be parsimonious. In domestic ungulates the proportion of unfused early-fusing epiphyses (such as the distal end of the humerus) gives an indication of juvenile mortality which can be compared with dental data (e.g. O'Connor 1991a, 248–54). At the other extreme, the proportion of fully fused vertebral centra gives us some information about an age group generally older than those represented by the latest-erupting teeth. A sample in which most cattle mandibles have the third molar in wear, yet over half of the vertebral centra unfused, would indicate quite a high mortality between the time of eruption of the third molar, and the time of fusion of the vertebral centra, maybe as much as two years later in cattle. That inference could then be compared with the state of attrition of the third molars: are most of them in wear but not heavily worn? Epiphysial fusion then becomes a useful cross-check for data derived from dental eruption and attrition. Anomalies between the two may be explicable in terms of castration of males delaying fusion, or may arise simply because the mandibles and the limb bones in the sample have each sampled a different population of individuals.

AND FINALLY . . .

Another age-estimation method which has mostly been applied to human remains is the examination of histological structure, in particular the degree of remodelling to form secondary osteons (Kerley 1965; Aiello & Molleson 1993; Stout & Stanley 1991). Jane Ruddle (1996) has applied this technique to roe deer, using a known-age series to test the accuracy of the technique in comparison with age estimation by dental eruption and attrition. By generating regression equations using histological data and the known age of the specimens, Ruddle was able to 'predict' the age of the specimens by a back-regression procedure. The differences between the known and 'predicted' ages gave a useful measure of accuracy, and showed histological analysis to be a little less accurate than analysis of dental eruption and attrition. More studies of this sort are needed before the value of histological analysis as a means of age-estimation for animals other than humans can be assessed, and the procedure validated. However, it clearly shows promise, despite being rather labour-intensive.

Most of this chapter has been about mammals, and age at death analysis is certainly most often applied to mammal bones in archaeological samples. Birds lack teeth, so are not amenable to some age-estimation techniques, and their limb bones do not develop epiphyses in the same way as those of mammals. Birds are skeletally immature for a remarkably short time, with some species capable of growing to near-adult body size in just a few weeks from hatching. In most species full ossification of the skeleton is attained at or soon after fledging (i.e. when the bird leaves the nest), so skeletally immature individuals are normally only present at or close to the nest-site, during the nesting season (Chapter 12). Because of the rapidity of skeletal development, it is only possible to note bird bones as immature or adult, or at best to define a couple of immature stages. During the earliest days of post-hatching development, the major wing and leg bones may only resemble undifferentiated rods of porous bone, with little of the morphology of a humerus, tibiotarsus or whatever. At this stage, the survival and recovery of the bones would seem to be highly improbable, but such immature bones can and do survive in archaeological samples, and clearly represent individuals at a very early stage of development. As adult size is approached, the bones take on more of the distinctive morphology of the element concerned, often with a relatively robust shaft but with porous articular ends.

The size of fish is related to their age, so size can be used to investigate the age distribution of the fish populations represented by the archaeological sample. For example, sardine bones from the fills of an amphora recovered from a Roman wreck at Randello, Sicily, gave a reconstructed size range inconsistent with the age pattern typical of a single shoal of sardines (Wheeler & Locker 1985). In this case the context of the bones makes it likely that they were preserved in some way, and so the fish in the sample could have derived from a number of different fishing events, perhaps at different times, or at different distances from the shore, thus sampling different shoals with different age structures, and giving the rather wide overall size range in the sample.

Age at death analysis can reveal a good deal about human decision-making, but our inferences along those lines are only as robust as the archaeological data and the modern analogue data. Modern studies show that cementum increments, dental eruption and attrition, and epiphysial fusion all have their weaknesses and failings. That is not a reason to reject these procedures and to give up trying, however, as the potential yield of archaeological information is considerable. Instead, we need to be as rigorous as our samples allow, and to be clear about the limitations of this line of research.

Estimation of age at death implicitly assumes that the animals were healthy, or at least not suffering a disease or trauma which would have influenced skeletal or dental development. Occasionally, the recording of dental attrition is complicated because teeth and jaws show signs of disease or injury. The next chapter reviews the study of signs of disease and trauma in archaeological bone samples.

NINE

PALAEOPATHOLOGY: UNDERSTANDING SICKNESS AND INJURY

Palaeopathology is the study of the signs of disease and injury in ancient hard and soft tissues. For the purposes of this chapter, the term is taken to cover the recognition and interpretation of such signs in the bones of animals, other than humans, recovered from archaeological deposits. The diseases concerned may have been diseases of the skeletal system itself, or may be secondary effects on the skeleton of diseases which primarily affected other tissues. The reason for studying palaeopathology in animal bones is quite simple: the diseases and injuries were obviously relevant to the lives of the animals concerned, and probably also to the people who lived with and hunted or husbanded them. Palaeopathology can also make a contribution to veterinary history, by showing that particular disorders can be recognized in ancient material, but it is mainly a source of information on the health of past animals, and hence on their interactions with past peoples and with their wider environment.

The palaeopathology of human remains is well advanced: a mature scientific discipline with largely agreed codes of practice and nomenclature (e.g. Ortner & Putschar 1985; Roberts & Manchester 1995). The same cannot be said of animal palaeopathology, which is an inchoate discipline, pursued by a relatively small number of analysts. The study of palaeopathology in animal bones differs from the study of human palaeopathology for two main reasons.

First, with animal bones we are only rarely dealing with the whole skeleton of a single individual. Human remains often, though not invariably, occur as whole or part skeletons, making it possible to attempt a differential diagnosis on the basis of pathological characters on several parts of the skeleton, or to map the extent of the effects of a condition. A simple example would be examining all the joint surfaces within one leg to see whether an obvious degenerative joint disease in the ankle had caused abnormal joint function in the knee or hip. Animals more generally occur as a mass of disarticulated bones from an unknown number of individuals, usually of a range of species. Examination and diagnosis has to proceed on a bone-by-bone basis, not skeleton-by-skeleton.

Second, there is less useful modern clinical literature available. Veterinary surgeons have little to do with animal skeletons, not least because diseases and injuries in domestic animals today are seldom allowed to develop to the point at which the skeleton is appreciably affected or modified. In domestic ungulates remedial action or slaughter usually quickly intervenes. Examples of bone pathology in the veterinary journals tend to be isolated cases of something really unusual, generally in dogs or cats, or older studies of bone pathology which has arisen as a consequence of experimentation related to feeding and growth rate. This last category has included some research which would not be considered morally acceptable today, but it is from these often grisly sources that we can obtain some useful information, and a number of them are cited below. Many of the references used in this chapter are from the 1960s and 1970s, and the references are to a remarkably diverse range of journals, including veterinary sources, agricultural journals and pathology journals. This reflects the diverse and rather patchy literature on which animal palaeopathology has to draw.

It would be easy for this chapter to consist of a presentation of interesting cases drawn from the archaeological literature, but that would say little about the methods and potential of palaeopathology. Instead, there is a selective review of skeletal pathologies reported in the clinical literature with the emphasis on those that we ought to be able to recognize even in disarticulated archaeological material. This is followed by an overview of the sort of conditions which are reported in archaeological material, and some recommendations for putting animal palaeopathology on a firm footing for the future. The aim of the chapter is to show the potential of research into animal palaeopathology, the extent to which that potential is (or is not) being realized at present, and ways in which such research can go forward.

AS REPORTED BY VETERINARIANS

One topic which has been relatively well reviewed in the clinical literature is joint disease. I use the general term *arthropathy* here to refer to all pathologies of joints, so as to avoid the more debatable definition of terms such as *arthritis* or *arthrosis*. Arthropathies are obviously of some economic significance, as lame animals neither feed nor breed optimally, quite apart from the fact that a lame animal is obviously in discomfort and so demands attention (Fig. 9.1). This makes the arthropathies important both in the modern clinical literature and in the archaeological context, as the detrimental consequence of lameness in domestic livestock would have been just as apparent in the Neolithic as today, even though the human response might have been different.

One particular arthropathy which has received close veterinary attention is lameness in pigs. This can be caused by a specific organism, *Erysipelothrix rhusiopathiae*, which can cause lymph and blood infections in humans, hence the need to diagnose the cause of arthropathies in pigs before infected meat is handled and consumed by people (Cross & Edwards 1981). In their report of apparently the same condition, Duthie & Lancaster (1964) described granular erosion of the joint surfaces in the elbows of affected pigs. Although this only affects the articular cartilage in mild cases, more advanced cases affect the underlying bone, and so should be recognizable in archaeological material. A confident diagnosis of *E. rhusiopathiae* as the causal agent in an archaeological case of arthropathy would require well-preserved material and the systematic exclusion of other causes, but the archaeological significance would be considerable. Other forms of pig lameness

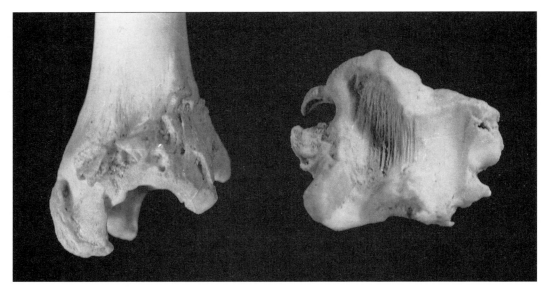

Fig. 9.1. The distal articulation of a sheep tibia from the Orkney Islands, showing lesions characteristic of osteoarthritis. The articular surface shows deep grooves, where the articular cartilages have been destroyed, allowing bone to abrade bone. Around the joint, a proliferation of new bone shows how the overall morphology of an arthritic joint can be severely modified.

include a condition in which the articular cartilage invaginates (i.e. is folded in and projects into the underlying bone), which ought to be recognizable in dry bone material (Grøndalen 1974). However, if the condition develops in young pigs, it sometimes appears to heal as the animal ages.

We should beware of expecting to find all modern arthropathies in ancient bones, as some conditions undoubtedly arise as a consequence of the rapid weight-gain and large adult size imposed by modern breeding and feeding regimes. Jensen *et al.* (1981) reported a high incidence of osteochondrosis in cattle, and proposed that rapid weight gain by cattle fattened for the butcher was a major cause. Advanced osteochondral pathologies (i.e. affecting both the articular cartilage and the underlying bone) ought to be readily identifiable in archaeological material, and the recognition of more than the occasional case in a large sample of, for example, medieval cattle would throw some doubt on Jensen *et al.*'s interpretation of their results. Some of the lesions illustrated in the modern clinical literature resemble the 'non-pathological depressions' reported in ancient cattle phalanges by Baker & Brothwell (1980, 109–11), in particular their Type 1 oval depressions (Fig. 9.2).

It is obviously dangerous to generalize about causes, as outwardly similar osteochondroses have been reported in horses, where rapid weight-gain is clearly not a factor (Trotter *et al.* 1982). Pascoe *et al.* (1984) give a particularly detailed account of osteochondral lesions in the distal femur in horses, though with little attempt at determining the aetiology. The better-known navicular bone disease seems to be related to an uneven weight distribution across the four legs, and may be reversible (Østblom *et al.* 1982). This is one condition that has been diagnosed with confidence in archaeological material (Baker & Brothwell 1980, 128–30), though its significance in terms of human utilization of the horse concerned is unclear. Before leaving osteochondral lesions, it is worth noting that they do not only occur in the large ungulates. Duff (1984) reported osteochondrosis dissecans in turkeys, where it might also be related to weight gain.

The possible association between weight, joint stress and joint pathology is particularly important, and is further discussed below. The association has long been mentioned in the clinical literature. Sokoloff (1960) reviewed 'arthritis' (using the term in a loose sense) in a range of species, paying particular attention to arthropathies of infectious origin. On joint stresses, he notes, 'In general, degenerative

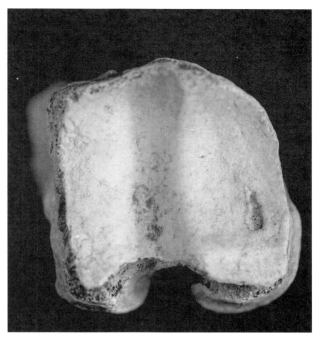

Fig. 9.2. *A minor lesion in the proximal articular surface of a cattle first phalanx. Are these lesions 'non-pathological', or are they a stress-related osteochondrosis, as reported in the clinical literature?*

changes in bulky mammals occur primarily in the parts of the skeleton where the brunt of the weight-bearing and jolt shock is sustained' (Sokoloff 1960, 220). We bulky mammals who jog for the supposed health benefits are familiar with this phenomenon.

Perhaps more obviously related to human utilization of livestock is the occurrence of skeletal pathologies which are directly attributable to levels of feeding. Evidence of chronic under-nutrition may also be relevant in the remains of hunted game, as the nutritional status of prey animals will obviously have been important both in terms of their vulnerability and of their value as a resource. Many older papers detail the consequence of experimentally induced under-nutrition, principally in pigs (e.g. Pratt & McCance 1964; Tonge & McCance 1965; Luke *et al.* 1981). Apart from a low growth rate and small attained adult size, under-nourished mammals typically show a low rate of skeletal maturity, with delayed epiphysial fusion, though there is very little effect on the timing of eruption of the teeth. The development of the jaws may be greatly affected, producing crowding of near-normal sized teeth into under-sized jaws, with resulting malocclusion. These are certainly effects which would be recognizable in archaeological material. However, these studies are probably rather poor analogues for us to use, as the degree of under-nutrition was quite extreme. Of more interest to us would be contrasts between just-adequately-fed and rather-well-fed populations of livestock. At the time of writing, just such a study is underway in Scotland, comparing populations of sheep with access to adequate grazing and to surplus feed over several years of growth. Nutrition may also be compromised by the presence of parasites in the alimentary canal, reducing the efficiency with which food is digested and interfering with the absorption of the products of digestion. Experimentally infesting lambs with different levels of one parasite shows that even a modest worm burden carried during the period of growth can reduce attained adult size, with an appreciable reduction in the degree of mineralization of the skeleton (Sykes *et al.* 1977).

More subtle nutritional deficiencies may produce quite distinctive skeletal effects, such as 'Bowie' or 'bent-leg' in sheep, which is outwardly similar to, but histologically distinct from, rickets (Fitch 1954; Baker & Brothwell 1980, 58). Rickets, apparently of nutritional origin, has been recorded in fast-growing cattle (Jonsson *et al.* 1972), and I have seen something similar in sheep subject to rapid weight gain (O'Connor 1982, 68–73). A nutritional deficiency may also have been the root cause of the abnormal angulation of the distal epiphysis of metapodials of fallow deer noted by Chapman *et al.* (1984), though it appears that mechanical stresses induced by the original condition then exaggerated the uneven loading of the affected joints, increasing the mis-angulation of the joint. More specifically, distinctive osteoporotic conditions have been noted in sheep which have grazed on land around former lead mines in northern England (Stewart & Allcroft 1956; Butler *et al.* 1957).

Reviews of the skeletal pathology of whole populations are relatively uncommon in the clinical literature, but would be of more obvious value to archaeology. An excellent exception is the review by Peterson *et al.* (1982) of two moose populations. Apart from describing arthropathies and forms of periodontal inflammation in the two populations, the authors tabulate the incidence of both conditions in different age categories in each of the two populations, allowing us to see the extent to which both conditions were age-related, and how far the demography of the population influenced the prevalence of the conditions. A population with a lot of old moose will show a higher prevalence of arthropathies than a relatively young population, a fairly unsurprising conclusion, but one which is seldom applied to archaeological material when the prevalence of arthropathies is considered (see below).

Another good review is Leader-Williams' (1980) study of mandibular swellings in reindeer in South Georgia. Despite the usual attribution of irregular mandibular inflammation to 'lumpy jaw' and thence to a specific infection of the bone (usually actinomycosis), Leader-Williams suspects quite a different aetiology in this case, associated with the unusual soil chemistry of the north-eastern part of South Georgia. That serves as something of a warning, given the connection which Baker & Brothwell (1980, 158) make between 'lumpy jaw' and two particular infective organisms. Rudge (1970) reported a similar survey of feral goats in the Kermadec Islands, comparing the prevalence and nature of periodontal disorders in particular with a control sample from mainland New Zealand. Differences between the two populations lay in the pattern of periodontal disease, which Rudge explains in terms of habitat. A high prevalence of periodontal disease, often accompanied by tooth loss, has been reported for roe deer in Bohemia and Moravia (Kratochvil 1984). In this instance, the author suspected an association with changes in agriculture and forestry in the region, reducing food diversity during the winter. Other pathologies of the jaws and teeth are more generally reported, not least in Colyer's encyclopaedic review (Miles & Grigson 1990), occasionally including such improbable animals as crocodiles (Hall 1985).

Periodontal disease in sheep, and its causes and consequences, has been a particular area of investigation. A condition known as 'broken mouth', in which the incisors and canine teeth become loosened and eventually fall out, has been widely reported (e.g. Page & Schroeder 1982, 165–70). The incidence of this condition varies markedly from flock to flock, and much research has gone into determining why this is so. The loss of teeth is sometimes associated with purulent gum infections (Page & Schroeder 1982), but can also be directly attributable to physical damage caused by the impaction into the gums and interdental spaces of the spiky awns of grasses such as *Bromus tectorum* (Anderson & Bulgin 1984). The consequences of periodontal disease may not be limited to the obvious damage around the teeth. Atkinson *et al.* (1982) have shown a loss of cortical bone density and marked porosity changes in the mandibles of 'broken mouth' sheep when compared with healthy individuals from the same population. Whether this could be sufficiently marked to have implications for the differential survival of specimens remains untested. Fig. 9.3 shows a sheep mandible from a Roman site in northern England with particularly marked bone loss around the third molar, which has none the less remained in situ in a sample in which much of the bone was highly fragmented.

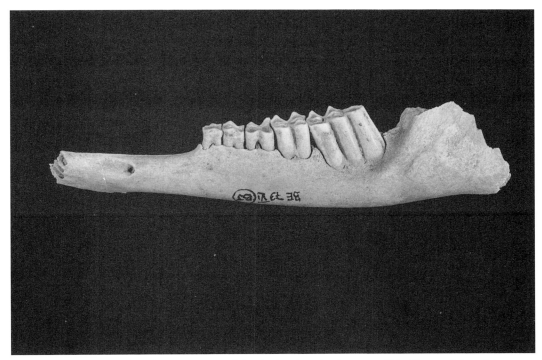

Fig. 9.3. Advanced periodontal recession around the third molar of a sheep mandible. The condition of the alveolar bone shows that the inflammation was not current at the time of death.

Faced with the clinical literature, it would be easy to become confused as to the significance of pathological specimens from archaeological samples. How much pathology should we expect to see? And at what point did a condition seen in the dry bones become significant to the animal, in terms of feeding, breeding or mobility? An important study in this regard is that undertaken by Caroline Richardson and colleagues in the 1970s (Richardson *et al.* 1979). These researchers acquired the heads of 481 culled ewes (female sheep sold off because they were no longer required as breeding stock) from the livestock market at Banbury, Oxfordshire. Of this large sample, only *two* could be described as having 'normal buccal morphology'. The other 479 exhibited a range of disorders, most often 'broken mouth', and including loose or missing teeth, inflammation and pocketing of the gums, often with impaction of food debris, and abnormal shearing of tooth occlusal surfaces. The results showed that incisors were the teeth most likely to be missing, with premolars more likely to be loose or missing than molars, a pattern which is familiar from archaeological material (Table 9.1). Minor but consistent differences in disposition to tooth loss or gum disease were noted between different breeds. Above all, though, Richardson *et al.* recorded the body condition of the sheep prior to slaughter, on a scale from emaciated to fat. Despite the high prevalence of dental and periodontal abnormalities, there was no correlation between dental disease and body condition. Some of the sheep were in much better condition than others, but this seemed to have little to do with their often ghastly teeth and gums.

Table 9.1. *The distribution of loose and missing teeth in the left mandibles of 481 adult female sheep.*

Note the particularly high frequency of absence of incisors and canines, and the higher frequency of loose premolars than molars. Data from Richardson *et al.* (1979).

Tooth location	loose %	missing %
I_1	13	40
I_2	14	39
I_3	14	39
C	8	54
PM_2	35	46
PM_3	37	14
PM_4	38	12
M_1	21	25
M_2	12	4
M_3	4	–

As Reported by Zooarchaeologists

Clearly there are some conditions well known in the clinical literature which ought to be recognizable in archaeological material. One of the first attempts to take an overview of animal palaeopathology both described archaeological specimens and sought to highlight those conditions which ought to be most readily diagnosed in disarticulated bone samples (Siegel 1976). Siegel particularly makes the point that texts from Middle Kingdom Egypt, the Babylonian Code of Hammurabi, and Late Bronze Age cuneiform tablets from Anatolia and Mesopotamia all show an appreciation of illness and injury in domestic animals, and means of avoiding and treating such conditions. The close association of people and animals obviously also allows plenty of opportunity for the exchange of infective organisms and parasites. Siegel's classification of disorders is largely followed by Baker & Brothwell (1980), currently the only major English-language synthetic account of the subject. Even so, much of the text is taken up with proposing what conditions might be recognized, then describing single examples of some of those conditions.

Some sources instead give a survey of the pathologies noted in archaeological assemblages. Feddersen & Heinrich (1978) review a series of pathological specimens from the early medieval site of Scharstork, eastern Holstein. They describe quite a range of specimens, including numerous arthropathies, and estimate that about 6 per cent of the individual animals in the sample showed some abnormal pathology. As this figure is based on estimated minimum numbers of individuals (Chapter 6), it should be treated with caution. None the less, this is at least an attempt at archaeological interpretation across the sample, not just case by case. Arthropathies were particularly common among the cattle bones, and the authors put this down to use and 'overstrain' as cattle were used for haulage. In the pig bones, pathologies seem more often to have had some traumatic origin: even the arthropathies seem mostly to have resulted from joint infection rather than mechanical stress. This brings us neatly back to the clinical literature relating to infections and lameness in pigs (above).

The theme of arthropathies as an indicator of joint stress was picked up by Higham *et al.* (1968), van Wijngaarden-Bakker & Krauwer (1979), and Armour-Chelu & Clutton-Brock (1988), who took the presence of certain lesions in cattle as evidence of the use of the cattle for ploughing. Subsequently, Bartosiewicz *et al.* (1993) have reviewed the consequences of prolonged haulage work in the metapodials of recent draught cattle. Their results give some support to the interpretations which have been made, though there remains the question of how far arthropathies are age-related (Fig. 9.4). Is a high prevalence in one sample an indication of heavy utilization of the cattle for haulage, or a reflection of the demography of that population?

The considerable assemblage of animal bones from the Iron Age hillfort at Danebury, Hampshire, included numerous pathological specimens, and Brothwell's (1995) review of 276 of them constitutes one of the most thorough published studies for a single site. Arthropathies and pathologies of the teeth and jaws comprise the most common abnormalities, though Brothwell draws attention to a dozen cases of possible congenital abnormality. Other research in palaeopathology still tends to be published as individual case studies; for example, a cranial trauma case involving the skull of an apparently female

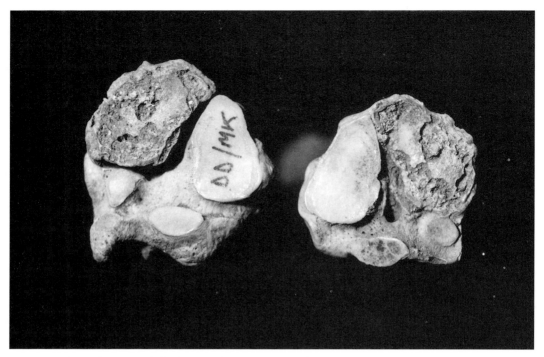

Fig. 9.4. Arthropathy in a cattle hock joint. The distal surface of the naviculo-cuboid and medial cuneiform (left) show marked degeneration of the joint surface of the cuneiform. The corresponding part of the proximal surface of the metatarsal (right) shows a similar degeneration, though the remainder of the metatarsal appears normal. See also Fig. 9.6.

cave bear of the extinct species *Ursus spelaeus* (Capasso 1998). The pathology was not lethal, and the bear may have died in hibernation. The lesion occupies much of the frontal part of the skull, between the orbits, with large areas of bone replaced by thickened, porous bone, which the author describes as resembling pumice-stone. There are large punctures located between the orbits and left of the interparietal crest. Capasso discusses the pattern of trauma and the subsequent inflammation of the bone, and notes other examples of injuries in cave bears, apparently attributable to fighting, which is frequently observed in extant large bear species. This is a particularly good example of a case-study, in that one short paper gives a full description of the lesion, discusses possible diagnoses, rejects some, and uses comparisons with other Pleistocene data and analogy with modern animals to test the plausibility of the conclusions. For a rather different view of ursids, incidentally, Blackmore *et al.* (1972) give a scholarly review of the incidence of trauma and disease in a large sample of teddy bears (*Brunus edwardii*), including a number of tragic case studies.

Dental palaeopathology has attracted appreciable research, not least because of the close analogies which can be drawn with the well-known dental pathology of humans. Major studies include reviews of particular species, such as the sabre-tooth cat *Smilodon californicus*, and the consequences of the stresses imposed on the teeth and jaws by the distinctive pattern of predation to which these remarkable animals were adapted (Shermis 1985). One unusually thorough review of a substantial Romano-British sample of mixed sheep and goats combined the recording of dental eruption and attrition with a detailed record of dental and paradontal abnormalities (Levitan 1985). This allowed analysis of, for example, the occurrence of periodontal disease in different age groups, and the frequency of involvement of different parts of the jaw. As well as recording conditions such as periodontal disease, Levitan also pointed out the need to record, for example, anomalies of occlusion and attrition.

Surveys of this kind are essential in palaeopathology as they not only allow detailed quantification of prevalence, but also allow us to question the boundaries between what is 'pathological' and what is 'normal'. In the case of periodontal disease, the development of porous bone around the margins of one or more alveoli might be taken as diagnostic, but close inspection of the alveoli of a series of mandibles will show a range of bone surface porosity. The ends of that range will define 'normal' and 'pathological', but numerous specimens will fall somewhere in between (Fig. 9.5). A similar issue arises with the recording and interpretation of dental calculus on the teeth of domestic ungulates. We can devise detailed forms of recording (e.g. Dobney & Brothwell 1987), and assume that the extent of mineralized calculus has something to do with diet and so with livestock management, but even this familiar condition suffers from poor definition of what is 'normal'.

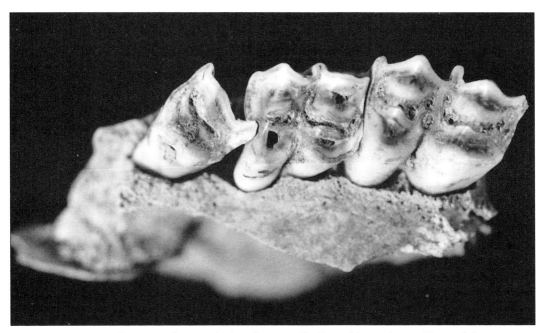

Fig. 9.5. Loosening and rotation of a premolar in a sheep maxilla. Does this constitute evidence of disease, or some other detail about the life of this sheep? Note that the movement of the premolar has caused it to abrade a groove into the adjacent molar.

Some conditions are commonly recorded on archaeological specimens, but defy consensus interpretation. One such is the occurrence of ante-mortem perforations on the posterior part of cattle skulls, usually close to the frontal eminence, where the frontal sinus is enclosed by a relatively thin layer of bone (Brothwell *et al.* 1996; Manaseryan *et al.* 1999). Several possible causes have been considered for these perforations, including developmental anomalies, infections, parasites, tumours and recurrent mechanical strain imposed by the cattle being yoked by their horns. All but the first and last have effectively been ruled out, leaving, as the authors nicely put it, a choice between yoke and genes. That takes us some way forward, but we are still short of an explanation for something which is quite familiar.

Similarly, Albarella (1995) reviews the depressions commonly seen on sheep horncores, using data from a modern series of sheep skulls. Although the depressions have previously been taken to indicate castrated males (Hatting 1974), Albarella found them on female skulls, so ruling out that possibility. Some of the individuals with horncore depressions also showed thinning of the cortical bone in their metatarsals, a condition which has been linked with calcium depletion, for example during pregnancy and lactation (Smith & Horwitz 1984; Horwitz & Smith 1990). Obviously this is just the sort of association which cannot be demonstrated in disarticulated archaeological material, and attempts to understand horncore depressions without reference to the rest of the skeleton have been unsuccessful. By examining the condition in modern material, Albarella may have hit on the solution. If horncore depressions are a feature of calcium-depleted individuals, then we might expect to see them more often in elderly females, particularly those that have been allowed to breed at an advanced age. This is an obvious line for further research, coupled with thin-section histology to confirm that the thinning of cortical bone really is consistent with calcium depletion.

SOME THOUGHTS ON THE WAY AHEAD

What recommendations can be made regarding the recording and analysis of animal palaeopathology? The first must be that it is looked for systematically. The corpus of published data will be inadequate if it consists only of isolated cases, noted either because the pathology is so severe as to demand attention, or because the sample was examined by an analyst with a particular interest in pathology. As things stand, one cannot tell whether the lack of mention of pathology in a report indicates a generally healthy population of animals, or the non-recording of what was, in fact, an appreciable amount of evidence. If it has not been possible to undertake full recording of the palaeopathology of a sample, the published report should state that pathology has not been recorded, and not merely pass over the topic without mention. The second recommendation must be that some indication is given of the prevalence of a condition in the sample concerned. A record of osteo-arthritic lesions in the acetabulae of cattle pelves from a sample is useful in itself, but more so if we can tell whether the affected joints comprised 1 per cent or 25 per cent of the cattle pelvic acetabulae in the sample.

A third recommendation is that the emphasis is put on *describing* and not simply *diagnosing* the lesions concerned. Our knowledge of animal palaeopathology is insufficiently complete for there to be a consensus on the diagnostic features of all major pathological conditions. In the example mentioned above, it would not be enough to report that 10 per cent of cattle pelvic acetabulae showed osteo-arthritic lesions: the diagnostic criteria should also be described and typical specimens illustrated. Description of a lesion needs to include a number of details. The location, given in conventional anatomical terminology, is obviously essential, as is the extent of the lesion. Most pathological lesions can be described in terms of whether they consist of an increase in bone at the affected site (*hyperostotic* or *blastic*), or a reduction in bone (often termed *lytic* or *clastic* lesions), or sometimes both, as when a central zone of bone destruction is surrounded by a hyperostosis. The effects may be apparent throughout the thickness of bone in the affected area, or may be restricted to the bone surface (*periostotic*). This much – location, extent, gain or loss of bone – gives an essential outline description of the lesion. Further detail will be necessary to describe, for example, whether new bone formed around a lesion is dense, compact bone, or whether it is distinctly porous, or granular in texture. There is scope here both for systematic use of a restricted terminology, and for the inspired use of metaphor. In the example of the cave bear pathology described above, Capasso (1998) describes the lesion as resembling pumice-stone. Though hardly a technical pathological term, this immediately conveys an impression of the texture of the bone, and the scale of the porosity which it exhibits. In short, the description needs to be sufficiently detailed to support any differential diagnosis which is offered, and to allow alternative diagnoses to be considered and tested. Illustration is also necessary, whether by photography or line-drawing, and the publication of radiographs may be helpful. My own preference is for the use of simple line drawings (e.g. Fig. 9.6) as a means of recording for archive the interpretation which has been made of photographs and,

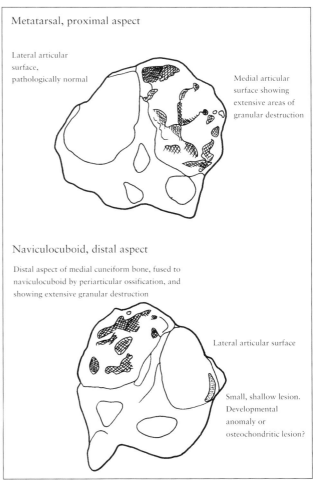

Fig. 9.6. An example of the use of a simple annotated line drawing to give both a record and an interpretation of a bone lesion, in this case the cattle bones pictured in Fig. 9.4.

109

especially, radiographs. Someone else's photograph or radiograph of a lump of bone can appear remarkably uninformative.

Apart from such straightforward methodological recommendations, what is the way forward for animal palaeopathology? Perhaps we need to go back to the beginning and make clear what it is we want to find out from studying palaeopathology. A major part of the rationale has to be the interpretation of past patterns of disease and injury in terms of human interactions with other vertebrate species. In that case, some pathological conditions are of more interest to us than others, such as the lower-limb arthropathies of cattle and horses. Palaeopathology is perhaps most effective when it is problem-driven, concerned to investigate a particular question to which the prevalence of a particular pathology might provide part of the answer, than when it is empirical and descriptive. An implication of that approach is that we must be willing to revisit samples of bones, to survey them for some previously overlooked condition, and not assume that any one record of a bone sample is definitive.

The problem of defining the boundaries of 'normal' bones has already been touched upon. Some pathological conditions will produce variations of size and shape which take a particular bone beyond the 'normal' range for that element and species. There will be variation in size and shape within populations, and variation within our archaeological samples. The next chapter tackles that variation and its recording and interpretation.

TEN

METRICAL AND NON-METRICAL VARIATION

If we take, for example, fifteen adult bison femora and lay them out on the bench, it will immediately be apparent that they are not all the same; indeed, probably no two of them will be entirely identical. The differences may not be substantial enough to make us doubt that the bones are all from one species, but they will reflect differences in the genetic make-up, including sex, of the animals, and further variation caused by the different environments and circumstances which they have experienced during life. Some will simply be larger than others, some will vary in the relative proportions of length and breadth, while others may vary in minor anatomical features such as the presence or absence of a particular foramen. Inherent in this variation there is information about the original animals and the populations from which they derive. Zooarchaeologists attempt to record at least some of this variation, and this chapter is about the recording and interpretation of metrical and non-metrical variation.

Metrical variation is often described as *continuous* variation; that is, an observation can take any value (or, at least, any that we can measure) between the extreme limits observed for that particular variable. Non-metrical variation is *discontinuous*; an observation can take only one of a fixed number of values. To put this into familiar terms, human body weight is a continuous variable: I can weigh 73.5kg or 80.11kg, or any other value which the bathroom scales are capable of resolving, and which does not exceed the physiological limits for an adult male human. However, the number of permanent molars in the mouth of an adult human is a discontinuous variable. The maximum is twelve – three molars in each quarter – and some people have only ten or eight. Barring somewhat exceptional trauma, one cannot have 9.3 molars: the range of possible values is discontinuous, and the number of molars per mouth constitutes non-metrical variation. Most of the recording and research which has gone on in zooarchaeology concerns metrical variation, and this chapter is largely concerned with that topic. Methodological considerations are discussed first, then a series of examples which show some of the ways in which metrical data are used. Finally, non-metrical variation is reviewed, with some examples that show this to be an unjustly neglected area of research.

MEASURING BONES: HOW?

Metrical data – the size and shape of bones – can easily be measured by applying some sort of accurate measuring device to the bones and simply reading off the measurements. The appropriate measuring device will depend upon the measurement concerned. For much zooarchaeological work, measurements are taken using calipers of the sort routinely used in engineering. These consist of a pair of jaws that slide apart along a finely graduated scale (Fig. 10.1). The distance between the jaws is usually given either by reading an approximate measurement from the scale and refining it by reference to a dial that enables, perhaps, the nearest 0.1mm to be read off, or by reading the measurement directly from a digital read-out. One can tell the approximate age of a zooarchaeologist by noting whether they can read calipers fitted with an old vernier scale!

Longer measurements, such as the length of limb bones of a large mammal, will be taken using what is sometimes called an osteometric box. Such a device merely allows two measuring points to be moved apart along a graduated scale, and is essentially a very large pair of calipers re-engineered to take measurements beyond the range of normal hand-held calipers. Exceptionally, it may be necessary to take measurements around a curved surface, as when recording the circumference of a bone, or the distance along an arc between two points on a skull. In these cases, a narrow measuring tape may be used, or the measurement may be taken using a piece of string or wire, which is then measured using calipers.

Whatever the technology involved, if the data are to be comparable between different analysts, then there has to be some agreement on what is measured. Two analysts studying the length of femora in bison might seek to use each other's data, only to find that they had each defined the length in slightly different ways, and so taken slightly different

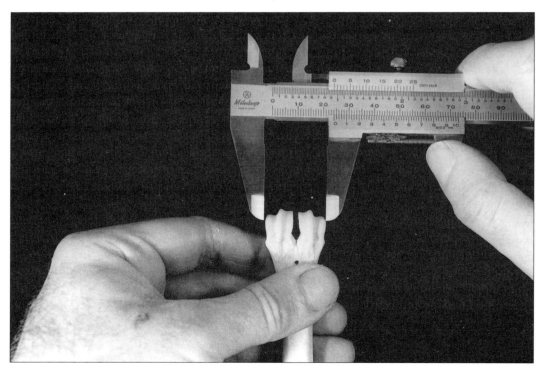

Fig. 10.1. Calipers, to illustrate their use in measuring bones. Note the vernier scale, indicative of the author's age!

measurements. To this end, a published series of standard measurements (von den Driesch 1976) is widely used. This source gives illustrations and definitions of hundreds of different measurements, intended to accommodate the range of mammal and bird taxa most often encountered in Old World archaeology, and is certainly adaptable to accommodate New World taxa as well (Fig. 10.2).

Any such guide needs to be comprehensive, but that does not mean that all of the measurements defined in it have to be taken if they are available. Many of them are very closely correlated with one another, and some are clearly included only because they have been published in earlier work. The point of measuring bones is in order to find something out, and the measurements which

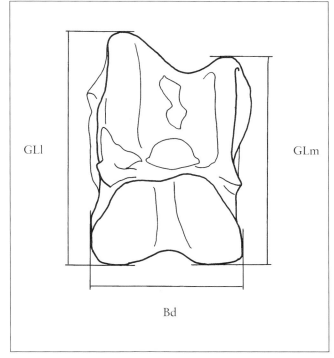

Fig. 10.2. An example of the illustration of standard descriptions of bone measurements. Here, three measurements are illustrated for the cattle astragalus. Obviously, the same definitions could be applied to any other ungulate species of sufficiently similar anatomy.

are taken should be those required for that investigation. They should conform as far as possible to some published standard, and if not they should be thoroughly and unambiguously defined, but can exclude measurements which are not immediately needed. Unused measurements taken just because a definition of that measurement has been published are redundant data, and redundant data are a waste of time.

Methods of summarizing and presenting biometrical data depend upon the use which is being made of them, and a certain amount of idiosyncratic preference on the part of the analyst. Personally, I prefer to tabulate summary descriptive statistics for each measured variable for each sample. To illustrate the point, Table 10.1 gives summary statistics for three measurements taken on cattle bones from one of the deposits from Caerleon that we have previously discussed.

The mean, standard deviation and number of cases could be regarded as an essential minimum, as they give the 'average' value for that variable, a measure of how the observations were spread around that average, and the size of the sample on which the figures are based. From those three statistics, one can calculate the standard error of the mean (a handy measure of how close the sample mean is likely to approximate the population mean), and the 95 per cent confidence intervals (a modified version of the same measure). For example, for the GLl measurement of the astragalus in Table 10.1, the confidence limits are 60.1 and 64.2mm; i.e. we can have 95 per cent confidence that had we measured all of the astragali of all of the cattle in the population from which that sample was derived, the population mean GLl would have fallen between those two values. Had we measured a sample of fifty, instead of just seventeen, the confidence limits would have been narrower – from 60.9 to 63.2mm. Some might also tabulate the minimum and maximum values, to show the extreme largest and smallest measurements obtained. That can be unhelpful, as the sample might happen to include an extremely large or small specimen so giving an outlying value for either the maximum or minimum. Among the metacarpal distal ends represented by the data in Table 10.1, there is a single specimen measuring 66.9mm – over 6mm broader than the next largest. That extreme specimen might be important in its own right, but measurements from it will artificially inflate the range (i.e. the difference between the minimum and maximum), and may give the impression that the sample was more variable than was actually the case. The standard deviation gives a better measure of the scatter of observations around the mean, and is less influenced by one or two outlying values.

Table 10.1. *Tabulated summary statistics for a sample of astragali and metacarpals of cattle from the late fourth-century sample B at Caerleon, to show what might be considered the useful minimum of descriptive statistics.*

The abbreviations given for the measurements follow von den Driesch (1976), and may be described as follows:

GLl	Greatest length, i.e. on the lateral side of the astragalus
Bd	Greatest medio-lateral breadth of the distal end (measured on the epiphysis of the metacarpal).

Measurement	Mean	Standard Deviation	Number of Cases
Astragalus			
GLl	62.06	4.13	17
Bd	39.82	3.16	17
Metacarpal			
Bd	54.93	4.95	14

Some people find tables such as Table 10.1 utterly repellent, and prefer to see biometrical data summarized in graphical form. A histogram such as Fig. 10.3 certainly gives a good impression of the overall distribution of observations, but needs to be combined with descriptive statistics if it is to be compared in any quantified way with data from another sample. Graphical presentation thus has to be accompanied by tabulated statistics which are effectively describing the same thing as the graphic, and that may not be the best use of publication space. What graphical representation can do is to show the relationship between two measurements, by plotting them together as a scattergram (Fig. 10.4).

The scatter of points on the graph conveys information about the closeness of the relationship between the two measurements (correlation), and whether the specimens represented on the graph vary only in size (points scattered along a line from bottom-left to

Fig. 10.3. An example of the use of a histogram to display metrical data, in this case the data in Table 10.1.

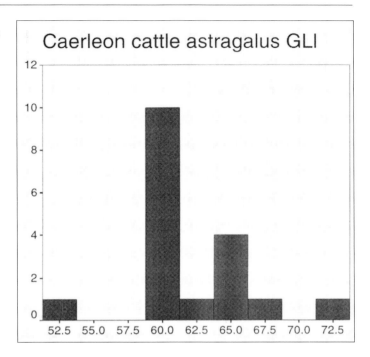

Fig. 10.4. An example of the use of a scattergram to show the relationship between two variables.

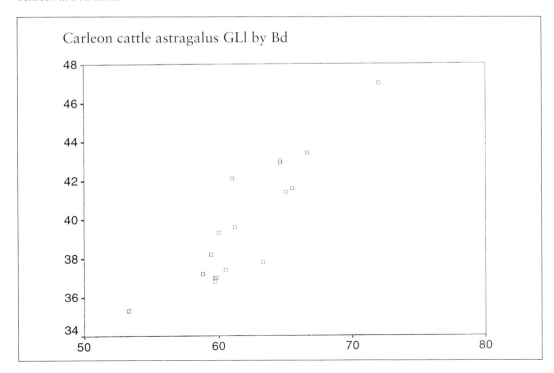

top-right), or in shape as well (points dispersed towards the top-left and bottom-right corners). The real skill in using scatter-grams lies in deciding which pair of measurements should be plotted together to investi-gate a particular question, and that requires under-standing the data as shapes of bones, and hence as animals.

So what do bone measure-ments represent, in terms of flesh-and-blood animals? The most obvious thing is the size of the animal, but size can be defined in a number of ways. The length of limb bones is obviously closely correlated with the height of the animal, usually expressed for quadrupeds as the shoulder (or withers) height. The reconstruction of shoulder height has been one of the major uses to which bone measurements have been put, using modern analogue data to show the relationship between a given bone length and the shoulder height of the animal. Von den Driesch & Boessneck (1974) recommended a series of factors derived from earlier publications which give a multiplier by which to convert, for example, the length of a sheep humerus to an estimated shoulder height for the animal. There are two main benefits to making such a calculation. The first is that the estimated shoulder height has some meaning in terms of whole, live animals, in a way that bone lengths do not. The largest cattle metatarsal in the Caerleon sample was 244mm in length. Converted to a shoulder height of 1.33m, that measurement immediately comes into perspective: its shoulders would have been level with my chest. The second is that conversion to estimated shoulder heights allows measurements of different elements to be directly compared. For example, if our sample has yielded length measurements for three humeri and four tibiae, those measurements have to be treated as two separate samples: converted to shoulder height estimates, they can be treated as one sample.

Size can also be defined in terms of weight, and this may be a more important parameter if our concern is with potential meat-yields of prey animals. Barbara Noddle (1973) investigated the relationship between a number of bone measurements on cattle and carcass weight, using modern animals to obtain reference data. It is important to note that we might expect this relationship to be a power relationship of the form $y = a.x^b$. Animals are three-dimensional objects. Their weight varies with their volume, and their volume varies with the cube of any linear dimension. Studies such as Noddle's, which attempt to find a linear relationship between bone measurements and weight, will thus only be partly successful, as the linear relationship should always give a less-good fit than a power relationship.

Fish add one more layer of complexity, as size in fish is an estimator of age, so that measurements of bones give both an estimate of size and therefore weight and meat yield, and also of the demography of the sampled population, topics which have already been discussed in Chapters 6 and 8. Modern reference samples of fish are used to derive linear regression equations for different species by means of which measurements of individual bones may be converted to estimates of body length (e.g. Smith 1995; Leach et al. 1997; Zohar et al. 1997).

Before moving away from methodological considerations, one more technique needs to be considered. One of the values of shoulder height estimation is that it allows measurements taken on different elements to be incorporated into the same analysis. Another means of doing this is to convert each measurement into a ratio between the observed value and the corresponding measurements taken on the skeleton of one individual animal of that species. This 'standard animal' approach is particularly valuable with small or fragmented samples, when no single element yields sufficient data to give a usable sample on its own. A disadvantage of the ratio figures is a tendency to exaggerate the variance of the sample, and it is customary to convert the ratios to their logarithms ('log-ratio method'; e.g. Reitz & Ruff 1994). For further discussion of the minutiae of this, and other related procedures, see Meadow (1999).

Log-ratio conversion of data maximizes the use of the available data, and has the advantage that the ratios characteristic of different elements can be examined separately. If, for example, the log-ratio values obtained from fore-limb measurements were consistently different from those obtained from hind-limb measurements, then one might conclude that the overall morphology of animals in the sample differed from that of the standard animal from which the baseline data were derived. Of course, this might be because the standard animal was somewhat exceptional, and there are advantages to taking a series of sample mean values as the standards against which to calculate log-ratio values.

MEASURING BONES: WHY?

Biometrical data are put to a range of uses in zooarchaeology. One of the most obvious is in the separation of skeletally similar species. Biometrical data can be both more sensitive and more objective than human judgement in determining whether a given specimen should be attributed to one taxon rather than another. An excellent example of this is with sheep and goat bones, the difficulty of separating which has biblical authority. Payne (1969) used two measurements on the distal end of the metacarpal of sheep and goats to separate the species. This work has recently been applied to bones from the Neolithic site at Arene Candide, Italy (Rowley-Conwy 1998). Rowley-Conwy also experimented with ratios of measurements around the proximal end of the metatarsal bone, and obtained quite satisfactory separation of apparent sheep and goat groups. His results indicated that both species were present at the site in the Middle Neolithic, but only sheep in the Early Neolithic, an inference which is of some importance in terms of inter-regional contact throughout peninsular Italy.

Another major topic to which biometric studies have made a contribution is in recognising the early stages of animal domestication. Domestication has induced morphological change within species, ultimately leading, some would argue, to separation into wild and domestic species. A size reduction seems to have accompanied the domestication of many species (e.g. Higham 1968). There is no general agreement as to why this size reduction happened, but the equation of small forms with domestic animals, in contrast to large wild forms of the same species, is well established in the literature. However, some species which did not undergo domestication early in the Holocene also show a marked size reduction around the same time, probably in response to climate change (Davis 1981).

The separation of wild and domestic pigs serves as a good example. Prehistoric European domestic pigs are appreciably smaller than modern wild boar (Teichert 1969). Only through recent selective breeding have domestic pig sizes (measured by Teichert as estimated shoulder height) attained those typical of wild boar, though with a much bulkier overall conformation. Lasota-Moskalewska *et al.* (1987) undertook a more thorough study of data from sites in Poland, and constructed an index to show the degree of dimorphism between wild and domestic pigs. This index increases gradually from the Neolithic through to the medieval period, and is more pronounced in some elements of the skeleton than in others. Payne & Bull (1988) reported a detailed analysis of metrical variation in a modern wild boar sample from Turkey, and proposed that particular measurements of the teeth and hind limbs showed less inherent variability and so constitute the best measurements for discriminating between wild and domestic pigs. The assumption that large pigs are wild pigs still passes largely unchallenged, though Rowley-Conwy (1995) has re-examined some claims for early domestic pigs and cattle from sites in southern Scandinavia and in Iberia, and has argued that the small individuals could just be outliers to the range of 'wild-sized' individuals.

By drawing together biometrical data from sites over a large geographical area, size variation through time and across regions can be examined. One particularly extensive survey has been conducted on cattle and sheep bone measurements from prehistoric to medieval sites across western and central Europe (Audoin-Rouzeau 1991a; 1991b; 1995). The scale of this survey has allowed some sweeping generalizations to be made, such as noting the consistently small size of sheep from medieval samples from England, compared with contemporary samples from continental Europe (Audoin-Rouzeau 1991b, 10–12). Other surveys have been more targeted, taking, for example, the few centuries during which sheep in England increased in size from the small medieval animals to the much bulkier sheep described by eighteenth-century agricultural writers (O'Connor 1995). This study showed that quite small sheep were still present in samples dated to the eighteenth century, suggesting that the agricultural writers were describing the more go-ahead livestock breeders, and not giving a useful overview of eighteenth-century livestock. Similarly, Reitz & Ruff (1994) have applied the log-ratio method to samples from European settlements in America to gauge the size and conformation of the cattle. Among other things, they note the large size of cattle from Puerto Real, Hispaniola, compared with cattle from the British settlement at Annapolis, Maryland, and suggest that the Spanish settlers of the Caribbean and Florida were introducing larger livestock than the British, and maintaining that difference in size. There may even be indications that the British settlers at Charleston acquired Spanish cattle for their herds.

Using bone measurements to trace phylogeny and affinities has been particularly important in investigations of dog skeletons from sites in the Pacific region. The metrical distinction of wolf and dog is one of zooarchaeology's more vexed questions. The distinctive differences, notably a greater tendency to crowding of the teeth in domestic dogs, have been extensively researched for over a century (e.g. Windle & Humphreys 1890). In some parts of the world there are no wild canids, such as wolves or jackals, which could have been domesticated, and so the spread of domestic dogs has been in association with people. In Australasia and the islands of Polynesia particular attention has been given to the different 'types' of dog characteristic of different mainland and island regions, and so of different human groups. Geoffrey Clark has gone to some lengths to define the skeletal characteristics which are typical of New Zealand dogs before European settlement (Clark 1997). An example of the value of this phylogenetic work concerns the skeleton of a dog from Pukapuka, in the Cook Islands of Polynesia. As first described, this dog was claimed to have skeletal traits typical of a dingo-type animal, indicating an origin in Australia, and therefore contact between Australia and Polynesia which had not previously been inferred (Shigehara 1993). Essentially, one dog skeleton was used to support major claims about human movement and cultural contact in the region. The affinities of the Pukapuka dog have since been categorically refuted by Clark (1998), using a complex multivariate analysis of skull shape to show that the dog has little affinity either with dingo-type dogs or with other early Polynesian dogs. Clark's conclusion, in fact, is that the Pukapuka dog's closest affinities are with European dogs, throwing into question the original dating of the find.

Biometrical data offer numerous lines of investigation, and this chapter can do little more than to scratch the surface and show a few examples. Two main points need to be made about biometrical investigations. The first is that it is all too easy for the collection and graphical presentation of biometrical data to become an end in itself, as if simply tabulating measurements constitutes a research activity. Biometrical data should be used to achieve pre-defined ends, and sufficient data published in whatever form is necessary to support and elucidate the research aim to which they contribute. The place for unused numerical data is the unpublished archive. The second point is that the division between metrical and non-metrical data may not be as clear-cut as this chapter has presented it. Some skeletal traits may be usefully recorded in the form of measurements, but might equally well be recorded as a non-metrical character. A good example is the form of the distal metacarpal in sheep and goats, referred to earlier in this chapter. The distinctly different forms typical of sheep and of goats are conventionally recorded as the ratio between pairs of measurements, but with a little experience it is quite possible to allocate specimens to 'sheep' and 'goat' categories by visually assessing the same skeletal features. When recording skeletal variation within one species, therefore, we need to decide which would be the more appropriate way to define the trait which we seek to record.

NON-METRICAL VARIATION

The investigation of non-metrical traits in animal skeletons is a poorly developed area of research, with little systematic published record and mostly rather speculative interpretation. None the less, a few traits occur with sufficient frequency to suggest that they are worth recording systematically, and may have some interpretive value when we understand them a little better. In particular, two dental traits occur in bovids and some cervids. The first is the congenital absence of the second permanent premolar in the mandible (LPM_2). Although this tooth is often lost during life (e.g. Table 9.1), it is sometimes completely absent, with no trace of the tooth or its alveolus developing in the mandible. This trait has been known about for some time, having been reported in the clinical literature in cattle (Garlick 1954; Ohtaishi 1972), and in goats (Rudge 1970). The prevalence in modern animals is not well known: less than 1 per cent of cattle in Garlick's survey showed congenital absence of LPM_2. Andrews & Noddle (1975) reported the same trait in cattle and sheep mandibles from archaeological sites, demonstrating that congenital absence of the tooth could, with care, be distinguished from cases where the tooth had been lost during life with subsequent resorption of the alveolus. A single instance of absent LPM_2 in roe deer has been reported from Neolithic material from Bulhory, southern Moravia (Kratochvil 1986). The trait has been sporadically reported in the archaeological literature, though often with no indication of prevalence.

As with pathological conditions, it is important to know how many 'normal' specimens were seen in the sample. Reviewing data for cattle mandibles from Roman to medieval

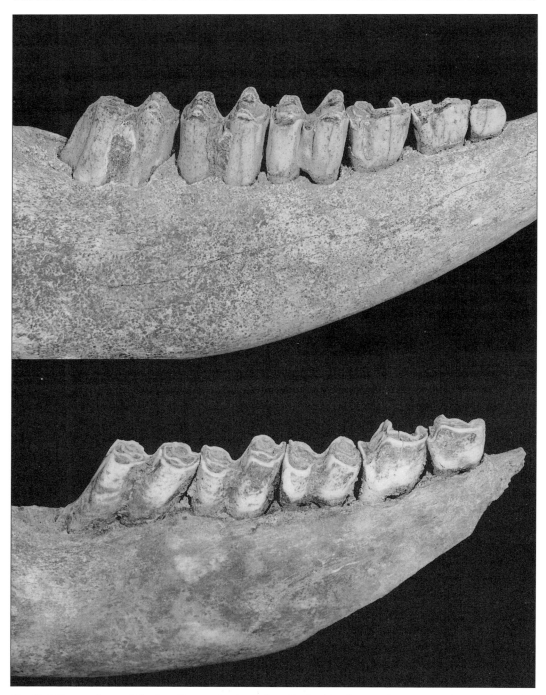

Fig. 10.5. Two cattle mandibles from Roman sites in northern England, to illustrate discontinuous traits. In both, the lower third molar (the tooth furthest to the left) has only two fully developed columns, and lacks the hypoconulid that normally comprises the distal part of the tooth. In the lower specimen, the lower second premolar (furthest to the right) is absent, and there is no trace of an alveolus, indicating that the tooth was congenitally absent.

samples from York, LPM_2 was congenitally absent from 6 to 8 per cent of specimens for which the appropriate part of the mandible could be examined (Bond & O'Connor 1998). This prevalence seems to be in accord with other published data for archaeological samples, but is remarkably high compared with the small amount of published work from modern cattle. To be honest, we cannot say why: the trait could be one against which there has been some degree of selection in modern cattle, though LPM_2 is almost redundant in the cattle jaw, and its congenital absence can hardly be a significant factor in feeding. Another possibility is that cattle in earlier times were maintained in smaller breeding groups, so that an uncommon genetic trait was more likely to be expressed in at least some herds. This may be an important line of argument. There are statistically significant differences in the frequency of absence of LPM_2 in sheep mandibles from different medieval sites in York, an observation which is consistent with other evidence that different parts of the city were acquiring sheep from different breeding populations (Bond & O'Connor 1998; see also Chapter 14). If nothing else, the prevalence of this trait may be useful as an indicator of genotype, particularly if supported by other evidence such as the prevalence of hornlessness in sheep and cattle.

Another dental trait which has received some attention is a distinctive malformation of the lower third molar (LM_3) in bovids and some cervids. This tooth normally consists of three distinct columns, of which the distal one is small but still makes some contribution to the occlusal surface of the tooth (Fig. 10.5). In a small proportion of cases, the distal column (anatomically, the talonid or hypoconulid) fails to develop completely or at all, sometimes being represented only by a small area of root coalescent with the roots of the adjacent column. This trait was noted by Guilday (1961) in a large sample of white-tailed deer (*Odocoileus virginianus*) from an early seventeenth-century Indian site at Washington Boro, Pennsylvania. Out of 297 mandibles, one had no third column at all on LM_3, and two more had the third column sufficiently under-developed to take the cusp out of occlusion. Reviewing my own data from York, this trait seems to be quite uncommon in sheep (less than 1 per cent), but shows a higher prevalence in cattle (around 3 per cent), with some indications of a particularly high prevalence in samples of Roman date (O'Connor 1989, 164–5). Again, we may not understand the full significance of this trait, but any sample which shows a high prevalence should be examined for other indications of a narrow or isolated genepool.

One other non-metrical trait which merits mention is the location of the major nutrient foramen in sheep femora. A branch of the femoral artery carries blood to the marrow cavity of the femur, passing through the cortical bone by way of a major foramen (Noddle 1978). In the great majority of sheep from most populations, this foramen is located on the anterior aspect of the bone, towards the proximal end (Fig. 10.6). In a minority of specimens, the foramen occupies one of two other positions: on the posterior aspect either around midshaft or towards the distal end. Exceptionally in adult sheep more than one position may be present. In most modern populations, the proximal position is predominant, with a few specimens showing the distal location, and fewer with the midshaft location. However, in some populations, the frequencies are quite different, and among British sheep breeds, the abnormal frequencies occur in breeds which are geographically restricted and which have been reduced to very small numbers, notably the Manx Loghtan, Ryeland and Portland breeds. A high frequency of midshaft or distal

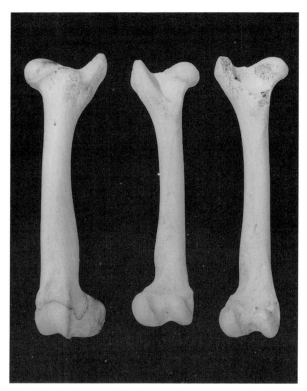

Fig. 10.6. Variation in the position of the major nutrient foramen in the sheep femur. The specimen on the left shows the foramen in the proximal anterior position, which is much the most common in most populations. In the middle specimen the foramen is just visible at midshaft on the posterior aspect, and in the right-hand specimen at a more distal position, also on the posterior aspect.

locations may thus convey some information about limited gene-flow or the gene-pool of the founder population. In archaeological material a high frequency of midshaft and distal locations has been noted in Neolithic material from the Skara Brae site in the Orkney Islands, a good candidate for breeding isolation (Noddle 1978). Furthermore, the same samples from medieval York which gave an unusually high frequency of absent LPM_2 in sheep mandibles also gave an unusually high frequency of occurrence of the distal location for this trait (Bond & O'Connor 1999).

It begins to look as if recording the location of nutrient foramina on sheep femora can tell us something about breeding groups within past sheep populations. No doubt there are other skeletal traits which we could also be recording, for a range of other species, which would enable us to study within-species variation in much the same way that blood group and eye colour can for humans. We have barely begun to scratch the surface of non-metrical variation, not least because there is so little clinical literature on which to base any interpretation of the archaeological data. However, this is one area where there is considerable potential for real advances to be made.

So far, this book has concentrated on bones, how they come to be deposited and recovered on archaeological sites, and some of the means of extracting useful information from them. The remaining chapters turn instead to some major topics which show animal bone data being used to address archaeological questions, and to understand people and their ecological role at various times and places. Obviously, the list of potential topics is long, and the selection given here is therefore a personal one. The intention is to show the analysis of animal bone samples of very different kinds, from very different archaeological contexts, and to show the connection of those animals with their human contemporaries.

ELEVEN

CLIMATE, ENVIRONMENT AND SMALL VERTEBRATES

This chapter is mostly about small mammals and herpetiles (i.e. amphibians and reptiles). These three groups of small-bodied, land-dwelling vertebrates tend to be recovered from archaeological deposits only when fine sieving is used, and then tend to be found together. They also have in common that their presence in archaeological deposits is usually interpreted as a death assemblage from the endemic fauna of the immediate vicinity, with minimal human involvement. People dig themselves a latrine pit, and the occasional mouse or frog falls into it and becomes a part of the forming deposit. However, there may be a more subtle association if the mouse was attracted to the human settlement by the prospect of food in the first place, or if the frog was attracted by the swarming invertebrates which were attracted by the latrine pit. When studying sites of past human settlement, we have to pay close attention to the taphonomy of the assemblage, and to the commensal behaviour of some species. Often, though, our assemblages come from deposits in caves or fissures, or from deposition in abandoned buildings, settings in which humans have had little direct influence on the species composition. Our main concern then is with the use of small vertebrates as indicators of past climate and environmental conditions. Ectothermic ('cold-blooded') taxa such as reptiles and amphibians are obviously quite sensitive to temperature changes, and so to climate change, and many rodents are highly adapted to particular habitats, and so to vegetation change as a consequence of climate change.

WHERE DID ALL THESE MICE COME FROM? UNDERSTANDING DEPOSITION

If we are to use small vertebrates as an indication of past environmental conditions, either in terms of large-scale climate or small-scale vegetation, it is essential that we understand the spatial and temporal catchment of the deposit in which the bones are found. Shipman's question 'What are all these bones doing here?' applies with force to small vertebrates. Although rodents, lizards and even snakes form a part of the human diet in some parts of the world, small vertebrates are generally more likely to be encountered in archaeological and recent geological deposits having been the food of something other than people. In particular, the pellets of undigested material ejected by various predatory birds, notably owls, are a potential source of small bones, and seem to be quite a common route by which small bones accumulate. The barn owl *Tyto alba*, in particular, has been implicated in the deposition of bones within abandoned buildings. Barn owls are creatures of habit, tending to take prey either to a nest site or to a preferred perch in order to consume and digest it. During the course of a night's hunting, several pellets of fur, claws and bones will be regurgitated on to the ground below the perch. If the pellets are not disturbed, or are quickly incorporated into a forming sediment, the more robust constituents, notably the bones, may survive as a closely packed clump of material. Identification and quantification of the taxa represented in the pellets will sometimes allow the assemblage to be attributed to a particular owl species, by analogy with the prey spectrum typical of that species today. This process of analogy has been used with confidence for many years, as examples in this chapter will show. We should exercise some caution, however. Studies comparing

Fig. 11.1. A typical example of small mammal and amphibian bones recovered by sieving. This sample was recovered from deposits overlying the floor of an abandoned Roman bath-house at Caerleon, in South Wales, and appears to be derived from pellets regurgitated by owls.

barn owl pellets from locations in Chile with pellets regurgitated by the same species in North America show quite substantial differences in species content and in the pattern of bone fragmentation (Saavedra & Simonetti 1998). Pellet composition is not simply a function of the owl species, but will vary between populations of the same species.

Table 11.1. *An assemblage of small mammal bones interpreted as having accumulated as the prey of a nocturnal bird, probably a barn owl.*

These specimens are from a sub-sample of an extensive deposit covering part of the floor of a Roman bath-house at Caerleon, in South Wales (O'Connor 1986b).
N is the number of mandibles attributed to each taxon; % is that number as a percentage of the total.

Taxon		N	%
Water shrew	*Neomys fodiens*	3	1.2
Common shrew	*Sorex araneus*	50	19.5
Pygmy shrew	*S. minutus*	8	3.1
Short-tailed vole	*Microtus agrestis*	55	21.5
Small vole sp.	*Microtus* sp.	62	24.2
Water vole	*Arvicola terrestris*	5	1.9
House mouse	*Mus* c.f. *domesticus*	15	5.9
Wood mouse	*Apodemus sylvaticus*	31	12.1
Mouse spp.	*Mus* or *Apodemus*	25	9.8
Harvest mouse	*Micromys minutus*	2	0.8

Where the presence of small bones can be used to argue for the presence of roosting owls, deductions may be drawn about the intensity of human activity at the site. For example, a deposit of small bones in one room of the Roman *basilica* in London was argued to be an accumulation of barn owl pellets, showing that the building was largely abandoned by people at the time of deposition of that layer (West & Milne 1993). Perhaps the most memorable aspect of the bones from Caerleon was a deposit consisting of many tens of thousands of rodent and frog bones on the floor of the abandoned bath house. Fig. 11.1 shows a small fraction of the deposit, and the reader might understand my initial reaction: where do I start? In fact, I started by extracting all mandibles and skulls from a sub-sample of the deposit, as these elements allow the most precise identification. Table 11.1 summarizes the species composition, which is most consistent with barn owl pellets. However, the significance in this case lay not so much in the indication of abandonment as in the implication that the building retained a roof at that point, protecting the slowly accumulating pellets from dispersal by rain and wind.

Not all small bone accumulations are from owl pellets, of course, and some authors have been particularly cautious about attributing bones to pellets. Before offering an interpretation of the small bones from fills of a late fifteenth-century well in London, Armitage & West (1987) carefully considered a range of depositional processes. The bones could have come from the droppings of some mammalian predators, and so could include prey captured some distance from the well. In that case, the bones would have been highly fragmented, and shown traces of acid corrosion from partial digestion. The bones could have come from owl pellets, with the same implication of prey being brought together from a large area. However, the samples included relatively intact skulls which would have been too big for any likely owl to have ingested in the first place, let alone eject again as part of a pellet, and the range of prey did not match that characteristic of any northern European owl. A third possibility was that the well just acted as a pit-fall trap, collecting animals which blundered into it. The high proportion of juvenile rodents was consistent with this interpretation, leading the authors to infer that the well had no superstructure around its edge, and that the sample represented the vertebrate fauna from the immediate vicinity of the well. This particular example shows how sorting out the taphonomy of the sample influences the interpretation, though, as Morales Muñiz & Rodriguez (1997, 623) warn, 'various accumulating agents can work in convergent ways . . . in the absence of reliable diagnostic criteria it might prove extremely difficult to assign specific remains to particular taphonomic groups'. Stahl (1996) details the criteria that we might look for to distinguish, for example, bones accumulated by predators from those accumulated by other thanatic processes.

Some amphibians hibernate in substantial numbers, and may not all survive the winter. This can result in quantities of bones of frogs and toads, especially, being deposited in close association. Where human activity, such as the construction of cairns, produces loose, rubbly conditions into which frogs and toads can insert themselves, there is the obvious potential for the intrusion of amphibian bones into a pre-existing structure. It is not uncommon to find clusters of bones of frogs and toads within and immediately beneath prehistoric burial mounds in Britain, particularly in upland regions where the body of the mound is composed of rock rubble rather than earth (e.g. Maltby 1983). Similarly, the fills of a well at the Roman villa at Dalton-on-Tees, in northern England, contained numerous frog and toad bones. In this case, the top of the well appears to have been deliberately filled with rubble and refuse that had accumulated in a nearby abandoned building. It appears that the rubble harboured large numbers of frogs and toads which were then dumped into the well. If the bones from Dalton-on-Tees had been studied without noting the other materials from the same deposit – tile, pottery, building stone – the frogs and toads might have been regarded as a death assemblage accumulated in the well as amphibians fell in and failed to escape. However, their stratigraphic position, high in the fills of a deliberately back-filled feature, and the associated debris pointed to the unfortunate creatures having been gathered up with the rubble in which they had sought shelter.

One approach to distinguishing the various sources of small vertebrate bones in archaeological deposits is that used at the Palaeolithic site of Douara cave, near Palmyra, in central Syria (Payne 1983). The vertical and horizontal distribution of bones of different taxa were plotted throughout the excavated deposits by mapping the location and concentration of different bones on to a cross-section of the excavated deposits. Bones of small rodents and of lizards showed quite marked concentrations which did not coincide with concentrations of lithic tools or other debris of human activity. Bones of larger mammals and of hedgehogs (*Hemiechinus* sp.) showed a closer spatial association with occupation debris, suggesting that these species were the remains of people's food. The small rodents and lizards were taken to have been deposited in owl pellets.

WHERE DID THIS TORTOISE COME FROM? SMALL VERTEBRATES AND CLIMATE

What of interpretation? A good example of the use of small mammal bones in the reconstruction of past habitats and climate change comes from Westbury-sub-Mendip, Somerset (Bishop 1982). Limestone quarrying over many years at Westbury gradually exposed a series of caves, in one of which was a bone-bearing deposit containing material apparently derived from the lair of an extinct bear, *Ursus deningeri*, a characteristic species of the Middle Pleistocene. Overlying the bear-den deposit was a thick deposit rich in small vertebrate remains, dominated by voles of the genus *Pitymys*, and apparently derived from owl pellets. *Pitymys* does not occur in Britain today, and so analogy with modern owl pellets could only be drawn with some caution. None the less, the small mammals seem to constitute a fauna of temperate conditions, and the deposit is taken to represent a warm stage in the complex and poorly understood oscillations of mid-Pleistocene climate.

At the cave site of l'Hortus, in the Langued'oc of southern France, a similar deposit shows a quite subtle shift in predominance of different rodents at different levels in the deposit (Chaline 1972). At some levels the vole *Microtus nivalis*, typical of rather dry and open terrain, is common, while at others the fauna consists of dormouse species and wood mouse *Apodemus sylvaticus*, apparently indicating more wooded conditions. As this is a relatively sheltered part of France, not subject to the extremes of temperature that affected northern Europe during the last Ice Age, the open grassland stages represented by *M. nivalis* probably correspond to periods of relatively cool climate, and the woodland stages to warmer periods, so allowing some correlation of this sequence with the climatic cycles of the later part of the Pleistocene.

One reptile which has been of some importance in assessing past climate change is the European pond tortoise *Emys orbicularis*. Although quite tolerant of cold winters, this species requires quite warm, dry summers if it is to breed successfully, conditions which do not prevail in north-western Europe today. Recoveries of this species from outside its present range may therefore give us some indication of warmer summers in the past. Just such an interpretation has been made of a specimen recovered from mid-Holocene deposits in the Netherlands, which is consistent with other evidence of slightly warmer summers in that region during the Neolithic period (van Wijngaarden-Bakker 1996). On a contemporary note, when talking about 'greenhouse effect' global warming with zooarchaeologist colleagues, it is notable how often the discussion turns to pond tortoises. Perhaps this well-known indicator of past climate change will serve as a useful indicator of current change if its breeding range extends back into north-western Europe.

Small mammals are particularly important habitat and climate indicators in arid parts of the world, where more direct evidence of vegetation change in the form of stratified deposits with pollen or plant macrofossils is unlikely to be preserved. The site of Klasies River Mouth, in South Africa, is important as one of the earliest sites with evidence of modern *Homo sapiens*, associated with Middle Stone Age cultural material. By plotting the abundance of small mammals typical of open terrain and of more closed vegetation through the thickness of the deposits, Avery (1987) was able to infer vegetation change in the region which appears to correlate with temperature fluctuations inferred from oxygen isotope analysis of deep-sea cores.

A particularly subtle interpretation of small mammal remains from Middle Pleistocene cave deposits comes from Gran Dolina, in the Duero Basin of Central Spain (Fernandez-Jalvo & Andrews 1992). Much of the analysis of these bones consisted of a detailed examination of the patterns of breakage, abrasion and partial digestion, in order to ascertain how much of the material was derived from owl pellets, and possibly from which species of owl. The authors conclude that at least three different owl species were involved in the accumulation at different levels in the 20m of deposition. One of the three, the long-eared owl (*Asio otus*) is a selective hunter, and so characteristically accumulates a more restricted diversity of prey in its pellets than would a more opportunistic hunter. One of the sedimentary units at Gran Dolina showed a distinctly low diversity of rodents compared with the others. This could have been taken to indicate some local change in vegetation, perhaps in response to worsening climatic conditions. However, bones from this unit had the characteristics of long-eared owl prey, so the reduced diversity is probably explained by the predator rather than by a change in climate: close attention to the taphonomy of the material was essential to the interpretation.

It is less common for small vertebrates to be used as indicators of climate and environment over the last few millennia. An important exception is the Monte di Tuda cave in northern Corsica, where very rich deposits derived from owl pellets have allowed a detailed study of vegetation change over the last 2,500 years (Vigne & Valladas 1996). Phases of cereal agriculture can be identified in the sequence, dated approximately to the Early Roman period and Early Middle Ages. Changes in the abundance of shrews and amphibians appear to mark periods of damper climate. The interpretation of data from Corsica is complicated by the presence in early to mid-Holocene deposits of endemic species which are now extinct, making it difficult to work from modern analogue faunas. For Monte di Tuda this problem was addressed by using a complex multivariate analysis to attribute the extinct species to faunal groups on the basis of the degree of association between extinct and extant species through the sequence of deposits. Thus the extinct vole *Tyrrhenicola henseli* showed a correlation with shrew species typical of rather open vegetation, and some correlation with the occurrence of house mouse, suggesting that this vole might have adapted quite well to the open fields around human settlements. In contrast, the extinct ochotonid *Prolagus sardus*, a relative of today's rabbits and pikas, seems to have been a species of low scrub, avoiding human disturbance. Samples dated to the fourth to second centuries cal. BC at Monte di Tuda record the arrival of black rat (*Rattus rattus*), of which more in Chapter 13.

Monte di Tuda is a good example of a site that has given information about the extinction of some species and extension of the range of another. Archaeological studies of small vertebrates make a useful contribution to the biogeographical study of present-day distributions, and sometimes throw up intriguing questions. One such concerns the water vole *Arvicola terrestris*, formerly common throughout Europe, and probably the inspiration for Ratty in *The Wind in the Willows*. In Britain today water voles are species of grassy river banks, yet bones of water vole are commonly encountered in archaeological deposits far from water, and are sometimes scarce in assemblages from riverside sites (e.g. in Yalden 1995). It looks as if water voles used to be not only much more abundant than is the case today, but also that they occupied a far greater range of habitats. In fact, if water voles were now extinct, and we were attempting to reconstruct their ecology from their correlation with other species in archaeological samples, we might think that they were a species of open upland habitats.

It is possible that water voles were displaced by a more competitive species, and suspicion falls on the pushy, versatile rat. Black rat is unlikely to be the culprit. As we shall see, this species is closely associated with human settlement, and has been predominantly an urban animal in Britain. However, the brown or Norway rat *Rattus norvegicus* occupies urban and rural habitats alike, and spread very rapidly after its introduction in the eighteenth century. Water voles might have been out-competed by brown rats, though if that were the case, their current concentration on river banks is hard to explain, as brown rats are common along rivers and are adept swimmers. Another possibility is that water voles lost out to rabbits. If water voles were formerly occupants of a grazing niche, avoiding competition with other voles by means of their larger body size, then the arrival of rabbits as a widespread feral animal could have had a serious impact. All of this is speculation based upon the archaeological data and some knowledge of the ecology of the species concerned. However, it highlights one instance in which the archaeological study of small mammal bones has raised interesting questions about the present distribution and abundance of familiar species, and about the conservation of a species in rapid decline.

Interpretation of small vertebrates in terms of large-scale change in climate and vegetation takes us away from human settlement and activities, and a lot of published work on small vertebrates seems to have more to do with Quaternary palaeontology than with archaeology. Small mammals and herpetiles comprise a challenging and technically problematic area of study, but a worthwhile one none the less. The use of small mammal sequences from caves as indicators of past vegetation and climate has tended to dominate the literature, but, as this brief survey has shown, there is also great potential in using small mammals and herpetiles as indicators of the conditions which people were creating around themselves. Rats and mice are the obvious commensal animals to study, but one might note the abundance in which frog bones are found around settlement sites of all periods in northern Europe. It is quite possible that this tells us something about, for example, the effect of human settlement in attracting and concentrating invertebrates, to which food source the frogs and perhaps other predators were then attracted. Or maybe the frogs themselves were sometimes used as food by the people: would we recognize that in the zooarchaeological record?

The topic of small animals as food is properly the subject of the next chapter, though if we fail to recognize that a particular species has been used for food by people, there can be odd consequences for the interpretation of small vertebrates as indicators of past environment (Fig. 11.2). For example, sites in the Cape region of South Africa commonly yield bones of the mole-rat *Bathyergus suillus*, and there has been something of a debate as to whether humans or eagle owls (*Bubo capensis*) were responsible for accumulating the bones, and therefore whether the considerable differences in relative abundance seen from site to site could be interpreted in environmental terms. The Blombos Cave site in the southern Cape has yielded mole-rat bones with distinctive patterns of charring, which are matched by the charring seen on specimens cooked by present-day people in the same area (Henshilwood 1997). In this case the debate seems to be shifting towards prehistoric collection and consumption of mole-rats, and thus to their interpretation in subsistence, rather than environmental, terms.

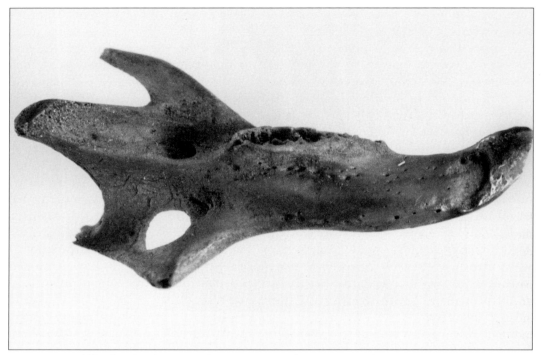

Fig. 11.2. Mandible of garden dormouse (Eliomys quercinus) *from Roman York (see Fig. 14.1). Was this animal a commensal pest, an unusual snack or a pet? (Photo courtesy of York Archaeological Trust)*

Even where the small mammals clearly were taken for food, there may be some environmental information. In northern Arizona, jackrabbits (*Lepus californicus*) and desert cottontails (*Sylvilagus audobonii*) were hunted in large numbers by Sinagua people living in the San Francisco Peaks region in the eleventh to fourteenth centuries AD. A comparison of the fragmentation pattern seen in Sinagua assemblages with that typical of contemporaneous assemblages from the Great Basin and Hohokam areas of southern Nevada shows the Sinagua material to have been less intensively processed, and these assemblages also show a higher proportion of jackrabbits. As jackrabbits are generally more common in open vegetation, while cottontails prefer low scrub, this difference could be taken to reflect differences in vegetation cover between the regions concerned. The Sinagua people grew crops and maintained fields, and might thus have created patches of habitat that particularly favoured jackrabbits (Quirt-Booth & Cruz-Uribe 1997).

The Sinagua example links us with the next chapter, which sets out to review the characteristics and diversity of bone assemblages from archaeological sites at which people lived primarily by hunting and foraging.

TWELVE

HUNTING AND FISHING: PEOPLE AS PREDATORS

It is a familiar assertion that people have been hunters and gatherers of food for most of the existence of our species, yet the archaeological record in the Old World, at least, is dominated by investigations of agricultural settlements, forts, castles and towns. Hunter-gatherer sites offer the opportunity to investigate humans acting directly as predators, perhaps in competition with other predatory species. Hunting is not a simple matter, nor do hunter-gatherer sites lack subtle complexity: as we shall see, some are very complex indeed. This chapter sets out to consider a few general points about the debris of human hunting activity, then reviews a series of case studies which show people targeting a particular prey species, people hunting a very wide range of prey, and hunting assuming a more social role in complex societies with an agricultural base.

In Chapter 11 we saw how death assemblages of small mammals can often be recognized as the remains of prey of other predators, such as owls. How do we recognize a bone deposit as the debris of predation by humans? In some circumstances the evidence will be direct and fairly unambiguous. The bone debris may have accumulated at a location where there are structures which clearly represent human activity of some kind. Hunting peoples are generally mobile, and seldom establish long-term settlements on the scale that agricultural peoples may. None the less a regularly used occupation site might have structures sufficiently substantial to survive as an archaeological site.

Even where structures are absent, the bone accumulations may include artefacts, most obviously the tools used to kill and butcher the prey. Many of the bison kill-sites of the American Plains, to which we return below, have yielded projectile points and other tools, and sometimes debris from the manufacture or finishing of stone tools. A good example is the palaeoindian Agate Basin site in the north-western High Plains in Wyoming, from which came several examples of elongated, fluted stone projectile points of the Folsom tradition (Frison & Stanford 1982). In 1970 at High Furlong, near Blackpool, Lancashire, the skeleton of an elk (*Alces alces*) was found in the sediments remaining from a Late Glacial lake. Careful excavation of the skeleton showed two barbed antler projectile points in position on the body, and the wounded animal may have blundered on to thin ice and subsequently drowned (Stuart 1982, 159–61). In the absence of artefacts, the bones may have cut-marks on them, showing that tools were used in the dismemberment of carcasses. This form of evidence has been used most strikingly in investigations of early hominid activity in Africa, though there is still some ambiguity in distinguishing the remains of animals killed and butchered by tool-using hominids from those of animals killed by some other predator and subsequently scavenged by hominids (e.g. Shipman 1983).

The boundary between hunting and scavenging can be a little hazy. In the case of a mammoth skeleton from Hallines, Belgium, disturbance and pursuit by humans may have driven the mammoth into swampy ground where it drowned and was subsequently butchered and utilized (Dennell 1983; Driver 1995, 28). Was that death by hunting or the scavenging of a natural death? At some bison kill-sites, such as the famous Olsen-Chubbuck site in Colorado, bison were actively driven towards a natural feature which would result in their stampede being abruptly halted (Wheat 1972). Many of the Olsen-Chubbuck bison were killed by the hunters, but many more died a 'natural' death as a consequence of falling into a dried-up stream bed, or as a result of the rest of the herd falling on top of them. In this case we would attribute the deaths to hunting, but where the disturbance of the animals by humans was less purposive and directional, it may still have increased the chance of animals dying and so being available to be scavenged. Taphonomic factors acting at each site may also produce patterns of surface damage which can mimic the consequences of human butchering of carcasses and deliberate modification of bones, making it important to consider the anataxic and perthotaxic processes acting at each site (Steele 1990).

Where structural associations, artefacts and cut-marks are all absent, human activity may still be inferred as the cause of death. We may note the association in the assemblages of species which are unlikely to have closely co-existed, most obviously, for example, fish and mammals, or mammal species characteristic of quite different vegetational environments. It has also been argued that other predators typically take prey only one at a time, whereas humans engage in multiple predation, killing several prey per hunt (Steele & Baker 1993). This observation probably holds as a general principle, with minor exceptions such as puffins (*Fratercula arctica*), which take beakfuls of fish per dive. However, the stratigraphical record at most sites is such that it is rarely possible to distinguish the debris from a hunt in which many prey have been killed from the debris from a series of hunts in each of which only a single prey has been taken. Owls, after all, swoop on small mammals one at a time, yet accumulate bone debris at roost sites which appears to have the characteristics of multiple predation.

An analysis of age at death may show a mortality pattern which is thought to be unlikely to be 'natural' attritional mortality, showing selective predation of particular age and sex groups. Reviewing Paleoindian bison kills, McCartney (1990) notes some evidence for the selective hunting of nursery herds, composed largely of cows and calves. However, given the seasonal division of bison into bull herds and nursery herds, any predator might appear to be selecting prey as a consequence of the demography of the animals encountered, rather than because of deliberate selection. In southern New Zealand, where introduced deer have become a pest, one means of culling deer is to shoot them from helicopters, with no particular regard for the age and sex of those shot. Because of the segregation of deer into different age/sex groups, this apparently 'random' hunting produces age at death distributions which look quite unlike 'natural' mortality (Wilkinson 1976). The behaviour of the prey population is thus one complicating factor in recognizing selective hunting by humans. Another is the conflation of different events in the archaeological record. As Driver (1995) points out, if a human population selectively preys on different age or sex groups through the course of a year, the death assemblage as recovered archaeologically could mimic an attritional mortality profile simply because the product of different kills would be merged in the recovered sample. We must proceed with some caution, therefore, though in most cases the role of humans in generating the death assemblage is fairly unambiguous, and our investigation of the hunting activity can proceed with confidence.

COMMUNAL BIG-GAME HUNTING

Some of the most dramatic bone accumulations generated by hunter-gatherers are those created when one prey species is the target of communal hunting. The ethnographic and historical literature abounds with descriptions of recent human groups who have, usually at a particular time of year, engaged in hunting large numbers of particular prey, often at locations which are used repeatedly (e.g. Driver 1990; 1995). The prey are often large ungulates, such as deer or bovids. As herbivores, these species often comprise a high proportion of the mammalian biomass, often associate in large herds for at least part of the year, and are less likely to regard humans as prey rather than predators. In parts of the world where large ungulates are rare or absent, their ecological replacements – large, herd-dwelling herbivores – have often been the subject of communal hunting, such as kangaroo (*Macropus* spp.) in Australia, and moa in New Zealand (Anderson 1983). The communal hunting of seals and small whales which is typical of many coastal regions of northern Eurasia and North America can be seen as an adaptation to environments where large herbivores are absent, but large carnivores either naturally congregate in circumstances in which they are disadvantaged (seals out of water), or can be made to do so (whales driven into shallow water).

Communal hunting characteristically involves the majority of adults in the human group, including individuals who would not otherwise be involved in hunting. The pros and cons of hunting communally rather than individually are not as obvious as they might at first appear. Put simply, if one hunter kills one deer, he or she will be better fed than if ten people kill one deer, but the deer is less likely to evade ten people than to evade one. This distinction becomes enhanced when prey are aggregated into dense clusters, with large gaps between the clusters. A single hunter will have to spend a lot of time searching to find the prey, but will then not be able to exploit fully the concentration of prey. A large group of hunters will be far better able to effect numerous kills, so optimizing the product of the hunt, and will be able to work cooperatively to locate aggregated prey. Essentially, communal hunting is a reliable way of procuring a lot of meat and fat in one go. The downside of this is that the quantity procured may exceed the capacity of even quite a large group of humans. Ethnographic study of people in the circum-Arctic regions of Asia show that the wastage of food may sometimes be considerable (Krupnik 1990).

Perhaps the best-known sites of communal hunting are the accumulations of bison (buffalo; *Bison* spp.) bones which occur on the Plains of North America from Texas north to Alberta. These accumulations are the archaeological record of an often highly organized utilization of bison by people from the early Holocene through to the period of European settlement (Frison 1978; Reeves 1990). The first point to make about communal hunting of bison is that it worked, not simply in terms of providing meat for a particular human population, but in terms of a predator–prey balance which was sustained over some ten thousand years. Although Paleoindian kill-sites extend as far south as Texas, by about eight thousand years ago, bison hunting seems no longer to have been economically significant in the southern Plains, probably as a result of climate change reducing the productivity of the southern grasslands (Reeves 1990). Further north, the record is more continuous, with the 'core area' extending from Wyoming north to Alberta and the Saskatchewan River. Reeves sees the classic Late Prehistoric period of communal bison hunting as being the result of a long development of technological innovations, including the bow and arrow around two thousand years ago, and the development of meat storage methods such as the manufacture of pemmican perhaps as early as five thousand years ago. (Pemmican is a concoction of flaked dried meat and fat, sometimes seasoned with berries. It lasts for months, has a very high calorific value, and may have been an important means of maintaining both people and dogs, the latter being vital as beasts of burden. Reeves rightly praises the importance of pemmican, though its pungent, often repulsive, taste and greasy texture have inhibited the adoption of pemmican into modern American cuisine!) The communal bison kill-sites thus range in date, and in size and frequency of use, and the few examples which can be described here should not be thought of as standing in for all such sites.

An early bison kill-site which shows many of the typical characteristics is the Olsen-Chubbuck site in eastern Colorado, dated to around ten thousand years ago (Wheat 1972). Largely excavated in 1958 and 1960, the site consisted of an infilled dry stream bed, locally termed an arroyo, in which were deposited the skeletons, part skeletons and disarticulated bones of about 190 bison (*Bison occidentalis*). Those lying at the bottom of the arroyo were almost complete, but often twisted and distorted, while the top of the bone deposit consisted largely of disarticulated bones, often apparently piled by body part or skeletal element. The overall impression was of a heap of bison carcasses, most of which had been systematically dismantled. A number of stone projectile points were found with the skeletons, often among vertebrae or ribs. Among the disarticulated bones, elements which carry little meat, such as metapodials and phalanges, were mostly lower in the deposit than those which carry substantial amounts of meat and marrow. Wheat's interpretation of the deposit is quite graphic. A small herd of bison appear to have been stampeded towards and into the arroyo, a declivity small enough not to be obvious to a panicking herd of short-sighted bison, yet big enough (around 2m wide and deep) to trip the leading animals, causing the rest of the herd to stumble into a helpless heap which the hunters could then set upon with spears and clubs. Butchering proceeded by laying the topmost carcasses on their bellies, cutting into the hide along the line of the backbone, then pulling the skin down to either side. Meat was peeled away from the back and ribcage, the shoulders were removed, the tongue and internal organs cut away and the hind limbs disarticulated and defleshed. As the butchering proceeded, horn was collected from cores broken off the skulls, and marrow was collected from the accumulating limb bones. Eventually the point was reached at which enough meat had been consumed and dried, and perhaps the remaining carcasses were beginning to go off, so the bison towards the bottom of the arroyo were hardly touched. The hunters moved on, now considerably more heavily laden, and rain water intermittently flowing in the arroyo brought sediment to bury the bones and rotting carcasses.

Olsen-Chubbuck appears to represent an opportunistic kill-site. The bones represent a single hunting event, and there is no indication that the arroyo had previously or subsequently been used for the same purpose. Slaughter, butchering and consumption all seem to have gone on at the same site. The different piles of disarticulated bones show that the carcasses were butchered very systematically, but the site does not show, for example, heavy, low-utility parts such as skulls and feet being left at the kill-site while more portable, meaty parts such as femora and ribs are taken away to a settlement. This contrasts with sites such as Arroyo Feo, in southern Patagonia, where there is a stratified sequence of occupation debris with copious bones of guanaco (*Camelus gunacoe*) (Borrero 1990). In the earliest deposits, around nine thousand years ago, the occurrence of mostly lower limb and head bones is consistent with a hunting camp at which animals were initially butchered and from which most of the meat was taken elsewhere. By Level 8, about 5,500 years BP, the bone assemblages are principally of major meat-bearing limb bones, indicating that the site was then a base camp to which meat was brought (Table 12.1). Possible guanaco kill- and processing sites have been described at Bloque Errática, in Tierra del Fuego (Borrero *et al.* 1985), and at Paso Otero I, in Argentina (Gutierrez *et al.* 1994). Differences in the behaviour of guanaco and bison mean that the major kill-sites seen in North America are unlikely to have close parallels in South America. Guanaco rarely aggregate in large enough numbers to require and support communal hunting.

Table 12.1. *Major butchering units of guanaco present in three occupation levels at the Arroyo Feo site in Patagonia.*

Data from Borrero (1990, 384). Note the predominance in Level 11 of parts with little meat value, likely to be left at a kill-site, in contrast with the more heavily meat-bearing parts in levels 8 and 9.

Level	Radiocarbon dates BP	Major butchering units present
8	5,550 ± 50	Foreleg (proximal humerus to distal radius) Hindleg (proximal femur to proximal metatarsal)
9	6,000 ± 60 4,900 ± 50	Foreleg, head and upper neck
11	9,410 ± 70 9,330 ± 80 8,610 ± 70 8,410 ± 70	Lower legs (metacarpals, metatarsals, phalanges), head

Some bison kill-sites show evidence of repeated use over a long period, particularly those from the Late Prehistoric period. The value of these stratified sites lies in the opportunity to observe the development of a hunting activity over a lengthy period of time, and in the significance which the place itself acquired in the cultural life of the hunters. One of the best-known examples is the Vore site, located in the Red Valley, in the Black Hills of north-eastern Wyoming (Reher & Frison 1980). Meticulously, though only partially, excavated in 1971 and 1972, the site consists of over 5m of cultural stratigraphy in a roughly circular sink-hole, some 30m in diameter. Within the deposits, a maximum of twenty-two separate deposits of bones could be identified, the thickest of them nearly 1m deep, representing between ten thousand and twenty thousand individuals. The site was in use between AD 1500 and 1800. It thus represents the last period of large-scale bison hunting in the Plains, at the beginning of European contact in what Reher & Frison aptly describe as 'the heart of the last free stronghold of native North America'. To the west of the site are the remains of drive-lines, lines of stone cairns probably marking lines along which to place brushwood, flags and people as a means of steering a herd of bison once they had been disturbed into movement (Brink & Rollans 1990).

Although the detail varied from one bone deposit to another, the excavated deposits showed the systematic butchering of bison, with carcasses being reduced to more portable butchering units (forelimbs, shoulder muscles, etc.) which could then be taken aside and processed further. There was much evidence of limb bones being broken up and processed for the extraction of marrow and fat, with the most productive bones apparently being removed from the kill-site altogether. The uppermost levels of the site, in particular, showed that butchering units were removed from the site, leaving largely processed skulls and blocks of vertebrae. Some deposits of selected elements were noted, including a dump of twenty-five mandibles. At three points in the deposits, rough circles of bison skulls were found, arranged with their noses pointing towards the centre of the circle. These are thought to have had some ceremonial significance. They are certainly too spatially organized just to be deposits of processed bones, and, as Reher & Frison take care to point out, the weight of a fresh bison head is such that the circles are unlikely to have been the work of children.

Dental development in the bison mandibles was studied in detail, in order to obtain information on the age at death of the animals, and thus the season of use of the sink-hole. The results indicated largely spring killing, though the seasonal pattern was not as clear as at some other sites in the region. The degree of wear seen on some of the older jaws, measured as tooth crown height, indicated that some of the bison survived to be over fifteen years old. Measurements of the teeth were then compared with data from other kill-sites distributed throughout the Holocene, including Olsen-Chubbuck, to show a general reduction in size of bison from the early Holocene through to the Late Prehistoric period. The study of the mandibles and teeth, of which we can only mention a few details here, thus contributed information about the human activity at the site, and about the biology of Plains bison as a whole.

In northern Europe in the Late Pleistocene and early Holocene, large ungulates such as red deer (*Cervus elaphus*) and reindeer (*Rangifer tarandus*) were the favoured prey of many human populations, though the communal hunting of these species does not seem to have attained quite the exclusive position that bison hunting occupied in at least some parts of the Plains at some times. In his discussion of the Palaeolithic site at Abri Pataud, in the Vézères region of France, Arthur Spiess (1979, 179–244) discusses the relative merits of reindeer and large bovids such as aurochs (*Bos primigenius*) and bison (*Bison priscus*) as prey for hunting bands, and predicts that if reliability of supply was the main requirement, then reindeer should comprise over three-quarters of the individual large mammals taken. From the site as a whole, and this is summarizing some fifteen thousand years of intermittent occupation, reindeer make up 69 per cent of the identified individuals. Apart from a few horses and red deer, most of the remainder were aurochs or bison, a result which suggests that hunters at Abri Pataud were approximating to Spiess' 'reliability' model. The season of hunting of the reindeer was inferred by examining the length of foetal bones, and the state of eruption and wear of teeth. We should note in passing that an attempt to examine incremental structures in the teeth (Chapter 8) failed because of the state of preservation of the teeth: only 11 successful sections were obtained out of 171 attempts. However, foetal bone length and dental data showed a predominance of hunting between October and March for all the occupation levels for which a satisfactory sample could be studied.

In some cases the interpretation of hunter-gatherer sites can be problematic. A case in point is Star Carr, in Yorkshire. This early Mesolithic site was excavated between 1949 and 1953, and is the best known of a series of sites dating from the very beginning of the Holocene which lie around the edges of what was then a diverse wetland area. The history of the study of Star Carr has been reviewed in some detail by the excavator, J.G.D. Clark (1972), and more succinctly by Legge & Rowley-Conwy (1988). An assemblage of just over a thousand identified mammal bones has variously been used to support interpretation of the site as a home base occupied from winter to late April (Clark 1972); a butchering station, possibly also a kill-site (Caulfield 1978); an antler and hide working site used intermittently throughout the year (Pitts 1979); an intermittently used butchering site (Andresen *et al.* 1981); and a hunting camp used in late spring and summer (Legge & Rowley-Conwy 1988). The mammal bones are predominantly of red deer, with elk, aurochs, roe deer and pig. For their re-interpretation, Legge & Rowley-Conwy went to the lengths of re-examining all the bones, and this led them to a number of re-identifications, for example attributing some alleged aurochs to elk, a claimed beaver as roe deer, and, most remarkably, noting part of a bear mandible which had previously been identified as pig. They also undertook a thorough study of the age at death of the roe deer mandibles, on which the spring–summer occupation was largely based. Subsequently, Richard Carter (1998) has re-examined the red deer and roe deer mandibles, and believes that some of them were killed during the winter. One fears that it can only be matter of time before yet another re-interpretation is proposed.

HUNTING TO EXTINCTION?

Our interpretation of sites such as Vore, Abri Pataud and Star Carr lean quite heavily on our understanding of the behaviour and population dynamics of the prey animals, allowing us to make informed statements about the seasonal movement of bison or the ability of reindeer populations to recover from heavy predation. In New Zealand the early Maori settlers, around AD 1000 and the succeeding few centuries, hunted to extinction a number of species of moa, flightless birds which ranged in size from a large chicken to nightmarish beasts over 2m tall (Anderson 1983). The archaeological study of moa hunting is constrained by the fact that we know very little about the ecology and behaviour of moa species: there are none for us to observe. The biology of moa is inferred in part from analogy with living species thought to be closely related to them, such as emu and cassowary, and in part from noting the distribution of moa remains with respect to environmental factors such as altitude, aspect and vegetation. Unlike the communal hunting methods used in Europe and North America, it appears that the early Maori may have used dogs to locate and hold moa which could then be speared and clubbed. Given the apparent size of the largest moa species, and noting the lethal ability of ostriches, the Maori dogs must have been remarkably bold and aggressive animals. The surviving archaeological record shows that moa were butchered and redistributed in much the same way as large mammals elsewhere, with low-meat parts such as the lower limbs being deposited at hunting sites, and the meatier parts taken away to cooking and consumption sites. Anderson (1983, 49) makes an interesting point, referring to the vulnerability of moa to extinction by the 'sudden impact of efficient *but inexperienced* hunters' (my emphasis).

Predators obviously have some impact on the population dynamics of their prey, and we might ask whether hunter-gatherers significantly reduced the range or population density of their prey. In some parts of the world, not least New Zealand, there is a clear correlation between the arrival of people and the extinction of elements of the local fauna. This observation led to the formulation of what has been called the 'Overkill Hypothesis' (Martin & Wright 1967; Reed 1970; Mosimann & Martin 1975; Spaulding 1983), a big, contentious subject which we can only briefly review here.

In North America it is certainly the case that a distinctive Pleistocene fauna (often called the Rancholabrean fauna, after the famous tar-seeps in California in which this fauna is particularly well represented) seems to have become extinct in the relatively short period of time during which people were colonizing the continent from north-eastern Asia. There are grounds for suspicion, but a strong defence case can be mounted none the less. Climate change may have been largely responsible for the Rancholabrean extinctions, with large, highly specialized species being unable to adapt to a rapidly changing environment, a point which has been well argued by Donald Grayson (1980). The same environmental changes allowed and encouraged the rapid expansion of human settlement, so producing an association between the two events. It has even been argued that humans could not have spread into North America until large Rancholabrean carnivores such as the bear *Arctodus simus* and the sabre-toothed cat (*Smilodon* sp.), became extinct (Geist 1989). The obvious forensic evidence which would clinch the case – remains of Rancholabrean species with unambiguous evidence of human involvement in their death – is scarce. There are a few such kill-sites, but not enough to prove the sort of wholesale massacre which the overkill hypothesis would require (Olsen 1990). Much of the discussion of the hypothesis has revolved around simulations which appear to show that humans *could* have effected such an overkill (Mosimann & Martin 1975), and debate over whether the end-Pleistocene environmental changes in North America were sufficient to have triggered such an extinction event (Spaulding 1983).

Typically, it was Charles Reed who widened the debate to consider the attitudes of different cultural groups in recent times to the wild animals around them (Reed 1970). He contrasts attitudes in China, where the killing of wild animals is traditionally permitted yet much less socially embedded than in Europe or North America, with the Judaeo-Christian principle of having dominion over other living things, which attitude European settlers imported to North America. Reed tells of encountering an eight-year-old boy in Arizona, who was shooting small lizards with a .22 rifle. On being asked why he was shooting such harmless creatures, the boy replied 'Ain't nothing else left'. Cultural differences in attitudes to wild animals certainly underlie the rather polarized debate concerning the Overkill Hypothesis, as does a desire on the part of some archaeologists to see hunter-gatherers as 'noble savages' living in equilibrium with nature. Perhaps, though, Reed's serial lizard-killer is a useful reminder that the attitudes of ancient human populations must have varied as well, and that the probability of a human population hunting some species to extinction has to do both with the biology of the prey, and with the history and culture of the people concerned.

SEASONAL FOWLING AND FISHING

Some prey animals, especially birds, may only be available seasonally, leading to the development of a highly organized seasonal exploitation. For example, in Tasmania, southern New Zealand and other islands in the region, the tradition of 'muttonbirding' involved the systematic collections of small procellariid sea-birds, mostly petrels, at their communal nesting sites (Anderson 1996). The antiquity of this exploitation remains uncertain. It definitely long pre-dates European contact in the region, although early European settlers engaged in muttonbirding. One settlement, on Norfolk Island, came close to starvation in 1790, and was saved by the arrival of huge numbers of the providence petrel *Pterodroma solandri*. Human need was clearly not tempered by gratitude, as providence petrels were extinct on Norfolk Island by 1800 (Anderson 1996, 408).

Bird bones can provide valuable information in recognizing the seasonal use of settlement or hunting sites. Because many bird species are highly seasonal in their breeding behaviour and movement within their range, the presence or absence of bones of adults or juveniles at a location can give a good indication of the time(s) of year at which the site was occupied. Birds are skeletally immature for a remarkably short time, with some small species capable of growing to near-adult body size in just a few weeks from hatching. In most species full ossification of the skeleton is attained as, or soon after, the bird leaves the nest, so skeletally immature individuals are normally only present at or close to the nest site, during the nesting season. Because of the rapidity of skeletal development, it is only possible to note bones as immature or adult, or at best to define a couple of immature stages. During the earliest days of post-hatching development, the major wing and leg bones may resemble undifferentiated rods of porous bone, with little of the morphology of a humerus, tibiotarsus, or whatever. At this stage the survival and recovery of the bones would seem to be highly improbable, but such immature bones can and do survive in archaeological samples, and clearly represent individuals at a very early stage of post-hatching development. As adult size is approached, the bones take on more of the distinctive morphology of the element concerned, often with a relatively robust shaft but with porous articular ends.

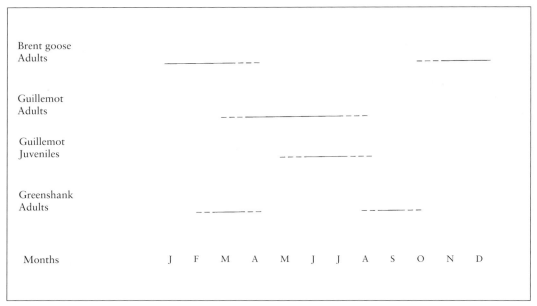

Fig. 12.1. Diagram to show how the presence of seasonal breeding bird species in an assemblage can be used to infer seasonal occupation of a site by humans. The presence of juvenile and adult guillemots, coupled with the absence of brent goose or greenshank bones, could be taken to indicate occupation of the site in mid-summer.

A simple example of the use of birds as seasonal indicators is Avery's (1977) study of the prehistoric Paternoster Midden site in the south-western Cape, South Africa. The predominant species in the midden deposit were jackass penguin (*Spheniscus demersus*) and Cape cormorant (*Phalacrocorax capensis*), including numerous immature specimens. Jackass penguins breed more or less throughout the year, but the other species fixed the deposition of the midden to the late summer to autumn period. Coastal Inuit sites in Greenland show considerable variation in the ratios of mammal to bird bones at different sites, with much seal, and sometimes caribou, bone at some locations (Gotfredson 1997). One early site, Nipisat I (Saqqaq culture, around 4,000–3,000 BP), included deposits with numerous bones of Brünnich's guillemot, including a high proportion of juveniles, thus confirming quite narrowly targeted summer hunting. Inuit sites in south-eastern Greenland typically show a much lower proportion of bird bones than those on the west coast. The East Greenland current brings drift ice and cold water inshore, making the east coast less capable of supporting bird populations in densities attractive to people.

A more subtle balancing of resources is suggested by Lefèvre (1997) for sites in southern Patagonia ranging in date from six thousand years ago to the seventeenth century AD. A survey of the Seno Skyring region produced fifty-seven sites, mostly shell middens with mammal and bird bones. The bird species were predominantly cormorant (*Phalacrocorax* spp.) and the charmingly named steamer duck (*Tachyeres pteneres*). Many of the Seno Skyring sites included juvenile bones, indicating collection during the nesting season, i.e. from the end of November to about mid-March. There were certainly mammals available:

some mammal bone occurs in most of the middens, and sea-lions would have been vulnerable to hunting at about the same season as the birds. Lefèvre points out that the sea-lions would have been in poor condition at this time of the year, and suggests that the collection of birds instead shows an emphasis on procuring meat with a good fat content. Incidentally, Lefèvre has undertaken similar work in Tierra del Fuego and on the Aleutian Islands, showing that zooarchaeologists will literally go to the ends of the Earth in pursuit of their research!

Many fish species show marked seasonality of movement, and so may only be available to a human population at certain times of year. The presence or absence of these seasonal species in archaeological samples may convey information about the way people moved around a landscape through the year. In the East Penobscot area of southern Maine, middens dated to the Ceramic period (broadly 2,700–1,200 BP) show probably year-round settlement on coastal sites extending to warm-season use of off-shore islands (Belcher 1994). The islands appear to have been used principally to take shallow-water, mudflat-dwelling fish. Two sites on islands in particularly sheltered locations appear to have been used in the colder seasons. Similarly, the Neolithic site of Hekelingen III, in the Netherlands, gave a range of fish remains consistent with year-round settlement (Prummel 1987). The site was located close to a freshwater creek, which probably yielded the majority of the fish represented at the site. Seasonal species included sturgeon (*Acipenser sturio*) and thin-lipped grey mullet (*Liza ramada*), the latter a marine species, but one which enters rivers and creeks during the summer.

In these examples, the pattern of seasonal exploitation was determined by the presence of fish species that show seasonal changes in distribution. Another source of such information is through the study of skeletal parts which show incremental growth, notably the otoliths, flattened calcareous elements which lie in the skull of fishes and serve to maintain balance and body alignment in the water (Fig. 12.2). Incremental growth shows in the otoliths as more or less dense bands of growth, which in turn may be seen in polished sections as light and dark bands. Incremental growth is obviously most marked in species living in temperate and near-Polar waters, where seasonal fluctuations of water temperature trigger alternations of rapid and slow, or negligible, growth.

In tropical waters fluctuations of water temperature tend to be lower, but here there may be links between growth rate and reproductive condition, which may in turn be linked to climatic variables such as dry/wet seasons. Daily growth increments have been noted in the otoliths of modern fish (Panella 1980), but rarely demonstrated in ancient material. An unusual exception is at the Late Palaeolithic site of Makhadma, Egypt, where circum-daily increments in the tilapid *Oreochromis niloticus* could be counted between sharp changes in growth rate which appeared to be linked with the seasonal inundation of the Nile. Van Neer *et al.* (1993) estimated that the majority of the fish were captured about forty to eighty days after the inundation, and so on a falling river level, presumably because the fish were then accessible in pools left on the flood plain by the falling river.

The size of the fish represented in an archaeological sample may also be related to the fishing technique used in their capture. If fish are taken in shallow water by spearing them, the catch will tend to exclude small individuals, for the simple reason that they are

Fig. 12.2. The otoliths of fish of the cod family, a source of information on seasonal growth and fishing strategies. (Photo courtesy of Andrew Jones)

more difficult to hit. Some Mesolithic sites in Denmark, for example, have produced bones of pike (*Esox lucius*) with a size (and therefore age) distribution quite unlike that expected of a pike population. The conclusion was drawn that the pike were hunted by spearing, so selectively predating the larger fish (Noe-Nygaard 1983). A close examination of the pike vertebrae indicated that most were taken between May and August, at which season pike are in shallow water. Unlike spearing, fishing with nets may tend to collect large numbers of small fish. This will depend upon the mesh size of the net, and also the precise means by which the net captures the fish. Gill-nets are especially selective. These nets are hung vertically in the water, and rely on the fish penetrating part-way into the mesh, so that the net becomes entangled behind the gill covers, preventing the fish from withdrawing. For any particular mesh size, small fish will not be caught, as they will pass right through the mesh, while large fish will not be caught because they will not penetrate far enough into the mesh. A gill-net will therefore tend to catch a rather narrow size-range of fish (Fig. 12.3). Fish-traps of netting or wicker-work, on the other hand, will tend to catch all fish above a certain size, so distinguishing a catch made by trapping from one made by gill-netting. Hook and line fishing will tend to catch the larger, predatory fish, though the simple equation of large hooks with large fish may be too simple. How large a fish a given hook size will take depends on the details of the jaw anatomy of the species involved (Owen & Merrick 1994).

Using criteria such as those outlined above, fish exploitation in later Mesolithic Denmark has been extended beyond spearing pike to include fishing by trapping and by hook and line (Enghoff 1994). A diversity of approach can also be seen in remains from sites on the barrier islands off the coast of Georgia, close to the Florida border. Here, middens dated between AD 1000 and the time of European settlement show a sophisticated year-round exploitation of estuarine and salt-marsh habitats, with different locations used for particular strategies. The middens include a lot of remains of small fish, indicating the use of fine nets and fish-weirs, rather than hook and line fishing. This in turn implies a collective effort, rather than individual fishing (Reitz 1982). The inferences which can be drawn from fishing techniques

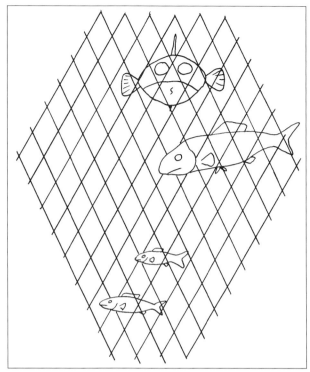

Fig. 12.3. Illustration of the size-selection that can result from fish capture by gill-nets. The large fish (above) is much larger than the mesh size, and does not become entangled in the net. The small fish (bottom) can swim through the mesh without becoming entangled. Only fish with a body cross-section close to the mesh size (middle) swim part-way through the mesh, and become trapped as the net is caught up behind the gill covers.

can sometimes be surprising. For example, sites in the lower Darling region of New South Wales, Australia, include extensive middens rich in the remains of golden perch (*Macquaria ambigua*) (Balme 1982). The size distribution of golden perch from at least two sites, Major Swale and North Casuarina Ridge, show the characteristics of gill-netting. This conclusion would be unremarkable, but for the fact that both sites are radiocarbon dated to around 25,000 years ago. The deductions made on the basis of the fish bones thus have important implications for the development of cordage and netting technology by this early date.

To some extent the interpretation of fish bones in terms of fishing technology relies upon ethnographic observations, and analogy from the present into the past. This is not the place to rehearse all the arguments which surround this process, though fish bones from elsewhere in New South Wales have raised interesting questions regarding ethnographic data. The first European settlers in the vicinity of modern-day Sydney recorded local people using essentially two methods of fishing: spears, and hook and line.

However, remains from excavated midden sites in the area, sites which represent the settlement garbage of the people encountered by those first settlers, show a very wide size-range of fish, more consistent with the use of nets or traps, or with small fish being caught by hand in rock-pools (Attenbrow & Steele 1995). In particular, the presence of numerous small sparid fish (sea-bream family) indicates the exploitation of shallow estuarine waters, ideal for the construction of fish traps. The archaeological results suggest that the observations made by the first settlers were partial, possibly in both senses. It may be that the European observers were unfamiliar with fishing methods other than the use of hook and line or spears, and so failed to recognize other methods, or failed to notice the incidental collection of small fish during shellfish collection.

HUNTING AND FARMING

The debris of hunting may be encountered at sites where agriculture or pastoralism was the economic mainstay, or in areas where hunters and farmers co-existed. The Saladoid site at Trants, Montserrat, provides a good example (Reitz 1994). The occupants of this site were growing plant foods in garden plots. The tropical island setting and the coastal location of the site offered a diverse range of land and marine resources. Among the animal bones, there is no obvious favoured prey. In samples sieved on a ⅛" (about 3mm) mesh, a total of thirty-nine taxa were identified from 2,154 bones, of which well over half were 'unidentified fish'.

A similarly diverse utilization of vertebrates is seen at many southern African sites, even after the introduction of domestic livestock. For example, the long sequence of deposits at Rose Cottage cave, in eastern Orange Free State, South Africa, yielded Late Stone Age bone samples with thirty-two taxa in just 330 identified specimens. Even in the uppermost levels, dated to around AD 1700 and with bones of domestic cattle, sheep and goat, there are still forty-two taxa in 1,914 identified bones (Plug & Engela 1992; Plug 1997). The bones from Rose Cottage cave may include some leopard prey, and there is some association in the deposits between bones of leopard (*Panthera pardus*) and of hyrax (*Procavia capensis*), a common prey of leopards. None the less the great majority of the diverse vertebrate fauna appears to be the result of hunting going on alongside pastoral farming.

Bone assemblages from Late Stone Age sites in Natal, South Africa, show how little impact farming had on local hunting peoples. At Mhlwazini Cave, two main phases of occupation, dated to 3000–2000 BP and after AD 1000, gave broadly similar assemblages showing some concentration on hunting small to medium-sized antelope species. The age at death of the antelopes showed them to be mostly adults, which indicates selective hunting, avoiding the juvenile animals. This in turn indicates that hunting was undertaken by bow-and-arrow rather than trapping, as trapping is unlikely to have given a predominantly adult catch (Plug 1990). The uppermost level at Mhlwazini Cave is contemporaneous with the presence of Iron Age pastoralists in the region, yet there is no trace in the archaeological record of contact with the pastoralists or of any change in the hunting strategy. At KwaThwaleyakhe Shelter, the upper levels include bones of sheep, showing some degree of contact between hunter-gatherers and pastoralists. Among bones derived from food debris were found a number of astragali from sheep and other small bovids which were polished and worn in a way indicating that they had been used in divination (Plug 1993). The use of bones to divine the future and the unseen is a practice generally associated with Bantu-speaking agriculturalists, and therefore with the Iron Age peoples moving into Natal at this time, rather than with the hunter-gatherers in whose cultural debris the bones were found. The contact therefore extended to more than just the occasional sheep, yet in other respects, hunter-gatherer subsistence appears to have continued much as before.

Another site in the Thakela Basin in Natal is Maqonqo Shelter, which appears to have been a site of some regional significance (Plug 1996). The site has a long early to mid-Holocene sequence, with some Late Stone Age material towards the top, including sheep in the bone assemblages. Samples from Maqonqo include appreciably more bones of aardvark (*Orycteropus afer*) and pangolin (*Manis temmincki*) than those from KwaThwaleyakhe Shelter and other sites in the region. These species are among those thought to have been of some 'ritual' significance to hunter-gatherers in Natal, and their presence in the Maqonqo samples may indicate that the site had some status beyond its role as a place to live. This is also borne out by the presence nearby of rock art panels.

The role of hunting in largely agricultural societies can be quite complex. A good example comes from Driver's work around Sand Canyon in south-western Colorado (Driver 1996). A series of large and small sites, broadly dated to AD 1150–1300, gave bone samples which consisted largely of three taxa: turkey (*Meleagris gallopavo*), lagomorph (mainly cottontail rabbit), and deer. From site to site the relative proportions of these three taxa varied appreciably. In particular, the large aggregated settlement at Sand Canyon pueblo gave a much higher proportion of deer than the smaller sites in the area, at which deer bones were infrequent, even though deer were evidently there to hunt. At the small, mostly chronologically late sites in the upper part of Sand Canyon, turkey bones were particularly abundant. Driver sees this as indicating that the people at these small settlements had little opportunity to hunt, and concentrated on raising domestic turkeys for meat, and that only the occupants of the large Sand Canyon pueblo had free access to deer. In effect, Driver postulates that the pueblo population had privileged access to a valuable resource, a situation which has echoes in medieval England.

When agriculture provides the food, hunting may still provide other resources. Two Neolithic sites in the Netherlands, Swifterbant and Hazendonk, have given evidence for the hunting of animals perhaps primarily for their fur (Zeiler 1987). Both sites were located in freshwater areas at the time of occupation (around 5,200 BP for Swifterbant, a little later for the main occupation at Hazendonk). Both sites gave samples with numerous bones of beaver (*Castor fiber*) and otter (*Lutra lutra*), with lesser amounts of bear (*Ursus arctos*), polecat (*Mustela putorius*), cat (*Felis silvestris*), fox (*Vulpes vulpes*), badger (*Meles meles*) and pine marten (*Martes martes*). The otter and beaver remains from both sites were predominantly of adult animals, over two years old in the case of the otters. Many of the bones showed fine cut-marks, especially at Swifterbant, which were consistent with the animals having been skinned and dismembered. Beaver mandibles, for example, often showed cut marks where the skin had been cut away from around the muzzle. Traces of burning were found on some of the bones, and this may indicate that the animals were eaten as well. None the less the bones from these two sites probably represent fairly selective hunting of fur-bearing animals, to obtain a resource which agriculture, well established in the Netherlands by this time, could not provide.

Even when the supply of resources is assured, hunting may continue to carry prestige value, and so be undertaken by some people within the population, but not all. In modern Britain the hunting of foxes and red grouse (*Lagopus scoticus*) is essentially limited to a land-owning minority, and fulfils no subsistence role ('The unspeakable in pursuit of the uneatable,' according to Oscar Wilde). The role now seems to be entirely that of a social status marker: one shoots grouse because one can afford to shoot grouse. In other cultures hunting has been sublimated in other ways, and perhaps the traditional Spanish bullfight can be seen as a highly ritualized form of hunting (Morales Muñiz & Morales Muñiz 1995). The origins of the bullfight are obscure and hotly debated – the authors write with evident feeling about the alleged sexual imagery and the insecurity of Spanish men – but ultimately the rite is one of control and slaughter of a potentially dangerous animal. It is a long way from the bison skull circles of the Vore site to the Spanish bullfight, though both represent the ceremonial elaboration of humans counterpoised with wild animals.

Although the relationship between hunters and their prey may be a close and complex one, that between farmers and their livestock is generally closer still. The next chapter reviews the study of early animal domestication.

Thirteen

Settling Down: the Domestication of Animals and People

This chapter reviews the bone evidence that may be recovered from sites formerly occupied by agricultural and pastoral peoples. We are concerned here more with domestic animals than with wild ones, and so the chapter begins with some discussion of domestication, and the recognition of domestic animals in the archaeological record, and the means by which husbandry practices can be inferred.

Understanding Domestication

The taking into domestication of animals such as sheep, pigs and llamas and the development of animal husbandry alongside the development of crop plants mark a major change in the economic and social activities of human populations (Table 13.1). The zoological status of domestic animals occupied the minds of Victorian naturalists such as Charles Darwin, as they tried to come to terms with the apparent mutability of species (Galton 1865; Darwin 1868). The variability of domestic animals, not to mention the capacity for man-made variation seen in, for example, domestic pigeons, was an obvious challenge to the notion of divine creation.

Later writers saw animal domestication as a part of the 'development' of human beings, an improving step along the road from our simian origins. To the brilliant Marxist writer V. Gordon Childe, the domestication of animals was one aspect of the 'Neolithic revolution', a great leap forward taken by people in the Middle East largely as a consequence of climatic changes which coaxed people and animals into proximity in shrunken areas of favourable habitat (Childe 1928; 1936; 1942).

Whatever the contemporary views on Darwin and Childe, and each has their supporters and detractors in roughly equal measure, the importance of animal husbandry as an alternative to hunting and foraging is fairly clear. It allows a greater concentration of prey (i.e. domestic livestock) to be maintained than would generally be possible in the wild, and it allows this concentration to be retained within easy reach of human settlement, either by keeping livestock close to permanent settlements, or by moving the settlement as the livestock are moved between seasonal grazing areas. Furthermore, the breeding behaviour of the animals can be influenced, perhaps giving preference to certain adult males in order to increase or decrease the frequency of some particular trait in the herd or flock. It is not necessary to understand the gene theory of inheritance in order to observe that some physical traits are more common in the offspring of adults which have that trait than those of adults which do not. Whether one attributes that to genes, to Lamarckian inheritance of acquired traits, or to the beneficence of the great goat god is unimportant. The inheritance still works, and no doubt early herders and farmers were observant enough to notice that fact and to make use of it, whatever mechanism they held to be responsible. It is debatable whether animal domestication was a purposive act on the part of people, or a mutualistic coming-together of people and animals which also had something to gain from the deal (O'Connor 1997). Whichever it was, animal domestication and the emergence of animal husbandry allowed people to live in different ways, and so had a marked effect on the settlement and pattern of human activity in some parts of the world.

Table 13.1.   *A summary of the origins and utility of some major domestic animals.*

This is by no means a comprehensive list, and is only intended to give a little background information about species discussed in this book.

Some major domestic animals summarised. Note that nomenclature follows Gentry *et al.* (1996) *Bulletin of Zoological Nomenclature* 53(1).

Cattle *Bos taurus* L.
Large ruminant (=cud-chewing), artiodactyl (=even-toed hoofed mammal). Apparently originates from wild *Bos primigenius* Boj., which was common throughout Eurasia in the early Holocene. Probably under domestication by 8,000 BP in North Africa and/or Near East, and became the principal domestic mammal of prehistoric Europe. Valuable for meat, hides, milk and traction-power. Less adaptable than sheep in areas of sparse, low-quality grazing, or arid regions, or in mountain regions. Quite susceptible to insect-borne disease in tropics.
Note also: domestic **gaur** *Bos frontalis* Lambert from wild *Bos gaurus* Smith, important in India, Burma, Malaya; domestic **water buffalo** *Bos bubalis* L. from wild *Bos arnee* Kerr, important in India and south-east Asia; domestic **yak** *Bos grunniens* L. from wild yak *Poephagus mutus* Przewalski, important in Tibet and neighbouring regions.

Sheep *Ovis aries* L.
Medium-sized ruminant artiodactyl, apparently originating from wild *Ovis orientalis* Gmelin, which was widespread throughout south-west Asia. Domesticated possibly as early as 10,000 BP in Zagros Mountains, perhaps with other local centres of domestication in Anatolia and Caucasus. The main domestic mammal of prehistoric Near East. Valuable for meat, wool and milk; very adaptable to food and climate, quite drought-tolerant.

Goat *Capra hircus* L.
Medium-sized ruminant artiodactyl, apparently originating from wild *Capra aegagrus* Erxleben, formerly widespread in south-west Asia and (probably) south-east Europe. Appears to have come into domestication with sheep: the similarity of their bones makes it difficult to be certain. Valuable for meat and milk; more drought-tolerant than sheep, and more adaptable to browsing bushes, woody material, discarded footwear . . .

Horse *Equus caballus* L.
Large perissodactyl (=odd-toed ungulate), originating from wild tarpan *Equus ferus* Boddaert, which is now extinct, but probably ranged from the central Asian steppe into western Europe. First domesticated around 5,000 BP in southern Russia, probably as a meat animal. Later more important for riding and traction. Tolerant of quite a wide climatic range, but not good on sparse or dry grazing.
Note also domestic **donkey** *Equus asinus* L., from wild ass *Equus africanus*, probably domesticated in north-east Africa by 5,000 BP.

Dromedary *Camelus dromedarius* L.
Large ruminant artiodactyl, originating from a wild form of the same species. Probably domesticated in the Arabian Peninsula around 5,000 BP, certainly by 3,500 BP. Valuable for meat, milk, wool and traction. Not tolerant of low temperatures, especially when cool and damp, and susceptible to insect-borne disease in tropics.

Bactrian camel *Camelus bactrianus* L.
Large ruminant artiodactyl, originating from a wild form *Camelus bactrianus ferus* Przewalski. Domesticated in the Turkestan-Mongolia region by 5,000 BP. Valuable for meat, milk, wool and traction. Not as good a load-carrier as dromedary, but more tolerant of cold.

Llama *Camelus glama* L., **alpaca** *Camelus pacos* L.
Two of the four 'South American camelids'; the other two being wild **guanaco** *Camelus guanicoe* Müller and **vicuña** *Camelus vicugna* Molina. Llama and alpaca were brought into domestication in the central Andes perhaps by 6,000 BP, from one or both of guanaco and vicuña. The relationships are currently completely unclear, and are the subject of ancient DNA investigations. Both llama and alpaca are useful for meat and wool, and both can be used to carry loads. Llama are better load carriers than alpaca, and work better at lower altitudes: alpaca tend to be kept at higher altitudes and produce better wool. Both are of a rather nervous disposition, especially when courting.

Pig *Sus domesticus* Erxleben
A medium-sized ungulate, developed from the wild boar *Sus scrofa* L., which is common throughout Eurasia. Domesticated by 7,500 BP in China, perhaps by 6,000 BP in northern Europe. Valued for meat and skins; will eat practically anything.

Fowl *Gallus domesticus* L.
A medium-sized bird, domesticated by 8,000 BP from wild jungle fowl *Gallus gallus* L. in south-east Asia, though older sources argue for domestication in the Indus Valley as late as 4,000 BP. Valued for meat and eggs, and as a handy household scavenger.

Guinea pig *Cavia porcellus* L.
A medium-sized rodent, domesticated from wild *Cavia aperea* Erxleben in central Andes, perhaps about 4,000–3,000 BP. Probably a household scavenger for much longer than this, first utilised then deliberately bred as a source of meat.

Dog *Canis familiaris* L.
A medium-sized carnivore, domesticated in the Near East and northern Europe by 10,000 BP, arguably from wolf *Canis lupus*, perhaps originally as an aid in hunting then increasingly as a companion animal.

Human beings *Homo sapiens* L.
A large primate, domesticated by cats before 7,000 BP as a source of food.

What is a domestic animal? Looking around us today, that might seem obvious. Cows are domestic, bison are wild; horses are domestic, zebras are wild; pussy cats are domestic, tigers are wild. Elephants are wild, except where Indian elephants are used as working animals, when they are tame, which may or may not be the same as being domestic. Guinea pigs are domestic, except in South America where they are still wild, though even there many populations live around people's houses, so they might be domestic. Trying to impose a definition that will serve to categorize all animals as wild or domestic becomes impossible, yet this is a necessary starting point for any archaeological investigation of the subject. We cannot go into the subject in detail here: a range of different views are given by papers in Clutton-Brock (1989), by Harris (1996) and by O'Connor (1997).

Some see animal domestication as a speciation event: people select and isolate some animals from a population, and 'maintains complete mastery over [the isolated group's] breeding, organization of territory, and food supply' (Clutton-Brock 1989, 7). As a consequence of this isolation, the attributes of the animals diverge from those of the population from which they were originally separated, and from those of other free-living populations. The genetic diversity of the isolated group might be less than, and differ from, that of the original population, so that they begin their isolation with a different gene pool (founder effect). Acting upon that gene pool will be a series of selection pressures which will be quite different to those acting on a free-living population: traits which were advantageous in the wild may be detrimental in captivity (Zohary et al. 1998). Add some degree of naïve selective breeding, and the divergence of free-living and controlled populations is easily understood. On this model, if we are to recognize early domestic animals in the archaeological record, we are looking for morphological differences. These may be differences of gross size, or more subtle differences of conformation – shape rather than size, or differences in the occurrence of particular non-metrical skeletal traits.

Others emphasize the social incorporation of the animals, rather than the genetic isolation. For example, Ducos (1978, 54) states that domestication only exists when living animals are 'integrated as objects into the socio-economic organization of the human group'. Whereas the speciation model gives us morphological change to look for in archaeological material, the behavioural model requires us to recognize the social incorporation of animals. This could involve a change in distribution of a species, as people move animals out of their previous range, requiring us to know the original distribution of the free-living populations. That distribution need not have been as it is today, so does an archaeological record from outside the modern range indicate a formerly wider range for free-living populations, or the existence of a domestic population? We return to that conundrum later in the chapter. Other aspects of social incorporation may be more obvious. The treatment afforded to the remains of the animals may differ from that afforded to wild animals; their spatial distribution around and within settlement areas may differ; there may be structures unambiguously associated with the keeping and management of a captive population; and the mortality profile may indicate a pattern of culling inconsistent with a free-living population. None of these features would be diagnostic of domestication on its own, but a coincidence of several, especially with some morphological evidence, might be quite persuasive.

If that seems a very lengthy way to introduce a review of the archaeological evidence for past animal husbandry, that is because the topic is complex and open to widely differing points of view. There is little to be gained from theorizing at length without recourse to the bone data, but it would be equally futile to plunge into the bones without first considering in some detail what it is that we are trying to recognize and comprehend.

RECOGNIZING DOMESTIC ANIMALS

Details of size and shape have been cited by some authors as *prima facie* evidence that a given bone sample is of domestic, not wild, individuals. At one extreme is the confidence of Bökönyi (1989, 25): 'With animal remains from prehistoric sites . . . decrease of size can only indicate domestication. As for crowded teeth, which are common in pigs and dogs, rare in cattle, and which I have seen in only one single horse skull, this is a reasonably sure proof of domestication.' Other authors are more cautious. Discussing Neolithic cattle remains from the UK and other parts of northern Europe, Grigson (1984) points out that the naive assumption of a size divergence from wild *Bos primigenius* failed to appreciate two things. First, Holocene *B. primigenius* seems to have been smaller than Pleistocene forms, so that some size reduction in the wild species appears to have occurred regardless of domestication. Second, there seems to have been quite a degree of sexual dimorphism in *B. primigenius*, though the species is extinct and cannot be studied directly. These two sources of size variation in the supposed wild progenitor has greatly complicated the discussion of early cattle domestication in Europe, and has led to repeated reassessment and re-attribution of some Neolithic material. Similarly, a proportional reduction in the length of the facial skeleton is often cited as a character which distinguishes domestic dog from wolf, yet Olsen (1979) notes the same trait in canids which cannot be other than wild. Of 404 skulls of dire wolf (*Canis dirus*) exhibited at the Rancho La Brea tar pits in California, at least 25, according to Olsen, exhibit the facial shortening supposedly characteristic of domestic dogs, even though the skulls date from a time in the Pleistocene before human colonization of the Americas. Olsen's paper is a good antidote to the confidence of Bökönyi (above). He poses the question, 'Archaeologically, what constitutes an early domestic animal?', and systematically shows that there is no simple answer. Fig. 13.1 underlines the point: here are two canid skulls, one smaller than the other and with a proportionally shorter face. That small one is the wolf.

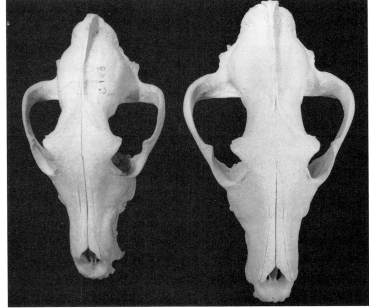

Fig. 13.1. Two canid skulls, to illustrate the difficulty of using size alone to diagnose wild or domestic status. The two skulls are similarly proportioned in terms of the ratio of muzzle length to overall length, but one skull is clearly smaller than the other. So which, if either, is the wolf? In fact, the left skull is from a female Canadian timber wolf, the right from an Alsatian dog.

Size change is better considered in the context of other attributes of the bone samples, such as changes in the relative abundance of potential domesticates. The Aceramic Neolithic site at Khirokitia, Cyprus, has produced abundant animal bone samples from the main occupation of the site, a period of a few centuries around seven to eight thousand years ago (Davis 1994). The main food species seem to have been sheep, pig and fallow deer, all of which were probably deliberate introductions to Cyprus. During the time that the site was occupied, the relative abundance of sheep increases, from less than 40 per cent to over 80 per cent of those three taxa, and there is also some indication of a size increase in the sheep. Taking those two observations together, we can postulate that there was intensified exploitation of the sheep, creating a selection pressure towards larger size. Davis suggests that there was some habitat degradation going on, wooded conditions shifting towards open grassland, so increasing the area of habitat suitable for sheep at the expense of the deer and pigs. Maybe, too, the three taxa were introduced as potential prey to hunt, despite one being a species which had been domesticated elsewhere by that time, and the change seen in the Khirokitia data reflects a move to husbandry of the sheep, replacing hunting of pigs, deer and feral sheep.

A similar case is seen on Gotland, a large island in the Baltic. Pigs appear to have been deliberately introduced to Gotland, probably early in the Neolithic, but was this as a domestic animal or as a wild resource to hunt? A recent study of pig remains from the Middle Neolithic site at Ajvide uses three lines of evidence to suggest that the pigs were wild (Rowley-Conwy & Storå 1997). There is the evidence of the size of the pigs, which lies within the range of modern European wild boar. Then there is the pattern of age at death, which indicates seasonal killing, predominantly in the autumn and early winter. That looks more like the seasonal exploitation of a wild population than the husbanding of a domestic pig population, which is more likely to have been cropped at regular intervals through the year. Finally, there is the question of niche. Middle Neolithic people on Gotland did not grow crops, and so were not generating a crop surplus or waste from crop production. In the absence of such materials, where is the niche for domestic pigs? Any one of these three lines of argument would not be wholly convincing on its own, but taken together, they well support Rowley-Conwy & Storå's case that the pigs were hunted wild animals.

The transition from hunting to herding is seen at a number of sites in the Middle East, not least at the major settlement at Tell Abu Hureyra, in northern Syria (Legge & Rowley-Conwy 1987). At this site, intensive exploitation of gazelles (*Gazella subgutterosa*) continued into the early Neolithic, by which time there is good evidence from the site for cultivation of a range of food plants, and small numbers of sheep and goat bones. It is suggested that Abu Hureyra had such a well-established system for big seasonal kills of migrating gazelles that animal husbandry simply was not necessary. The occasional sheep and goat bones may well represent animals kept for milking. Eventually, some factor (over-hunting, a change of migration patterns?) reduced reliable gazelle numbers below a certain threshold, and there seems to have been quite an abrupt switch to the husbanding of domestic sheep and goats.

Further east something similar is seen at Merhgarh, in the Indus Valley, Pakistan. Like Abu Hureyra, the site has an aceramic Neolithic period in which plants were cultivated yet the majority of meat seems to have been derived from hunting, especially of gazelle (*Gazella dorcas*) (Meadow 1984). By the end of the aceramic Neolithic, almost all the animal bones are of sheep, cattle and goat, though the wild ungulates which were formerly the major prey continue to be represented in bone samples, probably through the elimination of crop-robbing herbivores. From the end of the aceramic Neolithic onwards, there is a steady rise in the relative abundance of cattle, a nice contrast with the predominance of sheep and goat in Middle Eastern sites. The rise in relative abundance is paralleled by a reduction in the size of the cattle, especially in the earlier phases. This is the wild–domestic size reduction which has been used elsewhere to argue for the domestic status of cattle bones. This can be explained in terms of animals being kept under 'primitive conditions', deprived of their natural range and quantity of food. It is then assumed that the change in nutritional status would have affected phenotypic characters at first (i.e. underfed animals attaining only a reduced adult size), and in due course affecting the genotype of the cattle, there being some selective advantage to being small.

However, we might instead consider an alternative mechanism. Isolated populations of animals often vary in size from the population from which they were derived: at one time or another, the planet has housed isolated populations of all manner of giant or dwarf vertebrates, most familiarly on islands. Large mammals, in particular, tend toward smaller forms when isolated, and this has been explained in terms of a relaxation of the selection pressures for larger size (Zohary *et al.* 1998). In other words, perhaps early domestic cattle were smaller than their wild forebears simply because they no longer needed to be large, and not because of any specific pressure brought to bear by the conditions in which they were kept.

The age at death distribution of a sample has been used to argue for domesticated status. The simple case is put by Dexter Perkins Jr (1973). In a review of the sheep and goat remains from prehistoric sites throughout the Middle East, Perkins argues that a high proportion of juveniles is indicative of domestication. For example, at Zawi Chemi Shanidar, in the northern Zagros Mountains, the proportion of juvenile sheep in the upper levels would be unsustainable through the culling of a wild population, and the relative abundance of sheep rises in the upper levels. Perkins argues that this represents the introduction of domestic sheep locally, as Shanidar is not really in typical sheep country. The use of mortality profiles in this way is not uncontroversial, and high proportions of juvenile animals have been noted in samples of species which appear to have been wild. To return to the Middle Eastern gazelles, Davis (1983) has noted up to one-third juveniles in gazelle remains from the Natufian (i.e. Mesolithic) levels at Hayonim Terrace. Davis briefly considers and rejects the possibility that these gazelles were domesticated: the migratory and territorial habits of gazelles do not suit them to close control and captive breeding.

Occasionally, the evidence of size change and mortality profiles may conflict. The Aceramic Neolithic site at Asikli Hüyük, Turkey, has cattle, sheep, goat and pigs. The pigs are large, and, on those grounds, probably wild. The sheep and goats show the same large size as wild forms of those species do today, but the age at death data show a concentration on killing two- to four-year-olds, an age when we might expect mortality in the wild to be at a minimum, but domestic animals are at the optimum if killing for meat.

The size of the animals implies that they were wild, but the mortality profile more closely resembles what we might expect of a domestic population (Payne 1985b). The interplay of size and mortality profiles features in Tony Legge's survey of the evidence for early sheep and goat husbandry across a broad geographical sweep from Turkey to Iran (Legge 1996). Our interpretation requires both an understanding of the different degrees of sexual dimorphism in sheep and goats, and the possibility that, for example, preferential slaughter of young males, before the skeleton is fully fused, will remove them from the measured sample, and so suppress the sample mean. Thus at the early Neolithic site of Ganj Dareh, Iran, the mortality profile of the abundant goats suggests highly controlled culling, probably to utilize young males as meat while conserving adult females to breed. Such a strategy would indicate a domestic population, yet the Ganj Dareh goats are large in comparison to others from other Neolithic sites in the region, possibly because they represent a very early stage of domestication before substantial size reduction had occurred.

An example in which the different lines of argument come together is the investigation of the early domestication of the South American camelids. A conventional view has it that llama and alpaca are both wholly domestic animals, through speciation brought about by domestication from one or more wild ancestors, presumably either guanaco or vicuña. Llama and alpaca will interbreed under controlled conditions, and it is clear that the differentiation of these four taxa into 'good' species is a little questionable (Wheeler 1995). From the archaeological point of view, their similarity means that distinguishing their bones is problematic, and so recognizing a domesticated population is difficult.

The Junin *puna* (high montane grassland) of central Peru is a region where the wild species are still found, and from which the domestic forms are likely to have spread throughout montane South America. Early Holocene deposits in Junin, representing the first couple of millennia of human presence in the area, are typified by the hunting of deer and of the extinct equid *Parahipparion peruanum* (Wheeler *et al.* 1976). By about nine thousand years ago, camelids join the prey assemblages, constituting only about 26 per cent of the bones at Panalauca Cave, but 59 per cent at the broadly contemporary Lauricocha Cave. By about 7,000 BP, camelids markedly increase in abundance (over 80 per cent of bones), and domestic dog appears for the first time. Over the next few millennia, the concentration on camelids becomes still more marked, attaining over 90 per cent of identified bones at some sites in the *puna*. But is this targeted hunting, reminiscent of Middle Eastern exploitation of gazelles, or is it the herding of domestic camelids? In the absence of good morphological criteria, we might note the higher proportion of neonatal and juvenile animals in the later samples: is this evidence of domestic status? High infant mortality in camelids can be caused by close-herding in corrals, where the young are especially susceptible to enterotoxaemia, causing lethal diarrhoea (Wheeler 1984), though both wild and domestic camelids are susceptible to catastrophic infant mortality through unseasonal heavy snowfalls (Browman 1989). Morphological evidence for camelid domestication is limited to the rather ambiguous matter of size variation, and some fairly subtle differences in enamel distribution and cross-sectional shape between the incisors of alpaca and vicuña, differences which Wheeler (1984) has used to argue for the early presence of (presumably domestic) alpaca at Telarmachay Cave, in the Junin *puna*.

One part of the world where early animal husbandry is still somewhat unclear is China, from which much archaeological evidence has been obtained, but little of it has been published in an internationally accessible form. What is clear is that northern China had a vibrant Neolithic culture, with domestic dogs, pigs and chickens, by about 8,000–7,500 BP. The dogs and pigs are argued to be domestic on the conventional grounds of size and morphology, while the chickens are far removed from their modern geographical range (West & Zhou 1988). In this instance the chickens are also well outside the biome to which they are clearly adapted, so the counter-argument that the Neolithic chickens are just wild birds from a formerly much wider range is not convincing. The first, rather fragmentary evidence of domestic sheep and goats appears in northern China some two to three millennia later than the pigs and chickens (Ben-Shun 1984), with much the same pattern in southern China, where sheep seem never to have been a particularly important domesticate. The pattern of animal domestication in China is intriguingly distinctive, with 'backyard' species such as pigs and chickens being domesticated long before the herd ungulates which typify early domestication in the more familiar Middle East.

INFERRING HUSBANDRY PRACTICES

Through much of the temperate zone of Eurasia, the domestic status of livestock is not in doubt once settlement has acquired all of the characteristics of the Neolithic. Instead, our attention turns to using the relative abundance and mortality profiles of the domestic animals to derive information about husbandry practices. It is difficult to generalize about this process: each site is different, and presents quite different opportunities and challenges. However, two examples from the Middle East will be briefly reviewed, to show something of the process of inference.

The first is a small site in north-west Iran: Dinkha Tepe (Gilbert & Steinfeld 1977). This occupation mound spans the Bronze and Iron Ages, roughly from 1,900 BC to 800 BC, and yielded a modest bone assemblage, much of it from Bronze Age levels (1,900–1,600 BC). In many respects Dinkha Tepe is a very ordinary Middle Eastern prehistoric assemblage, and so constitutes a useful example. Of nearly 2,500 identifiable bones from the Bronze Age levels, cattle are the most abundant species; then sheep, pig and goat, with some horse, dog and deer bones. Note the use of 'species': in fact, the most abundant taxa were 'small ungulate', 'sheep or goat', and 'large ungulate'. If we allow some ingenious redistribution of the large and small ungulate categories, caprines (i.e. sheep and goats) probably outnumber cattle by about two or three to one. An estimate of age at death based on epiphysial fusion (there being too few mandibles), indicates that goats were killed off at an earlier age than sheep. That suggests that the goats were kept primarily for meat, with the sheep retained to a greater age for secondary products such as wool. It is possible that the goats were traded rather than husbanded, as the proportion of adults is too low to constitute a viable breeding population. The cattle bones include a high proportion of adults, indicating that they were kept principally as plough or dairy animals, not killed young for meat. In sum, Bronze Age Dinkha Tepe seems to have been a settlement of pastoral farmers who conserved most of their sheep and cattle to adulthood so as to crop milk, wool, pulling power and dung, while trading for young goats to provide meat.

A sharp contrast is provided by the site of Umm Qseir, in north-eastern Syria, close to the borders of Iraq and Turkey (Zeder 1994). This is a multi-period site, with particularly good representation of the Halafian cultural tradition (5,500–4,500 BC), and lies in the Khabur basin, a region with numerous known sites of this period. The Halafian settlement was evidently small – perhaps only two or three families – and the simple house structures lacked stones for milling cereals or sickles to cut them, and had little in the way of permanent hearths. The initial interpretation was of a temporary seasonal encampment, through which nomadic pastoralists passed regularly but briefly. However, although the bone assemblages include sheep, goat and pig, the majority of the Halafian assemblages are bones from wild animals, including gazelle, wild ass, aurochs and fallow deer. This can be made to fit with the transhumance model by assuming that the site was occupied in spring in order to utilize the lush banks of the Khabur river and the prey living along its banks, before retreating northwards as the pasture dried up in summer. Unfortunately for this model, the age at death distributions of the pigs represents a viable breeding population, not just a few animals, and is consistent with pigs having been killed at all times of the year. The age at death of the sheep and goats shows a concentration on killing two- to four-year-old animals, with the younger animals appearing to show a peak of killing from late summer to winter (i.e. seven- to twelve-month-old individuals, based on February to March births). In all, Zeder suggests that Umm Qseir was occupied year-round, with a highly opportunistic economic strategy. Sheep and goats saw the people through the later part of the dry summer and into the cold wet season. As the spring flush of grass attracted game, so the strategy shifted to hunting gazelles, a versatile means of making the best use of a region not ideally suited to farming.

UNINVITED GUESTS: THE SIDE EFFECTS OF SETTLING DOWN

Certain animals, notably rodents, have been closely associated with humans for millennia, as uninvited guests in our houses and barns, as companion animals, even as objects of veneration (i.e. consider Mickey Mouse!). Our relationship with the house mouse (*Mus domesticus*: taxonomy here will follow Marshall & Sage 1981) has been particularly complex, and the social incorporation of mice, as pets and as selected fancy forms, has a considerable antiquity in China (Berry 1981; Brothwell 1981). It is difficult to be confident about the stratigraphical position and therefore dating of bones of a species which burrows. None the less enough good records are made to show that mice have accompanied humans virtually since people have farmed and lived in villages. Some interesting information on the process of transportation of mice has been obtained from sites in the Duero Valley, Central Spain (Morales Muñiz *et al.* 1995). Iron Age sites in this area have produced some of the earliest western European records of house mouse and of house sparrow (*Passer domesticus*). There is some association of the remains of these two commensal species with those of donkeys and shellfish and other coastal animals. This suggests that mice were transported into Spain from a southerly direction by people, or with trade goods, with a North African or Near Eastern connection. Given the dating of these finds, it is possible that the spread of house mice through Spain was a consequence of Phoenician colonization and trade.

The other Old World (though now global) rodent which has attracted great archaeological interest is the black rat (or ship rat, or roof rat) *Rattus rattus*. This endearing creature has been ruthlessly pursued through the archaeological and historical records by several authors, in particular Philip Armitage (*et al.* 1984; 1993; 1994). The introduction of rats into Europe has been a matter of myth and legend, with the traditional view being nicely put by Matheson (1931, 7): the species was 'unknown to the Greeks and Romans . . . the returning ships of the Crusaders were probably largely instrumental in bringing the black rat to our shores'. In fact, archaeological records have shown black rat to have spread from a probable southern Asian origin to the British Isles by the second century AD (Armitage *et al.* 1984; O'Connor 1988b). These Roman rat populations may have died out with the end of urban living in the fifth century, only for rats to be reintroduced to north-western Europe during the Viking period (O'Connor 1991b; Armitage 1994). This does not indicate that the traditionally nasty hairy Vikings were also verminous. Rather, the expansion of trade in the eighth and ninth centuries from the Baltic region, along the Russian river systems, brought north-western Europe into contact with the Islamic world centred on Constantinople and Baghdad which in turn had trade contact with India and beyond. The Viking traders put north-western Europe back into contact with the homeland of the black rat, and the rats seem to have taken full advantage. The development of major routeways, linking expanding towns, certainly facilitated the spread and expansion of rats through the eleventh to thirteenth centuries (Audoin-Rouzeau & Vigne 1994). The black rat is, of course, traditionally linked with the spread of the Black Death through fourteenth-century Europe, though from an historical and epidemiological perspective, the case is far from proven (D. Davis 1986).

Given their facility for hitching a ride, it was inevitable that black rats would cross the Atlantic as Europeans settled in the Americas. In fact, Armitage (1993) reports what may have been one of the first black rats to reach the New World, represented by a single mandible from a site at En Bas Saline, in northern Haiti, which is thought to have been one of the settlements established by Columbus in December 1492. By the late 1500s rats had reached the west coast of South America, and by 1568 Spanish troops garrisoned at Fort Mateo, Florida, were complaining that the rats were a nuisance. The rapid early spread was not restricted to the warmer latitudes. Excavation of the Basque galleon *San Juan*, wrecked in Red Bay, Labrador, in 1565 has shown that there were black rats on board (Grenier 1985). Life on board ship was not necessarily wholly to the rats' benefit. The Emanuel Point wreck, Florida, yielded a minimum of twenty-one black rats and two house mice (Armitage, quoted at length in Smith *et al.* 1995). On six limb bones from these rats, Armitage noted growth abnormalities apparently diagnostic of rickets, which would indicate a severe deficiency of vitamin D and consequent disruption of the calcium-phosphorus metabolism essential for bone mineralization. In the Caribbean the importation of the guinea pig *Cavia porcellus* has been noted, and assumed to have been deliberate (Wing 1989). Given the ease with which rats accompanied people around the Old World, perhaps guinea pigs, as the New World commensal rodent, were also successful in hitching a ride?

Some bird species have exploited people with great success, and one of the most successful of synanthropic birds is the house sparrow. It is clear that sparrows adopted people in the Middle East in the early Natufian, more or less as soon as there were villages (Tchernov 1993). From that beginning, sparrows obviously spread quite rapidly in their new niche: Ericson *et al.* (1997) report house sparrow from a Late Bronze Age site in central Sweden. This record pre-dates the arrival of domestic fowl in that region, and Ericson *et al.* thus discount the theory that sparrows spread across Europe as the keeping of domestic fowl provided scattered and spilt grain. The spread of house sparrows through North America in recent times raises an interesting point. One of the factors in the deliberate introduction of house sparrows to North America from the 1850s onwards was the desire of European immigrants to the American cities to see something familiar living around them (Long 1981, 375). It is possible that the same desire during earlier periods of human expansion and colonization facilitated the spread of other synanthropic birds around the world. We return to the association between towns and birds in Chapter 14.

OURSELVES AND OTHER ANIMALS

So what does the archaeological record reveal about the origins of animal husbandry, and our adoption by pets and pests? A number of animals quite clearly entered into a domesticatory relationship with humans – cattle, sheep, goats, pigs, llama, water buffalo and turkeys, to name but a few. However, that leaves us with the problem of distinguishing domesticated animals from those that are tamed. As Charles Reed points out, Egyptian illustrations show all manner of animals behaving in ways which indicate them to have been tamed, not least hyenas (Reed 1980, 18). Despite Reed's charming exegesis on the topic of hyenas as a potential man's-best-friend, rolling limply on one's back while being hand-fed does not necessarily constitute domestication. Presumably the tamed status of those hyenas would be inferred from finding their remains among the day-to-day human occupation debris, or finding them to have been buried with some care.

Taming an animal to provide an amiable companion and taming one in order for it to do useful work are obviously two different processes. Asiatic elephants (*Elephas maximus*) have some two thousand years of history as a tamed and utilized work animal, yet breed only rarely in captivity. People thus lack close control over the breeding of the species, and so the status of elephants cannot be described as domesticated, despite the very close working relationship (Baker & Manwell 1983). The nature of this relationship is known largely through Sanskrit and recent historical sources: it is debatable whether we would understand the status of working elephants if we had only their bones in archaeological samples and no supporting history. Another interesting point which Baker & Manwell make concerns the role of bravery and 'dare' in the catching and subduing of elephants. To be the one who catches a wild elephant and breaks it to your will conveys status, and it is tempting to wonder whether something similar might have been a factor in the early domestication and social incorporation of horses and cattle (which takes us back to the subject of bullfights – Chapter 12!).

In conclusion, perhaps what we have to ask is whether it is more important to be able to point to a piece of bone and say 'Dog, not wolf', or to point to the bone and its archaeological context and say 'Large canid, apparently tame companion animal'. The former statement has the merit of zoological clarity, but the latter probably tells us more in archaeological terms. What it requires, of course, is that we look at more than just the bones, and we might note that there is as much genetic divergence between different populations of modern dogs as there is between dogs and wolves (Tsuda *et al.* 1997).

Whatever the early story, humans and animals developed a range of relationships, which allowed sheep to spread far beyond the Middle East, gave water buffalo a niche among Asian padi-fields that might otherwise have crowded them to extinction, and allowed cats to take over the world. This process also facilitated the settlement of humans in ever greater numbers in focal settlements which sometimes became towns, which in their turn sometimes became cities. Some animals followed humans into the cities, while others remained conveniently on the periphery, whence they could be procured as required. Humans in the towns and cities developed varying degrees of social and economic complexity, some of which came to be reflected in what they ate and where – and how – the garbage was disposed of. The next chapter looks at archaeological bone samples from towns and cities, and how this complexity may be reflected in the bones.

FOURTEEN

URBAN GARBAGE: ON DROVERS, BUTCHERS, WEALTH AND RATS

At various times and places over the last five thousand years or so, people have gathered in the accumulations of population and housing which we refer to as towns. Where people are concentrated, so too are the processes of food preparation and consumption, and the disposal of refuse. Ancient towns and cities sometimes yield very large quantities of archaeological animal bones, and this may itself be a distinctive characteristic of what we can briefly describe as urban bone assemblages. In addition, the social and economic characteristics of towns give to those assemblages characteristics which can be quite different to those from hunter-gatherer or agrarian sites, and which can be a valuable source of information about the social and economic activities of the people concerned.

There is a wealth of literature surrounding the origins and functions of towns and cities. This is not the place to go into the topic in great detail, but some of the political and economic theory on towns has a bearing on the interpretation of urban bone assemblages, and the archaeological information which we might hope to extract from them. One strand of opinion derives from Marx and Engels, who essentially saw the emergence of city-states in the protohistoric Middle East as a means of institutionalizing inequalities of control of the means of production (Engels 1891). Gordon Childe saw cities as evolving to utilize the surplus production which he believed would inevitably have resulted from increasingly efficient agriculture, allowing the emergence of agriculturally unproductive craftspeople, who in turn required a ruling elite with powers of tithe or taxation by which to finance construction and to patronize craft specialization (Childe 1950; 1957). For Mesoamerica Sanders & Price (1968) proposed that the surplus agricultural production which allowed the development of non-productive specialists was actively induced and managed by the ruling elite, rather than the inevitable outcome of agrarian development. There has been a shift of emphasis away from the overtly political analysis of Engels, and more recent models tend to see towns largely in terms of the specialization of craft production, and thus a high degree of segregation of economic activities, in terms of personnel, timing, and location (e.g. Wright 1977).

What does all of this have to do with bones? Possibly quite a lot. As nucleations of population, towns need to draw in food from a large area, requiring control of acquisition, droving, marketing and butchering, and possibly the provision of 'holding' areas in or near the town. The bones recovered from a town may be of livestock which began their lives many kilometres away. Whether or not one accepts Engels' analysis regarding inequalities of economic control, a proportion of the population was agriculturally unproductive, and so had to be fed in some way. Some form of marketing or redistribution was necessary, and this creates the potential for substantial differences in the animal products acquired by different families or neighbourhoods. These differences may reflect the degree of control and influence (or 'wealth') exercised by a particular segment of the urban population. We might see this reflected in the distribution of different taxa, or of different joints of meat, or of different age classes.

The disposal of refuse, and therefore the location and characteristics of deposits of bones, may carry valuable information about the tolerance of refuse at different periods and in different places, or about the deposition of mostly household debris rather than the garbage from larger-scale butchering activity (Fig. 14.1). Among the debris of human subsistence, there will also be the bones of the urban vertebrate fauna, whether of

Fig. 14.1. A view of waterlogged Roman deposits and structures in York, UK. The deposits will include bones and other objects from activities within and around the timber buildings, and debris from elsewhere around the city deposited as 'landfill' at this low-lying riverside site. The dormouse immortalized in Fig. 11.2 came from the deposits depicted here. (Photo courtesy of York Archaeological Trust)

companion animals such as dogs and cats, or of opportunistic commensal species such as mice and crows. Urban bone assemblages can thus give us information about the social and economic relations between the town and its hinterland and between different parts of the town, about where and when it was felt appropriate to deposit refuse, and about the wider urban ecosystem. In any investigation, it is essential that the town or city as a whole is seen as the 'site', not just the individual excavation, as even a very large excavation will reflect only the characteristics of one neighbourhood.

Published examples of urban archaeology obviously mostly come from those parts of the world where there is a long history of urban development, and where there has been active archaeological investigation. It is inevitable, then, that this chapter deals mostly with examples from the Middle East and Europe, and perhaps excusable that my own work on Roman and medieval towns in England provides some of the more detailed examples.

SUPPLY AND DEMAND

A useful starting point is to consider the economic relationship between the town and its hinterland. Did towns in the past rely upon a rural hinterland population to generate a surplus which could be supplied to the towns, or did some towns actively manage production on lands directly owned and managed by the urban population? This question has been investigated for two major Roman towns in southern England: Dorchester and Winchester (Maltby 1994). Contemporary documents and inscriptions give grounds to believe that land around at least some of the Roman towns in Britain was farmed by the inhabitants of the town, and excavations in some Roman towns have located what appears to be housing for livestock, as at Silchester (Boon 1974). The results of Maltby's comparison are somewhat ambiguous, but a couple of points should be noted. The pigs at Dorchester and Winchester were significantly larger than those from the nearby large rural site of Owslebury. It appears that the pigs slaughtered in the towns did not come from the rural populations represented by Owslebury, but were a different, larger form of pig, perhaps raised in sties in and around the towns. The size distribution of the cattle bones from the towns indicates a predominance of adult females, and one excavation at Dorchester has produced a quantity of bones of young calves (Maltby 1993). Putting these data together, Maltby suggests that the urban population might have maintained milking herds, hence the age distribution, and hence too the deposition of culled, presumably male, calves within the town rather than at some rural location.

Maltby's discussion of Dorchester and Winchester raises the big question of supply and demand. At its simplest, we might ask whether a particular town generated such demand that the rural hinterland was geared to meet that demand, or whether agricultural settlements in the surrounding area simply continued farming as they saw fit, and supplied a surplus to the towns as and when they could. In other words, did the town get what it wanted, or what the hinterland wanted to supply? Melinda Zeder has investigated this question for the Bronze Age town at Tal-e-Malyan, in the Kur River region of Iran (Zeder 1991). For the Banesh phase (about 3,400–2,800 BC), there is a marked difference in the age distribution of goats and of sheep, and a high ratio of goats to sheep. Zeder points out that sheep generally yield more meat, whereas goats have a higher reproductive capacity. If livestock were being raised largely to feed the town, we might expect a higher ratio of sheep to goats. The high proportion of goats suggests that the animals were supplied by pastoralists who had other priorities. Furthermore, the goats were generally slaughtered as immature animals, while the sheep were generally older. Zeder's interpretation is that the sheep were mainly kept for their secondary products of wool and milk, with surplus young goats being supplied to the town, rather like the interpretation offered for Dinkah Tepe (Chapter 13). Rural availability, rather than urban demand, seems to have directed the process. The Middle Bronze Age urban site at Tell Jemmeh, Israel, also seems to show that sheep and goats were supplied from surplus pastoral stock. The sheep and goats at this site were killed either as young animals approaching one year old, or as adults around five years old. Measurements of the adults were consistent with most of them being female, so giving the impression that the town was fed with animals surplus to milk production (Wapnish & Hesse 1988).

My own interpretation of samples from medieval York makes the same point. The cattle supplied to the town were largely adult, though not particularly elderly, and the sheep were predominantly adult (O'Connor 1989; 1991a; Bond & O'Connor 1999). The data are consistent with a hinterland in which the priorities were to raise cattle to draw the plough, and sheep for wool, with animals being traded into the city only when they had worked for a few years, or produced some young or a couple of years' worth of wool. Even one of the major cities of medieval England does not seem to have generated enough demand to justify the specialized production of animals for meat alone. In fact, the large-scale droving of cattle to London, in order to feed the burgeoning urban population, seems only to have begun in the seventeenth century (Armitage 1978).

Historical sources will not necessarily lend support to the interpretation of bone assemblages in matters of supply and demand. Gill Clark (*et al.* 1989) reports material from what appears to have been a relatively affluent household in late fourteenth-century Tarquinia, Italy. The bones are principally those of old cattle and mature, probably female, sheep. The meat supply to this household appears to have been obtained from worn-out working oxen, and sheep surplus to the needs of a pastoral economy based on wool production. Contemporary Italian written sources class the beef from former working cattle as of very low value indeed, fit only for manual workers and those with a strong stomach. Either the interpretation of this household as affluent is seriously wide of the mark, or the written sources are describing things as the writer would wish them to be, rather than the harsh reality of life. On the other hand, documentary sources can provide information on the minutiae of supply and demand, not least seasonal availability, which will not be detectable in the archaeological samples, but which is none the less relevant to the interpretation of the archaeological data (Clark 1992). In the end, we tend to assume that urban supply and demand was economically rational, while accepting that social attitudes and tastes might create patterns of demand that are unexpected precisely because they are not (O'Connor 1992a).

SOURCES AND BUTCHERING

One approach to the analysis of economic relations between town and country is to attempt to 'source' the livestock: in other words, to determine the likely place of origin of the animals whose remains are found in the town. This is fraught with difficulties. At Roman Winchester and Dorchester Maltby (1994) suggested that the town pigs were of a different size to contemporary country pigs, and further suggested that two different types of sheep were recognizable in Winchester. One was a relatively small, horned type, consistent with the sheep typical of Iron Age sites in the region, and the other was a much larger, hornless type, which appears in small numbers on rural sites such as Owslebury much later than in Winchester.

My own analyses have detected the same large morphology in Roman sheep from Winchester and other sites in southern and eastern England (O'Connor 1982), and Noddle (1998) has noted large hornless sheep from Roman deposits at Wroxeter, in western England. Assuming for the moment that Roman Winchester was supplied with sheep of two very different types, does that necessarily imply provisioning from two different areas, or were the small sheep and the large sheep each typical of different locations within the catchment of Winchester? There is no reason why two different types of sheep should not

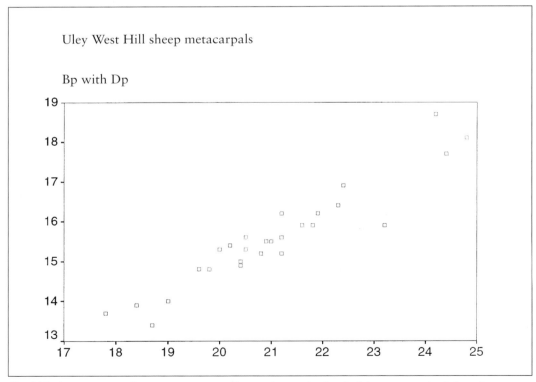

Fig. 14.2. A scattergram of two measurements taken on the proximal end of the metacarpals of sheep from a Roman site at Uley West Hill, Gloucestershire, to illustrate the presence of a few particularly large specimens. Size distributions like this one have been noted from a number of Roman sites in southern England.

have been kept in separate flocks, but in the same locations, throughout southern England through the Roman period.

Apart from biometrical data, other evidence may be used to suggest diversity of type in livestock. In York, the sheep represented in near-contemporaneous samples from two different medieval sites within the city wore down their teeth at different rates, indicating some difference in the grazing environment (Bond & O'Connor 1999, 390–1; see also Chapter 8). Furthermore, other samples from medieval York include sheep with quite different frequencies of two non-metrical traits than are typical of the rest of the city (Bond & O'Connor 1999, 409–10; see also Chapter 10). Taking these data together, we seem to have good grounds for saying that the city was drawing in sheep from several different areas. The different attrition rates might represent the difference between flocks grazed largely on the chalk pastures of the Yorkshire Wolds, to the east of York, and those grazed on the often sandy soils closer to the city. The samples with unusual frequencies of non-metrical traits come from an ecclesiastical enclave within the medieval city, so may represent flocks accessible only to that particular segment of the population. If the ecclesiastical sheep were a relatively small population, with a high degree of in-breeding, then founder effect followed by drift within an isolated population could have brought about the distinctive frequency of non-metrical traits. However, that is quite speculative, and frankly gets us no nearer to being able to say that these sheep came from *here* rather than from *there*.

Livestock and meat products move around a town, not just into it. Given the concentration of mouths to feed, it is unsurprising that towns often show the development of specialist butchers, and of areas where the killing and subdivision of carcasses took place. Apart from the bone assemblages produced during the initial subdivision of carcasses, intermediate stages of exchange and butchering of joints might produce distinctive assemblages, before the domestic processes of cooking and consumption lead to the deposition of yet another, distinctively patterned assemblage (O'Connor 1993b). With ungulates such as cattle and sheep, it is generally assumed that the low food utility of the heads and feet will lead to them being deposited close to the site of slaughter and initial butchery, potentially producing assemblages which mimic those typical of hunter-gatherer kill-sites. Two medieval sites in Exeter, in south-west England, serve as good examples (Levitan 1987). At Exe Bridge thirteenth-century deposits gave samples in which cattle horncores were predominant, overlain by later medieval deposits with abundant cattle horncores, metapodials and phalanges. This is clearly debris from the initial butchering of carcasses, and the location of the deposits – dumped in riverside muds – is consistent with the disposal of a large amount of noxious refuse. In contrast, samples from St Katherine's Priory include the major meat-bearing bones of cattle, and are, if anything, rather depleted in head and foot bones. This bias is more pronounced in the sheep bones from St Katherine's Priory, in which the great majority are from the fore and hind limbs, and the limb girdles. Levitan's conclusion is that the sheep, and probably the cattle, mostly arrived at the priory as butchered joints, not 'on the hoof', though it is possible that livestock came to the priory on the hoof, but that the heads and feet were subsequently deposited well away from the priory. Other examples of cattle 'heads and feet' deposits have been identified from Roman towns in Britain (Maltby 1984). One such deposit, in riverside muds in Lincoln, contains such a quantity of bone as to show that large-scale butchering of cattle, and the economic organization which that implies, was still going on in the city in the late fourth century AD, a time by which some authors have suggested that Roman towns in England were in economic decline (Dobney *et al.* 1998).

The marks left on bones by the butchers' tools may also reveal something about the ways in which carcasses were treated. Butchering procedures may be strongly influenced by custom and practice. For example, a comparison of the butchering marks on cattle bones from Roman towns in central-southern England with those from rural settlements of the same date shows big differences in practice. Cattle bones from the towns bear the marks of heavy-bladed chopping tools, such as axes and cleavers, while those from the rural sites bear fine cut-marks, indicating that the carcasses were taken apart with the aid of a knife (Maltby 1989). It is tempting to interpret this observation in cultural terms, with the more Romanized towns adopting one practice while the 'natives' use another. On the other hand, the difference could be purely functional. The careful dismantling of a cattle carcass with a knife probably maximizes the amount of meat which is recovered from the skeleton, but is relatively slow and requires considerable skill. Taking a dead cow apart with an axe may be more wasteful in terms of recoverable meat, but it is quicker and less demanding of experience. Use of the axe and cleaver in the towns may therefore have been a compromise which allowed speedy butchering of cattle on the scale which the urban demand necessitated.

A similar contrast was noted by Rosemary Luff in her study of bones from a quarry-workers' village outside the Egyptian city of Amarna (Kemp *et al.* 1994). The cattle carcasses seemed to have been dismembered rather haphazardly with a cleaver, whereas pig and caprine (mostly goat) bones from the same samples showed only fine knife-marks. Given that the village was an artisan's settlement adjacent to a city which was both a royal and a religious centre, Luff suggests that the pigs and goats were kept and butchered by the villagers, while the cattle were butchered in the city, probably by temple priests, having come in as offerings which were subsequently redistributed. Pig and goat remains from the village lacked bones from the hind limbs, so perhaps hams and legs of goat were either traded with the city or sent to it as offerings.

It does not follow that we shall find the bone refuse typical of a specific stage of butchery at the place at which that butchering was carried out. In the examples mentioned above, it should not be supposed that the cattle in medieval Exeter or in Roman Lincoln were actually slaughtered and butchered on the banks of the rivers Exe and Witham, only that the riversides offered a convenient place at which to dump the refuse. Given the often crowded conditions of towns in the past (and today), disposal of large volumes of smelly debris must have been a problem. A convenient river would no doubt have made a useful sewer, and surrounding farmland might have benefited from a top-dressing of urban waste, taking this debris out of the urban archaeological record.

Some quantification of the extent of such disposal is given by West (1995), in a delightful study of seventeenth- to early eighteenth-century samples from the Royal Navy Victualling Yard, London. Archaeological evidence from the site showed the presence of pens and stockyard areas, and historical sources refer to the slaughter of, among other things, forty oxen *per day* in order to keep the Navy fed. West points out that this would generate around 880kg of cattle bone per day, yet the Early phase at the site, representing around seventy-five years of use, yielded only 38kg of cattle bone. Even adding to this all of the 'cattle-sized' bones gives a total of just 62kg – enough to make three cows, and a vanishingly small percentage of the total originally generated (about .0004 per cent, making due allowance for no slaughter on Sundays and Holy Days). The remainder presumably largely went into landfill dumps along London's fast-developing waterfront, though West ingeniously adds another possibility, namely fashions in Dutch furniture and the accession of William of Orange. The later part of the seventeenth century saw a sharp change from the heavy, dowelled furniture of earlier decades to more refined forms with glued joints, and often with delicate marquetry. In short, there was a considerable increase in the demand for glue, and glue was manufactured from hides, hooves and bones. Lest this should seem too speculative, West notes that the earliest records of glue manufacture on an industrial scale are from late seventeenth-century Holland, with introduction to England in the eighteenth century. Furthermore, records from 1910 show that even at that late date, the Netherlands imported 7,000,000kg of bones for glue-making. Apart from shedding useful light on the volumes of bone debris generated by industrial-scale butchery, West's study of the Victualling Yard material stands as one of the most audacious, yet plausible, interpretations of animal bone data in the English-language literature!

RECOGNIZING THE RICH AND FAMOUS

Turning to the question of wealth and status among the urban population, this brings us back to the various political paradigms reviewed at the beginning of this chapter, and the issue of access to resources. Terms such as 'wealth', 'prosperity' and 'socioeconomic status' are somewhat intangible. In urban archaeology we tend to equate such terms with the occurrence in particular buildings or parts of a town of high value artefacts or uncommon food items, consumables of one form or another to which not everyone in the population seems to have had access, so that the possession or consumption of them seems to denote social or economic power. Differences in status might account for some of the differences which Reitz (1986) noted between rural (mixed slave and planter) and urban (middle-class and blue-collar) sites of mid-eighteenth to mid-nineteenth-century date on the Atlantic coasts of South Carolina and Georgia. Reitz observes that the urban samples probably 'summarize' debris from dozens of individual houses and shops, so blurring the detail of individual wealth and status. To some extent this is almost an inevitable characteristic of urban archaeological deposits, especially where refuse has been collected and redeposited on to riversides and waste ground. Occasionally, though, the excavation of individual house plots and their associated refuse pits and dumps allows very detailed interpretation.

Excavations in 1981 and 1983 at the Waterlooplein and Oostenbergermiddenstraat sites in Amsterdam, Holland, uncovered a total of about one hundred cess pits (latrine pits) dated to the seventeenth and eighteenth centuries. At Waterlooplein the sites of 110 houses were excavated, in a part of the city known to have been particularly settled by Portugese Jews (Ijzereef 1989). Apart from a few cess pits, the Oostenberger site included a refuse deposit dated to the end of the sixteenth century, the bones in which were a mixture of skulls and horncores, domestic food debris and refuse from a manufacturer of bone buttons (MacGregor 1989). Ijzereef set about distinguishing Jewish from non-Jewish (or non-kosher) households on the basis of the amount of pig bone in the cess pits: in most cases there was a negligible amount (less than 1 per cent) or an appreciable amount (more than 5 per cent; usually around 15 per cent) (Ijzereef 1989, 45–6). The no-pig deposits were also characterized by the absence of hind legs of cattle and sheep. This joint is not kosher unless the sciatic nerve is removed, and it may be that the simple alternative was to sell on the hindquarters to non-kosher butchers. No-pig deposits also lacked calf bones, showed a high relative abundance of chicken bones (in contrast to the common duck bones in apparently non-Jewish contexts), and lacked eel bones. Eels are not kosher.

The clarity with which the refuse from Jewish and non-Jewish households could apparently be identified at Waterlooplein shows that urban bone samples can retain a remarkable degree of resolution of detail. From the same Amsterdam sites Ijzereef was able to draw up a scale of apparent wealth. At one end lay an eighteenth-century sample with a relatively low proportion of cattle bones, and those only the most meat-bearing elements, and a high proportion of chicken, turkey, goose and fish bones, the latter including tuna (*Thunnus thynnus*). Add to that salmon, oysters and lobster, and the appearance of wealth is quite convincing. At the other end of the scale lay another eighteenth-century sample, predominantly of highly fragmented cattle and sheep bones, among which head and foot elements were common. Ijzereef suggests that this family lived on the charity of the local butcher. Between these extremes, a total of six wealth categories were defined on the basis of the bone samples. Plotting these categories through time, this part of Amsterdam seems to have been relatively rich in the early 1600s, with a gradual decline to about 1700, by which time most households were generating 'poor' refuse. The second half of the eighteenth century is marked by a division of the data into either rich or poor, with few examples in between (Ijzereef 1989, 51).

In the example above, tuna seems to have been an indicator of comparative wealth. We need to draw a distinction between species which were simply exotic and uncommon, perhaps such as tuna in seventeenth- and eighteenth-century Amsterdam, and those which were not uncommon but to which access was restricted. A good example of the latter is the status of, and degree of access to, deer in medieval Europe. York is fairly typical of tenth- to sixteenth-century towns across northern Europe in yielding few specimens of red deer and fallow deer. Tenth- to twelfth-century deposits sometimes contain fragments of red deer antler, where this valuable raw material has been brought into the town to be worked into combs and pins, but bones from the meat-bearing parts of the carcass are uncommon. Both species were maintained on estates as animals to be hunted for the amusement of the landed classes, rather than as food for urban merchants and artisans. Thus in the Netherlands, for example, red deer bones are commonly found at castle sites, but only rarely at town or monastic sites (Groenman-van Waateringe 1994). One site in York, the ecclesiastical enclave at the Bedern, has yielded modest numbers of fallow deer bones, and those predominantly bones of the hind limb (Bond & O'Connor 1999). This appears to represent the donation of haunches of venison to the ecclesiastical college, and is paralleled by samples from some English castles, notably Launceston Castle, Cornwall (Albarella & Davis 1996).

On a smaller scale, rabbits also seem to have been restricted in medieval England. Though present in the country at least from the eleventh century onwards, and one of the most familiar 'wild' animals in the countryside today, rabbits were kept on estates under quite controlled conditions. They were hunted as an alternative to deer and other large game, a form of management seen elsewhere in northern Europe (Groenman-van Waateringe 1994). The scarcity of rabbit bones in medieval samples from York is thus no surprise, but seventeenth-century deposits at the 1–5 Aldwark site (currently unpublished) did produce quite large numbers of rabbit bones. Does this indicate that the neighourhood in question had privileged access? The rest of the assemblages included a lot of sheep bones, principally from the fore and hind limbs, and a diverse range of birds and fish, including species not found so far elsewhere in the city. Like some of Ijzereef's samples from Waterlooplein, the post-medieval samples from Aldwark give the impression of wealth. However, there may be an alternative explanation, at least for the rabbits. It is possible that by the seventeenth century sufficient rabbits had escaped from managed estate populations to have established feral populations which would have been more generally available. Certainly, the Aldwark households had a varied, good quality meat diet, but access to rabbits may not have been a matter of privilege by that date.

The intensity of archaeological activity in north-western Europe means that fish bones have been intensively studied in this region, allowing quite complex questions of regional trade and supply, and biogeographical questions to be addressed. The introduction of the carp (*Cyprinus carpio*) to western Europe has been investigated as an indicator of the development of fish ponds and the cultivation of captive stocks (Hoffman 1994). There are problems of identification among the carp family, but reliable records of carp outside what is thought to be its Holocene range have been obtained at Leeuwarden, Netherlands (Brinkhuizen 1979), and at monastic sites in Belgium (van Neer & Ervynck 1994). At some medieval sites it has been possible to follow fish exploitation through time, showing marked changes from century to century. At York, for example, sites dated to the ninth and tenth centuries AD (the Anglo-Scandinavian period) give assemblages with abundant cyprinids (carp family), pike, eels and herring. Through the eleventh and twelfth centuries there is a marked change to fewer cyprinids and pike, and more cod (*Gadus morhua*). Within the cyprinids, there is also something of a change from clean water species, such as chub (*Leuciscus cephalus*) and barbel (*Barbus barbus*), to more tolerant species such as roach (*Rutilus rutilus*) (Jones 1988; Bond & O'Connor 1999, 398–401).

PETS AND PESTS

Among the food debris deposited in towns, it is not uncommon to find the remains of the companion animals, notably dogs and cats, that lived in and among the human habitation, and the various vertebrate species that took advantage of the town as a source of food and shelter. Where livestock are kept, dogs have an obvious function, either to assist in herding the animals or to deter other potential predators. The dogs that we find in urban deposits are less obviously working animals, though they may have been important as guard dogs, and utility is a somewhat subjective parameter (O'Connor 1992b). Cats pose still more of a problem, adept as they are at establishing feral populations (Tabor 1983). Age at death estimates for cats from medieval urban sites in Britain and Ireland indicate quite a high mortality of juveniles, and it is not unusual to find knife-cuts on cat bones indicative of skinning (McCormick 1988; O'Connor 1992b; Luff & Moreno-Garcia 1995). Does this indicate that cats were raised specifically for their skins, and 'cropped' as soon as a useful body size was attained? That remains possible but unproven, and it is equally likely that young cats were particularly vulnerable as juveniles newly independent of their mothers, and that people in medieval towns opportunistically used the fur from dead cats.

We interpret the remains of dogs and cats as companion animals because that is their role today. Some of the other species that occur in urban archaeological samples may have fulfilled the same role in the past. For example, the remains of jackdaw (*Corvus monedula*) are commonly found in most medieval towns in northern Europe. This familiar bird is a common scavenger, an intelligent and versatile inhabitant of towns and cities, and we generally assume that the medieval jackdaws occupied that niche. However, jackdaws, in common with other corvids, make good pets, readily adapting to a domestic life, and forming close attachments with humans. At least some of the jackdaws that we find in medieval deposits may have been companion animals, not scavengers: only the context of a particular find would show that distinction.

The importance of towns in facilitating the spread of rats and mice has already been touched upon in Chapter 13. The deposition of large volumes of organic refuse by urban dwellers provides the bones on which we develop our archaeological interpretations, but the deposition of it in the first place may have been of considerable importance in providing food for a wide range of urban vertebrates. Some species no doubt fed directly on the refuse itself, while others preyed on the vertebrate and invertebrate animals attracted by the refuse, and still others predated the invertebrates attracted by the distinctive nitrophile vegetation which would have developed around refuse deposits of any age. We can see urban refuse as forming the basis of a complex community, many of the species in which were vertebrates, the bones of which can be recovered from samples of the refuse deposits (Fig. 14.3). To some extent this is true of any human occupation site, but towns and cities are characterized by the nucleation of people, and thus the deposition of refuse in large concentrations, making these refuse-dependent animal communities particularly typical of urban archaeological sites.

One last source of bones in urban archaeological deposits merits mention. From time to time we encounter what appear to be deliberate burials of one or more animals, often closely associated with structures. In one example from York, the bodies of several cats and chickens had been placed in a shallow pit dug immediately below the foundations of a wall. It was difficult to escape the conclusion that the animals were some kind of a foundation deposit, a superstitious gesture to someone or something intangible. On a larger scale, excavations in House 11 at Pompeii have uncovered deposits of cremated cockerel bones, which appear to be some form of votive offering, dating to around thirty years earlier than the eruption which destroyed Pompeii in AD 79 (Fulford & Wallace-Hadrill 1998). Perhaps the offering was successful only in the short term?

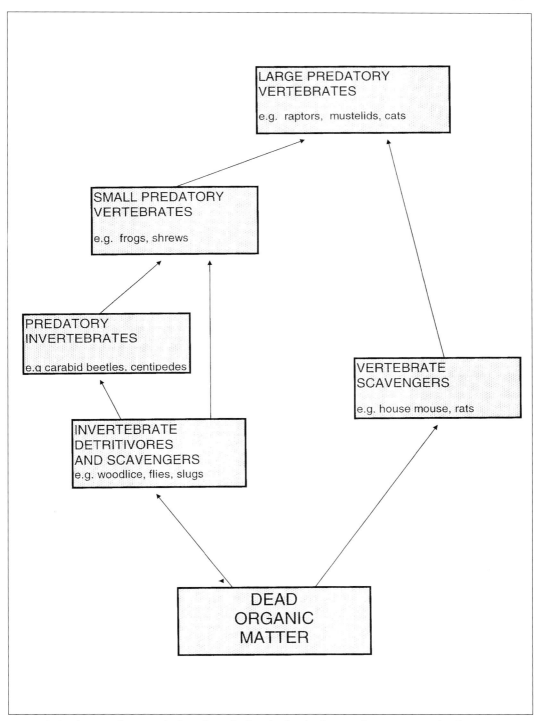

Fig. 14.3. A schematic diagram of a hypothetical urban food-web, showing the importance of garbage as a source of energy and nutrients on which many species depend either directly or indirectly.

Having worked on animal bone samples from urban sites for a number of years, it is difficult to stand back and regard their archaeological significance with an objective eye. I find the complex sources and taphonomy of urban bones an irresistible challenge, and the occasional recovery of samples which can be closely linked to a particular building or a particular suite of activities gives the bones a close link to the human activities which are, in the end, the subject of archaeology. However, that is a personal point of view. The intention of this chapter has been to keep it on a scale commensurate with the importance of the topic, and not to try the patience of the reader!

FIFTEEN

MORE THAN JUST OLD BONES

When colleagues ask 'What's your area of research?', it is all too easy to reply 'Animal bones'. Defining what we do by the raw material of our research is a convenient form of academic shorthand. In this case, it is an unfortunate lapse of judgement, and somewhat misleading. Although this book has been about the study of animal bones, it has also been about the archaeology of the relations between people and other animals and that rather cumbersome phrase better expresses the aim of the research. 'Very well,' a persistent colleague might say, 'But isn't that the same thing as studying animal bones?' The purpose of this brief closing chapter is to suggest otherwise.

By defining our research aims in terms of the relations between people and other animals, we move away from focusing the research on the animals themselves. This helps to overcome the divide that often seems to exist between those who study ancient animal bones as palaeozoology – bones as fossils of animals – and those who study them as archaeological remains – bones as the debris of human activity. Instead, we focus on a series of processes going on between and within human populations and those of other species that were in some way affected by, or in some way affected, people in the past. Processes are, of course, more nebulous and intangible than animals or lumps of bone, but their study does not presuppose any particular source of data. That is an important point, because it encourages us to define research aims in terms of what we actually want to know, rather than in terms of what we think we can find out from a particular data source.

To explain this point more fully, let us consider some of the major questions which have already been reviewed in this book. If we return to domesticated animals, the act of domestication itself can be seen in (at least) two ways. On the one hand, it is a process of behavioural co-evolution on the part of people as much as the domestic animal. That process can be studied by examining animal bone assemblages from the early stages of domestication, looking for changes in size and shape that might indicate breeding isolation from the original free-living populations, or changes in distribution that might indicate active human interference with the biogeography of the species (Chapter 13). The behavioural aspects of domestication can also be examined by studying the behaviour of modern populations of sheep, guinea pigs, water buffalo and so on, generating data that are the equivalent of the ethnographic records used to good effect elsewhere in archaeology. On the other hand, domestication of animals is also a human social phenomenon, so our investigation of it would benefit from the ethnographic study of pastoral peoples, and from the archaeological study of cultural processes and evidence of social negotiations going on in parallel with the acquisition of domestic animals. To study the archaeology of animal domestication thoroughly, then, we need to bring together the study of animal bones with the wider cultural context, and to illuminate the whole by reference to studies of modern populations of people and their domesticates. The bones alone are not enough.

Once animals have been domesticated, our attention turns to questions of husbandry and the management of supply and demand. People establish priorities in terms of the production of resources, priorities that will be based on a complex integration of subsistence needs, exchange opportunities or obligations, and social perceptions derived from the history of that particular human population. Those priorities lead to decisions regarding the management of herds and flocks, decisions that may in turn lead to a particular age or sex group being conserved while another cohort is preferentially slaughtered. The mortality profile that results may be apparent in the archaeological samples (Chapter 8). However, to understand the decision-making fully, we would need to go beyond the bones to examine, for example, evidence from artefact assemblages that might show whether or not some resource derived from the animals was being processed intensively. If our samples of sheep mandibles show a mortality profile that we believe to be consistent with an emphasis on milk production, we might look for supporting evidence in the form of artefacts suited to the production or storage of dairy produce such as cheese or yogurt, or the survival of biochemical traces of dairy produce on and in the fabric of pottery containers.

The production of animals is often intimately linked with the production of crops, and this is particularly true of the Eurasian 'package' of cattle, sheep, barley and wheat. A simple consideration of energy flows shows that plant production depends upon the animals for dung to maintain fertility and traction power to pull ploughs and carts. Producing a crop surplus and allowing animals to graze off stubble and weeds after harvest might allow more animals to be kept than could otherwise be maintained by grazing alone. In Europe and the Middle East the study of field systems and plant remains can make a contribution to the archaeology of domestic livestock. Our study of the animals may benefit from surveying ancient field systems, or from the chemical and physical analysis of ancient soils. (For a more detailed discussion of this approach, see van der Veen & O'Connor 1998).

One could cite further examples: the point is that a full archaeological investigation of people and animals requires us to be willing to look beyond the bones to see the articulation of our research with that of other archaeologists, and the ways in which specialist studies of other archaeological materials and objects might contribute to our research, and ours to them. It matters that the archaeology of people and other animals is investigated fully and rigorously, because no human group has ever lived independently of other vertebrate species. We utilize them and are utilized by them, and we socially incorporate them, whether directly as pets and companions, or iconically as heraldic lions or Dreamtime snakes. This is, therefore, one of the few topics within archaeology that can be explored cross-culturally and for any period, a breadth which this book has set out to reflect.

So where do we go from here? It is one thing to set out a paradigm for research frameworks, but quite another to define objectives to take that research forward. Further developments in animal bone studies could take off in many different directions, but one can suggest several that are likely to be of particular importance.

The first of these is the investigation of genotype. Although there are many studies in the literature in which speculation is made about different 'types' or 'breeds' of animal, much of this is based on an assessment of phenotypic characters such as size and shape. Obviously, these traits are at least in part genetically controlled, but the growth environment and life history of the animal concerned can have a very marked impact too, and it may not be a simple matter to disentangle the two. If we are to resolve this problem, for example to understand the different populations of livestock utilized by a major settlement, then we need to access the genotype more directly. One way is through the analysis of ancient DNA, and there is no doubt that ancient DNA analysis will be a tool of increasing importance in the near future. However, we should take care not to expect too much too soon. The genetic material that survives in bone usually consists of short lengths of DNA, much less than a single gene. Remarkable though it is that such material survives at all, let alone that it can be extracted, amplified and sequenced, this is still a long way from being able to read the genotype of the animal concerned. By careful selection of the questions that we ask, these short fragments can be made to yield evidence that the animal carried a particular gene, or carried a base-pair sequence characteristic of a male or a female individual, or was more or less closely related to some extant species or deme.

The second means of investigating genotype is through a better understanding of the aetiology of the numerous non-metrical skeletal traits that we see on the bones of most species. A few of these have been discussed in Chapter 10, and it has been possible to use non-metrical traits to show that contemporaneous medieval sites within York were sampling different populations of sheep (Chapter 14). However, most non-metrical traits go unrecorded, if only because we would not be sure what to do with the records if we made them. Further progress will probably only be made by targeting one species at a time, and working through large numbers of modern specimens from a number of different populations, in order to gain some indication of the degree of inter-population variation seen in some of the traits. This is slow, meticulous work, and one can well imagine that it would have less appeal to the ambitious researcher than the glamorous world of ancient DNA. However, DNA fragments survive only in a minority of even freshly excavated bones, and material that has been in store in a museum for several decades is likely to be regarded with some suspicion. Non-metrical traits at least have the merit of being accessible on a much higher percentage of specimens, being technically simple to record, and of not degrading with prolonged storage, at least not unless the bone itself is destroyed.

Another area that merits further investigation is the gross histology of animal bone. There have been many investigations of the survival of histological detail, mostly undertaken as a means of understanding the decay of bone in the ground, and the extent to which the overall condition of the specimen represents the preservation of bone structure at a microscopic scale. The survival of histological detail has also been shown to be a good means of predicting the survival of recoverable DNA (Colton et al. 1997). Inherent in features such as the degree of organization into secondary osteons and the thickness of endosteal lamellar bone (Chapter 2), there is information about the state of skeletal growth and health of that individual animal at the time of death. Although case-by-case diagnosis might not be realistic, consistent differences between samples might reveal differences in growth rate, or might, for example, allow the conclusion that one herd of cattle had been routinely milked while another had not. Thin cortical bone in sheep bones from prehistoric sites in Israel has been interpreted as indicating milking flocks (Smith & Horvitz 1984). However, the cortical bone was assessed for thickness by examining x-ray images, and one feels that it would be more productive to examine the bone directly and minutely to determine the cause of the reduction in thickness. Examination by light microscopy would reveal some of the surviving information, though use of the scanning electron microscope to produce backscattered electron images would probably give more information, especially where deposition of minerals from the surrounding sediment obscures histological detail.

We are losing ourselves in minutiae. Ancient DNA and bone histology are sources of information about long-dead animals, but ultimately archaeology is about us. Whatever information we can extract by such technical investigations has to be linked back to the topic of the relations between past people and the animal populations with which they shared the planet. That set of relationships is obviously of great antiquity, and extends into the present day. That gives our study of animal bones an immediate modern relevance. We have a contribution to make to modern conservation biology, by giving a considerable time-depth to contemporary studies of how well, or badly, different animal species accommodate themselves to the almost ubiquitous presence of humans, and the many different things that we do (e.g. see Yalden 1999). Animal ecologists can observe the current state of affairs, and reconstruct the last couple of centuries from historical sources, but by studying the archaeology of animals, we can add a much longer timescale of observations, and so observe much slower processes and circumstances that no longer pertain. Admittedly, our observations will be dependent upon the survival and competent archaeological retrieval of the evidence, and will never be more than fragmentary. None the less, for much of the human career, it is the only direct source of evidence that we have.

I said that archaeology is about us. It is also about the present. Together with biology and the earth sciences, archaeology is a discipline that seeks to understand and explain the world around us. Just as that world contains Sand Canyon pueblo and the pyramids of Egypt, so it contains domestic guinea pigs, rats almost everywhere and moa absolutely nowhere. All of those things require an explanation if we are to have a full understanding of the world in which we live. Our study of the archaeology of vertebrate animals is thus as much a study of the familiar world in which we live today as it is a study of the remote and unfamiliar past.

BIBLIOGRAPHY

Aaris-Sorensen, K. 1983. 'A classification code and computerised database for faunal materials from archaeological sites', *Ossa* 8, 3.29

Adams, L. & Watkins, S.G. 1967. 'Annuli in tooth cementum indicate age in California ground squirrels', *Journal of Wildlife Management* 31, 836–9

Ahnlund, H. 1976. 'Age determination in the European badger *Meles meles* L.', *Zeitschrift für Säugetierkunde* 4, 119–25

Aiello, L. & Molleson, T. 1993. 'Are microscopic ageing techniques more accurate than macroscopic ageing techniques?', *Journal of Archaeological Science* 20, 689–704

Aitken, R.J. 1975. 'Cementum layers and tooth wear as criteria for ageing roe deer (*Capreolus capreolus*)', *Journal of Zoology, London* 175, 15–28

Albarella, U. 1995. 'Depressions in sheep horncores', *Journal of Archaeological Science* 22, 699–704

Albarella, U. & Davis, S.J.M. 1996. 'Mammals and birds from Launceston Castle, Cornwall: decline in status and the rise of agriculture', *Circaea* 12, 1–156

Alexander, R. McN. 1975. *The chordates*. Cambridge, Cambridge University Press.

Alexander, R. McN. 1994. *Bones. The unity of form and function*. London, Weidenfeld & Nicolson

Alexander, R. McN., Jayes, A.S., Maloiy, G.M.O. & Wathuta, E.M. 1979. 'Allometry of the limb bones of mammals from shrews (*Sorex*) to elephants (*Loxodonta*)', *Journal of Zoology, London* 189, 305–14

Amorosi, T. 1989. *A postcranial guide to domestic neo-natal and juvenile mammals*. Oxford, British Archaeological Reports International Series 533

Anderson, A. 1983. 'The prehistoric hunting of moa (Aves: Dinornithidae) in the high country of southern New Zealand', in C. Grigson & J. Clutton-Brock (eds) *Animals and archaeology: 2. Shell middens, fishes and birds*. Oxford, British Archaeological Reports International Series S183, 33–51

Anderson, A. 1996. 'Origins of Procellariidae hunting in the southwest Pacific', *International Journal of Osteoarchaeology* 6, 403–10

Anderson, B.C. & Bulgin, M.S. 1984. 'Starvation associated with dental disease in range ewes', *Journal of the American Veterinary Medical Association* 184, 737–8

Andresen, J.M., Byrd, B.F., Elson, M.D., McGuire, R.H., Mendoza, R.G., Staski, E. & White, J.P. 1981. 'The deer hunters: Star Carr reconsidered', *World Archaeology* 13, 32–46

Andrews, A.H. 1973. 'A survey of the relationship between age and the development of the anterior teeth in cattle', *The Veterinary Record* 92, 275–82

Andrews, A.H. & Noddle, B.A. 1975. 'Absence of premolar teeth from ruminant mandibles found at archaeological sites', *Journal of Archaeological Science* 2, 137–44

Andrews, P. 1990. *Owls, caves and fossils*. London, Natural History Museum

Arge, S.V. 1995. 'Mersogin bein – ein aldargamal matsiður', *Frøskaparrit* 43, 59–65

Armitage, P.L. 1978. 'Hertfordshire cattle and London meat markets in the 17th and 18th centuries', *The London Archaeologist* 3(8), 217–22

Armitage, P.L. 1993. 'Commensal rats in the New World, 1492–1992', *Biologist* 40, 174–8

Armitage, P.L. 1994. 'Unwelcome companions: ancient rats reviewed', *Antiquity* 68, 231–40

Armitage, P.L. & West. B. 1987. 'Faunal evidence from a late medieval garden well of the Greyfriars, London', *Transactions of the London and Middlesex Archaeological Society* 36, 107–36

Armitage, P.L., West, B. & Steedman, K. 1984. 'New evidence of black rat in Roman London', *The London Archaeologist* 4(14), 375–83

Armour-Chelu, M. & Clutton-Brock, J. 1988. 'Evidence for the use of cattle as draught animals at Etton', *Antiquaries Journal* 65, 297–302

Ascenzi, A. 1969. 'Microscopy and prehistoric bone', in D.R. Brothwell & E.S. Higgs (eds) *Science in archaeology*. Bristol, Thames & Hudson, 526–38

Attenbrow, V. & Steele, D. 1995. 'Fishing in Port Jackson, New South Wales – more than met the eye', *Antiquity* 69, 47–60

Atkinson, P.J., Spence, J.A., Aitchison, G. & Sykes, A.R. 1982. 'Mandibular bone in ageing sheep', *Journal of Comparative Pathology* 92, 51–67

Audoin-Rouzeau, F. 1987. 'Medieval and early modern butchery: evidence from the monastery of La Charité-sur-Loire (Nievre)', *Food and Foodways* 2, 31–48

Audoin-Rouzeau, F. 1991a. 'La taille du boeuf domestique en Europe de l'Antiquité aux temps modernes', *Fiches d'Osteologie Animale pour l'Archaeologie. Serie B. Mammiferes* 2, 3–40

Audoin-Rouzeau, F. 1991b. 'La taille du mouton en Europe de l'Antiquité aux temps modernes', *Fiches d'Osteologie Animale pour l'Archaeologie. Serie B. Mammiferes* 3, 3–36

Audoin-Rouzeau, F. 1995. 'Compter et mesurer les os animaux. Pour une histoire de l'élevage et de l'alimentation en Europe de l'Antiquité aux temps modernes', *Histoire et Mesure* 10, 277–312

Audoin-Rouzeau, F. & Vigne, J.-D. 1994. 'La colonisation de l'Europe par le rat noir (*Rattus rattus*)', *Revue de Paléobiologie* 13, 125–45

Avery, D.M. 1987. 'Late Pleistocene coastal environment of the southern Cape Province of South Africa: micromammals from Klasies River Mouth', *Journal of Archaeological Science* 14, 405–21

Avery, G. 1977. 'Report on the marine bird remains from the Paternoster midden', *South African Archaeological Bulletin* 32, 74–6

Baker, J.R. & Brothwell, D.R. 1980. *Animal diseases in archaeology*. London, Academic Press

Baker, C.M.A. & Manwell, C. 1983. 'Man and elephant. The "dare theory" of domestication and the origin of breeds', *Zeitschrift für Tierzüchtung und Züchtungsbiologie* 100, 55–75

Balme, J. 1982. 'Prehistoric fishing in the lower Darling, western New South Wales', in C. Grigson & J. Clutton-Brock (eds) *Animals and archaeology. 2. Shell middens, fishes and birds*. Oxford, British Archaeological Reports International Series 183, 19–33

Barrett, J.H. 1993. 'Bone weight, meat yield estimates and cod (*Gadus morhua*): a preliminary study of the weight method', *International Journal of Osteoarchaeology* 3, 1–18

Barrett, J.H. 1994. 'Bone weight and the intra-class comparison of fish taxa', in W. van Neer (ed.) *Fish exploitation in the past*. Tervuren, Annales du Musée Royal de l'Afrique Centrale, Sciences Zoologiques 274, 3–15

Bartosiewicz, L., van Neer, W. & Lentacker, A. 1993. 'Metapodial asymmetry in draught cattle', *International Journal of Osteoarchaeology* 3, 69–75

Beatty, M.T. & Bonnichsen, R. 1994. 'Dispersing aggregated soils and other fine earth in the field for recovery of organic archaeological materials', *Current Research in the Pleistocene* 11, 73–4

Behrensmeyer, A.K. 1978. 'Taphonomic and ecologic information from bone weathering', *Paleobiology* 4(2), 150–62

Behrensmeyer, A.K. & Hill, A.P. (eds) 1980. *Fossils in the making: vertebrate taphonomy and palaeoecology*. Chicago, Chicago University Press

Belcher, W.R. 1994. 'A regional approach to fish remains and seasonality in East Penobscot Bay, Maine', in W. van Neer (ed.) *Fish exploitation in the past*. Tervuren, Annales du Musée Royal de l'Afrique Centrale, Sciences Zoologiques 274, 115–22

Bement, L. & Masmajian, S. 1996. 'Epiphysial fusion in *Bison antiquus*', *Current Research in the Pleistocene* 13, 95–7

Ben-Shun, C. 1984. 'Animal domestication in Neolithic China', in J. Clutton-Brock & C. Grigson (eds) *Animals and archaeology: 3. Early herders and their flocks*. Oxford, British Archaeological Reports International Series 202, 363–9

Berman, E. 1974. 'The time and pattern of eruption of the permanent teeth of the cat', *Laboratory Animal Science* 24(6), 929–31

Berry, R.J. 1981. 'Town mouse, country mouse: adaptation and adaptibility in *Mus domesticus* (*Mus musculus domesticus*)', *Mammal Review* 11(3), 91–136

Binford, L.R. 1978. *Nunamiut ethnoarchaeology*. London, Academic Press

Binford, L.R. 1983. *In pursuit of the past*. London, Thames & Hudson

Binford, L.R. & Bertram, J.B. 1977. 'Bone frequencies and attritional processes', in L.R. Binford (ed.) *For theory building in archaeology*. New York, Academic Press, 77–153

Bishop, M.J. 1982. *The mammal fauna of the early Middle Pleistocene cavern infill site of Westbury-sub-Mendip, Somerset*. London, The Palaeontological Association, Special Papers in Palaeontology no. 28.

Blackmore, D.K., Owen, D.G. & Young, C.M. 1972. 'Some observations on the diseases of *Brunus edwardii* (Species nova)', *Veterinary Record* 90, 382–5

Bloom, W. & Fawcett, D.W. 1975. *A textbook of histology*. Philadelphia, Saunders

Blumenschine, R.J., Marean, C.W. & Capaldo, S.D. 1996. 'Blind tests of inter-analyst correspondence and accuracy in the identification of cut marks, percussion marks, and carnivore tooth marks on bone surfaces', *Journal of Archaeological Science* 23, 493–507

Boessneck, J., Müller, H.-H. & Teichert, M. 1964. 'Osteologische Unterscheidungsmerkmale zwischen Schaf (*Ovis aries* L.) und Ziege (*Capra hircus* L.)', *Kühn-Archiv* 78, 5–129

Bökönyi, S. 1970. 'A new method for the determination of the number of individuals in animal bone material', *American Journal of Archaeology* 74, 291–2

Bökönyi, S. 1978. 'The vertebrate fauna of Vlasac', in *Vlasac – a mesolithic settlement in the Iron Gates. Vol. II Geology, Biology, Anthropology*. Belgrade, Serbian Academy of Sciences and Arts Monographs 62, 35–50

Bökönyi, S. 1989. 'Definitions of animal domestication', in J. Clutton-Brock (ed.) *The walking larder*. London, Unwin Hyman One World Archaeology, 22–7

Böhme, G. 1977. 'Zur Bestimmung quartärer Anuren Eurpas an Hand von Skelettelementen', *Wissenschaftliche Zeitschrift der Humboldt-Universität zu Berlin Math-Nat.* 26/3, 283–300

Bond, J.M. & O'Connor, T.P. 1999. *Bones from Coppergate and other medieval sites*. York, Council for British Archaeology, Archaeology of York 15/5

Boon, G.C. 1974. *Silchester, the Roman town of Calleva*. Newton Abbot, David & Charles

Borrero, L.A. 1990. 'Fuego-Patagonian bone assemblages and the problem of communal guanaco hunting', in L.B. Davis & B.O.K. Reeves (eds) *Hunters of the recent past*. London, Unwin Hyman One World Archaeology, 373–99

Bourque, B.J., Morris, K. & Spiess, A. 1978. 'Determining the season of death of mammal teeth from archaeological sites: a new sectioning technique', *Science* 199, 530–1

Brain, C.K. 1967. 'Hottentot food remains and their bearing on the interpretation of fossil bone assemblages', *Scientific Papers of the Namib Desert Research Station* 32, 1–11

Brain, C.K. 1969. 'The contribution of Namib Desert Hottentots to an understanding of australopithecine bone accumulations', *Scientific Papers of the Namib Desert Research Station* 39, 13–22

Brain, C.K. 1981. *The Hunters and the hunted: an introduction to African cave taphonomy.* Chicago, Chicago University Press

Brink, J.W. & Rollans, M. 1990. 'Thoughts on the structure and function of drive lane systems at communal buffalo jumps', in Davis, L.B. & Reeves, B.O.K. (eds) *Hunters of the recent past.* London, Unwin Hyman One World Archaeology, 152–67

Brinkhuizen, D.C. 1979. 'Preliminary notes on fish remains from archaeological sites in the Netherlands', *Palaeohistoria* 21, 83–90

Brothwell, D.R. 1976. 'Further evidence of bone chewing by ungulates: the sheep of North Ronaldsay, Orkney', *Journal of Archaeological Science* 3, 179–82

Brothwell, D.R. 1981. 'The Pleistocene and Holocene archaeology of the house mouse and related species', *Symposia of the Zoological Society of London* 47, 1–13

Brothwell, D.R. 1995. 'Study 8: the special animal pathology', in B.W. Cunliffe, *Danebury. An Iron Age hillfort in Hampshire. Volume 6. A hillfort community in perspective.* York, Council for British Archaeology Research Reports 102; pp. 207–33

Brothwell, D.R., Dobney, K. & Ervynck, A. 1996. 'On the causes of perforations in archaeological domestic cattle skulls', *International Journal of Osteoarchaeology* 6, 471–87

Browman, D.L. 1989. 'Origins and development of Andean pastoralism: an overview of the past 6000 years', in J. Clutton-Brock (ed.) *The walking larder.* London, Unwin Hyman One World Archaeology; pp. 256–68

Brown, W.A.B. & Chapman, N.G. 1990. 'The dentition of fallow deer (*Dama dama*): a scoring scheme to assess age from wear of the permanent molariform teeth', *Journal of Zoology, London* 221, 659–82

Brown, W.A.B. & Chapman, N.G. 1991. 'The dentition of red deer (*Cervus elaphus*): a scoring scheme to assess age from wear of the permanent molariform teeth', *Journal of Zoology, London* 224, 519–36

Buitenhuis, H. 1995. 'A quantitative approach to species determination of Ovicapridae', in H. Buitenhuis and H.-P. Uerpmann (eds) *Archaeozoology of the Near East II.* Leiden, Backhuys, 140–55

Bull, G. & Payne, S. 1982. 'Tooth eruption and epiphysial fusion in pigs and wild boar', in B. Wilson, C. Grigson & S. Payne (eds.) *Ageing and sexing animal bones from archaeological sites.* Oxford: British Archaeological Reports British Series 109, 55–72

Bullock, D. & Rackham, D.J. 1982. 'Epiphysial fusion and tooth eruption of feral goats from Moffatdale, Dumfries and Galloway, Scotland', in B. Wilson, C. Grigson & S. Payne (eds.) *Ageing and sexing animal bones from archaeological sites.* Oxford: British Archaeological Reports British Series 109, 73–80

Burke, A. & Castanet, J. 1995. 'Histological observations of cementum growth in horse teeth and their application to archaeology', *Journal of Archaeological Science* 22, 479–93

Butler, E.J., Nisbet, D.I. & Robertson, J.M. 1957. 'Osteoporosis in lambs in a lead mining area I. A study of the naturally occurring disease', *Journal of Comparative Pathology* 67, 378–96

Cannon, D.Y. 1987. *Marine fish osteology. A manual for archaeologists.* Burnaby, B.C., Dept of Archaeology, Simon Fraser University Publication no. 18

Capasso, L. 1998. 'Cranial pathology of *Ursus spelaeus* Rosenmüller & Heinroth from Chateau Pignon, Basque Territories (Spain)', *International Journal of Osteoarchaeology* 8, 107–15

Carmines, E.G. & Zeller, R.A. 1979. 'Reliability and validity assessment', *Sage University Paper, Quantitative Applications in the Social Sciences 07-17.* Beverly Hills, Sage Publications

Carter, R.J. 1998. 'Reassessment of seasonality at the early Mesolithic site of Star Carr, Yorkshire, based on radiographs of mandibular teeth development in red deer', *Journal of Archaeological Science* 25, 851–6

Casteel, R.W. 1972. 'Some biases in the recovery of archaeological faunal remains', *Proceedings of the Prehistoric Society* 38, 382–8

Casteel, R.W. 1978. 'Faunal assemblages and the "Wiegemethode" or weight method', *Journal of Field Archaeology* 5, 71–7

Caughley, G. 1965. 'Horn rings and tooth eruption as criteria of age in the Himalayan thar *Hemitragus jemlahicus*', *New Zealand Journal of Science* 8, 333–51

Caulfield, S. 1978. 'Star Carr – an alternative view', *Irish Archaeological Research Forum* 5, 15–22

Chaix, L. & Méniel, P. 1996. *Eléments d'Archeozoologie*. Paris: éditions Errance

Chaline, J. 1972. 'Les rongeurs du Würmien II de la grotte de l'Hortus', *Etudes Quaternaires Mémoire* 1, 233–40

Chaplin, R.E. 1971. *The study of animal bones from archaeological sites* London, Seminar Press

Chapman, D.I., Chapman, N.G. & Jeffcott, L.B. 1984. 'Deformities of the metacarpus and metatarsus in fallow deer (*Dama dama* L.)', *Journal of Comparative Pathology* 94, 77–91

Chase, P.G. & Hagaman, R.M. 1987. 'Minimum number of individuals and its alternatives: a probability theory perspective', *Ossa* 13, 75–86

Child, A.M. 1995a. 'Microbial taphonomy of archaeological bone', *Studies in Conservation* 40, 19–30

Child, A.M. 1995b. 'Towards an understanding of the microbial decomposition of archaeological bone in the burial environment', *Journal of Archaeological Science* 22, 165–74

Childe, V.G. 1928. *The most ancient East: the Oriental prelude to European prehistory*. London, Kegan Paul

Childe, V.G. 1936. *Man makes himself*. London, Watts

Childe, V.G. 1942. *What happened in history*. Harmondsworth, Penguin

Childe, V.G. 1950. 'The urban revolution', *Town Planning Review* 21, 9–16

Childe, V.G. 1957. 'Civilisation, cities and towns', *Antiquity* 31, 36–8

Clark, G. 1992. 'Town and countryside in medieval Italy: a critical evaluation of the sources for understanding the mechanisms of supply and demand', *Anthropozoologica* 16, 75–82

Clark, G., Constantini, L., Finetti, A., Giorgi, J., Jones, A., Reese, D., Sutherland, S. & Whitehouse, D. 1989. 'The food refuse of an affluent urban household in the late fourteenth century: faunal and botanical remains from the Palazzo Vitelleschi, Tarquinia (Viterbo)', *Papers of the British School at Rome* 57, 200–321

Clark, G.R. 1997. 'Osteology of the Kuri Maori: the prehistoric dog of New Zealand', *Journal of Archaeological Science* 24, 113–26

Clark, G.R. 1998. 'Prehistoric contact between Australia and Polynesia: the Pukapuka dog re-examined', *International Journal of Osteoarchaeology* 8, 116–22

Clark, J. & Kietzke, K.K. 1967. 'Palaeoecology of the Lower Nodule Zone, Brule Formation, in the Big Badlands of South Dakota', in J. Clark, J.R. Beerbower & K.K. Kietzke (eds) *Oligocene sedimentation, stratigraphy and palaeoclimatology in the Big Badlands of South Dakota*. Fieldiana Geology Memoir 5; pp. 111–37

Clark, J.G.D. 1972. *Star Carr: a case study in bioarchaeology*. Reading, Mass., Addison-Wesley Modular Publications

Clason, A.T. 1972. 'Some remarks on the presentation of archaeozoological data', *Helinium* 12, 139–53

Clason, A.T. & Brinkhuizen, D. 1978. 'Swifterbant, mammals, birds and fishes', *Helinium* 18, 69–82

Clason, A.T. & Prummel, W. 1977. 'Collecting, sieving and archaeozoological research', *Journal of Archaeological Science* 4, 171–5

Clutton-Brock, J. (ed.) 1989. *The walking larder*. London, Unwin Hyman One World Archaeology

Clutton-Brock, J., Dennis-Bryan, K., Armitage, P.L. & Jewell, P.A. 1990. 'Osteology of Soay sheep', *Bulletin of the British Museum of Natural History* 56(1), 1–56

Cohen, A. & Serjeantson, D. 1996. *A manual for the identification of bird bones from archaeological sites* (2nd edn). London, Birkbeck College

Collins, M.J., Riley, M.S., Child, A. & Turner-Walker, G. 1995. 'A basic mathematical simulation of the chemical degradation of ancient collagen', *Journal of Archaeological Science* 22, 175–83

Colton, I.B., Bailey, J.F., Vercauteren, M. & Sykes, B. 1997. 'The preservation of ancient DNA and bone diagenesis', *Ancient Biomolecules* 1(2), 109–18

Crockford, S., Frederick, G. & Wigen, R. 1997. 'A humerus story: albatross element distribution from two northwest coast sites, North America', *International Journal of Osteoarchaeology* 7, 287–91

Cross, G.M. & Edwards, M.J. 1981. 'The detection of arthritis in pigs in an abattoir and its public health significance', *Australian Veterinary Journal* 57, 153–8

Curgy, J.-J. 1965. 'Apparition et soudure des points d'ossification des membres chez les mammifères', *Mémoires du Muséum National d'Histoire Naturelle. Série A. Zoologie* 32(3), 175–307

Cutress, T.W. & Healy, W.B. 1965. 'Wear of sheep's teeth II. Effects of pasture juices on dentine', *New Zealand Journal of Agricultural Research* 8, 753–62

Darwin, C. 1868. *The variation of animals and plants under domestication*. London, John Murray

Davis, D.E. 1986. 'The scarcity of rats and the Black Death: an ecological history', *Journal of Interdisciplinary History* 16, 455–70

Davis, P.G. 1997. 'The bioerosion of bird bones', *International Journal of Osteoarchaeology* 7, 388–401

Davis, S.J.M. 1980. 'A note on the dental and skeletal ontogeny of *Gazella*', *Israel Journal of Zoology* 29, 129–34

Davis, S.J.M. 1981. 'The effects of temperature change and domestication on the body size of Late Pleistocene to Holocene mammals of Israel', *Paleobiology* 7, 101–14

Davis, S.J.M. 1983. 'The age profile of gazelles predated by ancient man in Israel: possible evidence for a shift from seasonality to sedentism in the Natufian', *Paléorient* 9, 55–62

Davis, S.J.M. 1987. *The archaeology of animals*. London, Batsford

Davis, S.J.M. 1992. *A rapid method for recording information about mammal bones from archaeological sites. Ancient Monuments Laboratory Report 19/92*. London, English Heritage

Davis, S.J.M. 1994. 'Even more bones from Khirokitia: the 1988–1991 excavations', in A. Le Brun (ed.) *Fouilles récentes à Khirokitia (Chypre) 1988–1991*. Paris, éditions Recherches sur les Civilisations, 305–33

Deniz, E. & Payne, S. 1982. 'Eruption and wear in the mandibular dentition as a guide to ageing Turkish Angora goats', in B. Wilson, C. Grigson & S. Payne (eds) *Ageing and sexing animal bones from archaeological sites*. Oxford, British Archaeological Reports British Series 109, 155–205

Dennel, R. 1983. *European economic prehistory*. London, Academic Press

Dhingra, L.D. 1976. 'A preliminary radiographic study on the time and sequence of fusion of ossification loci in crossbred (Banuur X Nali) sheep', *Indian Journal of Animal Health* 15, 1–4

Dobney, K. & Brothwell, D.R. 1987. 'A method for evaluating the amount of dental calculus in teeth from archaeological sites', *Journal of Archaeological Science* 14, 343–51

Dobney, K., Kenward, H.K., Ottaway, P. & Donel, L. 1998. 'Down but not out: biological evidence for complex economic organisation in Lincoln in the late 4th century', *Antiquity* 72, 417–24

Dobney, K. & Rielly, K. 1988. 'A method for recording archaeological animal bones: the use of diagnostic zones', *Circaea* 5, 79–96

von den Driesch, A. 1976. *A guide to the measurement of animal bones from archaeological sites*. Cambridge, Mass., Peabody Museum of Archaeology and Ethnology, Bulletin no. 1

von den Driesch, A. & Boessneck, J. 1974. 'Kritische Anmerkungen zur Widerristhohenberechnung aus Langenmassen vor- und frühgeschichtlicher Tierknochen', *Säugetierkundliche Mitteilungen* 22, 325–48

Driver, J.C. 1990. 'Meat in due season: the timing of communal hunts', in L.B. Davis & B.O.K. Reeves (eds) *Hunters of the recent past*. London, Unwin Hyman One World Archaeology, 11–33.

Driver, J. 1992. 'Identification, classification and zooarchaeology', *Circaea* 9, 35–47

Driver, J.C. 1995. 'Social hunting and multiple predation', *MASCA Research Papers in Science and Archaeology* 12, 23–38

Driver, J.C. 1996. 'Social complexity and hunting systems in southwestern Colorado', in D.A. Meyer, P.C. Dawson & D.T. Hanna (eds) *Debating complexity. Proceedings of the twenty-sixth annual Chacmool Conference*. Calgary, Archaeological Association of the University of Calgary, 364–74

Ducos, P. 1978. '"Domestication" defined and methodological approaches to its recognition in faunal assemblages', in R.H. Meadow & M.A. Zeder (eds) *Approaches to faunal analysis in the Middle East*. Harvard University Peabody Museum Bulletin 2, 53–6

Duff, S.R.I. 1984. 'Osteochondrosis dissecans in turkeys', *Journal of Comparative Pathology* 94, 467–76

Duthie, L.F. & Lancaster, M.C. 1964. 'Polyarthritis and epiphyseolysis of pigs in England', *Veterinary Record* 76, 263–73

Efremov, J.A. 1940. 'Taphonomy: new branch of palaeontology', *Pan-American Geologist* 74, 81–93

Emara, M. 1937. 'Some observations on epiphyseal union of long bones in young Egyptian cattle and its aid in the estimation of age', *The Veterinary Record* 49, 1,534–7

Engels, K.F. 1891. *The origin of the family, private property, and the State*. New York, International Publishers

Enghoff, I.B. 1994. 'Fishing in Denmark during the Ertebo[/]lle Period', *International Journal of Osteoarchaeology* 4, 65–96

d'Erico, F., Villa, P., Pinto Llona, A.C. & Ruiz Idarraga, R. 1998. 'A Middle Palaeolithic origin of music? Using cave bear bone accumulations to assess the Divje Babe I bone flute', *Antiquity* 72, 65–79

Ericson, P.G.P., Tyrberg, T., Kjellberg, A.S., Jonsson, L. & Ullén, I. 1997. 'The earliest record of house sparrows (*Passer domesticus*) in northern Europe', *Journal of Archaeological Science* 24, 183–90

Farquarson, M.J., Speller, R.D. & Brikley, M. 1997. 'Measuring bone mineral density in archaeological bone using energy dispersive low-angle X-ray scattering techniques', *Journal of Archaeological Science* 24, 765–72

Feddersen, D. & Heinrich, D. 1978. 'Anomalien und Pathologien an Haustierknochen aus einer frühmittelalterlichen Siedlung und deren Bewertung im Hindblickauf die Tierhaltung', *Zeitschrift für Tierzüchtung und Züchtungsbiologie* 94, 161–70

Fernandez-Jalvo, Y. & Andrews, P. 1992. 'Small mammal taphonomy of Gran Dolina, Atapuerca (Burgos), Spain', *Journal of Archaeological Science* 19, 407–28

Fick, O.K.W. 1974. *Vergleichend morphologische Untersuchungen an Einzelknochen europäischer Taubenarten.* Unpublished doctoral dissertation, University of Münich

Fieller, N.R.J. & Turner, A. 1982. 'Number estimation in vertebrate samples', *Journal of Archaeological Science* 9, 49–62

Fitch, L.W.N. 1954. 'Osteodystrophic diseases of sheep in New Zealand. II – "Bowie" or "Bent-leg"', *New Zealand Veterinary Journal* 2, 118–22

Fisher, J.W. 1995. 'Bone surface modifications in zooarchaeology', *Journal of Archaeological Method and Theory* 2(1), 7–68

Franklin, M.C. 1950. *The influence of diet on dental development in the sheep.* Melbourne: Commonwealth Scientific and Industrial Research Organisation, Bulletin 252

Frison, G.C. 1978. *Prehistoric hunters of the High Plains.* New York, Academic Press

Frison, G.C. & Reher, C.A. 1970. 'Age determination of buffalo by teeth eruption and wear', in G.C. Frison (ed.) *Glenrock Buffalo Jump.* Plains Anthropologist Memoirs, 46–50

Frison, G.C. & Stanford, D.J. 1982. *The Agate Basin site. A record of the paleoindian occupation of the northwestern High Plains.* New York, Academic Press

Frost, H.M. 1973. *Bone remodeling and its relationship to metabolic bone diseases.* Springfield, Illinois, Charles C. Thomas

Fulford, M. & Wallace-Hadrill, A. 1998. 'Unpeeling Pompeii', *Antiquity* 72, 128–45

Fumihito, A., Miyake, T., Sumi, S.I., Takada, M., Ohno, S. & Kondo, N. 1994. 'One subspecies of the red junglefowl (*Gallus gallus gallus*) suffices as the matriarchic ancestor of all domestic breeds', *Proceedings of the National Academy of Sciences of the USA* 91(26), 12,505–9

Galton, F. 1865. 'The first steps towards the domestication of animals', *Transactions of the Ethnological Society of London* 3, 122–38

Garlick, N.L. 1954. 'The teeth of the ox in clinical diagnosis. III. Developmental abnormalities and general pathology', *American Journal of Veterinary Research* 15, 500–8

Gautier, A. 1984. 'How do I count you, let me count the ways? Problems of archaeozoological quantification', in C. Grigson & J. Clutton-Brock (eds) *Animals and archaeology: 4. Husbandry in Europe.* Oxford, British Archaeological Reports International Series 227, 237–51

Gehr, K.D. 1995. *Bones: a field and laboratory guide for identification of the postcranial bones of the mammalian skeleton.* Auburn WA, Bare Bones Publications

Geist, V. 1989. 'Did large predators keep humans out of North America?' in J. Clutton-Brock (ed.) *The walking larder.* London, Unwin Hyman One World Archaeology, 282–94.

Gibson, P.M. 1993. 'The application of hybrid neural network models to estimate age of domestic ungulates', *International Journal of Osteoarchaeology* 3(1), 45–8

Gilbert, A.S. & Steinfeld, P. 1977. 'Faunal remains from Dinkha Tepe, Northwestern Iran', *Journal of Field Archaeology* 4, 329–51

Gilbert, A.S. & Singer, B.H. 1982. 'Reassessing zooarchaeological quantification', *World Archaeology* 14(1), 21–40

Gilbert, A.S., Singer, B.H. & Perkins, D. jr. 1982. 'Quantification experiments in computer-simulated faunal collections', *Ossa* 8, 79–94

Gilinsky, N.L. & Bennington, J.D. 1994. 'Estimating numbers of whole individuals from collections of body parts: a taphonomic limitation of the palaeontological record', *Paleobiology* 20, 245–58

Gleed-Owen, C.P. 1998. *Quaternary herpetofaunas of the British Isles: taxonomic description, palaeoenvironmental reconstructions and biostratigraphic implications.* PhD thesis, University of Coventry, UK

Gordon, B.C. 1993. 'Archaeological tooth and fine seasonal increments: the need for standardized terms and techniques', *Archaeozoologia* 5(2), 9-16

Gordon, C.C. & Buikstra, J.E. 1981. 'Soil pH, bone preservation and sampling bias at mortuary sites', *American Antiquity* 46, 566–71

Gotfredson, A.B. 1997. 'Sea bird exploitation on coastal Inuit sites, west and southeast Greenland', *International Journal of Osteoarchaeology* 7, 271–86

Grant, A. 1982. 'The use of tooth wear as a guide to the age of domestic ungulates', in B. Wilson, C. Grigson & S. Payne (eds.) *Ageing and sexing animal bones from archaeological sites.* Oxford: British Archaeological Reports British Series 109, 91–108

Grayson, D.K. 1979. 'On the quantification of vertebrate archaeofaunas', in M.B. Schiffer (ed.) *Advances in Archaeological Method and Theory vol 2.* New York: Academic Press, 199–237

Grayson, D.K. 1980. 'Vicissitudes and overkill: the development of explanations of Pleistocene extinctions', *Advances in Archaeological Theory and Method* 3, 357–403

Grayson, D.K. 1981. 'The effects of sample size on some derived measures in vertebrate faunal analysis', *Journal of Archaeological Science* 8, 77–88

Grayson, D.K. 1984. *Quantitative Zooarchaeology.* London, Academic Press

Grenier, R. 1985. 'Excavating a 400-year-old Basque galleon', *National Geographic* 168, 58–67

Grigson, C. 1978. 'Towards a blueprint for animal bone reports in archaeology', in D.R. Brothwell, K.D. Thomas & J. Clutton-Brock (eds) *Research Problems in Zooarchaeology.* London, Institute of Archaeology Occasional Publications 3, 121–8

Grigson, C. 1984. 'The domestic mammals of the earlier Neolithic in Britain', in H. Schwabedissen (ed.) *Die Anfänge des Neolithikums vom Orient bis Nordeuropa. Teil IX. Der Beginn der Haustierhaltung in der "Alten Welt".* Cologne, Böhlau Verlag, 205–20

Groenman-van Waateringe, W. 1994. 'The menu of different classes in Dutch medieval society', in A.R. Hall & H.K. Kenward (eds) *Urban-rural connexions: perspectives from environmental archaeology.* Oxford, Oxbow Monographs 47, 147–69

Grødalen, T. 1974. 'Osteochondrosis and arthrosis in pigs. I: incidence in animals up to 120kg weight. II: incidence in breeding animals', *Acta Veterinaria Scandinavica* 15, 1–42

Grupe, G. 1995. 'Preservation of collagen from dry, sandy soil', *Journal of Archaeological Science* 22, 193–9

Guilday, J.E. 1961. 'Abnormal lower third molar in *Odocoileus*', *Journal of Mammalogy* 42, 551–3

Gustafson, G. 1966. *Forensic Odontology.* London, Staples Press

Gutierrez, M., Martinez, G., Johnson, E., Politis, G. & Hartwell, W.T. 1994. 'Nuevos analisis oseos en el sitio Paso Otero 1', *Actas y Memorias del XI Congreso Nacional de Arqueologia Argentina* 14, 222–4

Habermehl, K.-H. 1961. *Die Alterbestimmung bei Haustieren, Pelztieren und beim jagdbaren Wildtieren.* Berlin, Paul Parey

Hall, P.M. 1985. 'Brachycephalic growth and dental anomalies in the New Guinea crocodile (*Crocodylus novaeguineae*)', *Journal of Herpetology* 19, 300–3

Halstead, L.B. 1974. *Vertebrate hard tissues.* London, Wykeham

Harder, W. 1975. *Anatomy of fishes.* Stuttgart, Schweizerbartische Verlagsbuchhandlung

Harris, D.R. 1996. 'Domesticatory relationships of people, plants and animals', in R. Ellen & K. Fukui (eds) *Redefining nature: ecology, culture and domestication.* Oxford, Berg, 437–63

Hatting, T. 1974. 'The influence of castration on sheep horns', in A.T. Clason (ed.) *Archaeozoological Studies*. Amsterdam, Elsevier, 345–51

Hatting, T. 1983. 'Osteological investigations on *Ovis aries* L.', *Dansk Naturhistorisk Forening* 144, 115–35

Haynes, G. 1983. 'A guide for differentiating mammalian carnivore taxa responsible for gnaw damage to herbivore long bones', *Paleobiology* 9, 164–72

Healy, W.B., Cutress, T.W. & Michie, C. 1967. 'Wear of sheep's teeth IV. Reduction of soil ingestion and tooth wear by supplementary feeding', *New Zealand Journal of Agricultural Research* 10, 201–9

Healy, W.B. & Ludwig, T.G. 1965. 'Wear of sheep's teeth I. The role of ingested soil', *New Zealand Journal of Agricultural Research* 8, 737–52

Hedges, R.E.M., Millard, A. & Pike, A.W.G. 1995. 'Measurements and relationships of diagenetic alteration of bone from three archaeological sites', *Journal of Archaeological Science* 22, 201–9

Helmer, D. & Rocheteau, M. 1994. *Atlas du squelette appendiculaire des principaux genres Holocènes de petits ruminants du nord de la Méditerranée et du Proche-Orient*. Juan-les-Pins, CNRS Fiches d'Osteologie Animale pour l'Archaeologie no. 4

Hemming, J.E. 1969. 'Cemental deposition, tooth succession, and horn development as criteria of age in Dall sheep', *Journal of Wildlife Management* 33(3), 552–8

Henshilwood, C.S. 1997. 'Identifying the collector: evidence for human processing of the Cape Dune mole-rat *Bathyergus suillus*, from Blombos Cave, Southern Cape, South Africa', *Journal of Archaeological Science* 24, 659–62

Hesse, B. & Wapnish, P. 1985. *Animal bone archaeology*. Washington, Taraxacum Press

Higham, C.F.W. 1968. 'Size trends in prehistoric European domestic fauna, and the problem of local domestication', *Acta Zoologica Fennica* 120, 3–21

Higham, C.F.W., Kijngam, A., Manly, B.F.J. & Moore, S.J.E. 1981. 'The bovid third phalanx and prehistoric ploughing', *Journal of Archaeological Science* 8, 353–65

Hillson, S.M. 1986. *Teeth*. Cambridge University Press

Holzman, R.C. 1979. 'Maximum likelihood estimation of the fossil assemblage composition', *Paleobiology* 5(2), 77–89

Horwitz, L.K. & Smith, P. 1990. 'A radiographic study of extent of variation in cortical bones thickness in Soay sheep', *Journal of Archaeological Science* 17, 655–64

Hufthammer, A.K. 1995. 'Age determination of reindeer (*Rangifer tarandus* L.)', *Archaeozoologia* 7, 33–42

Ijzereef, F.G. 1989. 'Social differentiation from animal bone studies', in D. Serjeantson & T. Waldron (eds) *Diet and crafts in towns*. Oxford, British Archaeological Reports British Series 199, 41–54

Jackson, H.E. 1989. 'The trouble with transformations: the effects of sample size and sample composition on weight estimates based on skeletal mass allometry', *Journal of Archaeological Science* 16, 601–10

Jensen, R., Park, R.D., Lauerman, L.H., Braddy, P.M., Horton, D.P., Flack, D.E., Cox, M.F., Einertson, N., Miller, G.K. & Rehfeld, C.E. 1981. 'Osteochondrosis in feedlot cattle', *Veterinary Pathology* 18, 529–35

Johnsson, K. 1997. 'Chemical dating of bones based on diagenetic changes in bone apatite', *Journal of Archaeological Science* 24, 431–7

Jones, A.K.G. 1983. 'A comparison of two on-site methods of wet-sieving large archaeological soil samples', *Science and Archaeology* 25, 9–12

Jones, A.K.G. 1986. 'Fish bone survival in the digestive systems of pig, dog, and man', in D. Brinkhuizen & A. Clason (eds) *Fish and Archaeology*. Oxford, British Archaeological Reports International Series 294, 53–61

Jones, A.K.G. 1988. 'Provisional remarks on fish remains from archaeological deposits at York', in P. Murphy & C. French (eds) *The exploitation of wetlands*. Oxford, British Archaeological Reports British Series 186, 113–27.

Jonsson, G., Jacobsson, S.-O., Strömberg, B., Olsson, S.-E. & Björklund, N.E. 1972. 'Rickets and secondary nutritional hyperparathyroidism. A clinical syndrome in fattening bulls', *Acta Radiologica* 319 Supplement, 91–105

Keay, J.A. 1996. 'Accuracy of cementum age assigments for black bears', *California Fish and Game* 81(3), 113–21

Kemp, B.J., Samuel, D. & Luff, R. 1994. 'Food for an Egyptian city: Tell el-Amarna', in R. Luff & P. Rowley-Conwy (eds) *Whither environmental archaeology?* Oxford, Oxbow Monographs 38, 133–70

Kemp, R.L. 1996. *Anglian settlement at 46–54 Fishergate. Archaeology of York 7/1*. York, Council for British Archaeology

Kenward, H.K., Hall, A.R. & Jones, A.K.G. 1980. 'A tested set of techniques for the extraction of plant and animal macrofossils from waterlogged archaeological deposits', *Science and Archaeology* 22, 3–15

Kenward, H.K. & Hall, A.R. 1995. *Biological evidence from 16–22 Coppergate. The Archaeology of York 14/7*. York, Council for British Archaeology

Kerley, E.R. 1965. 'The microscopic determination of age in human bones', *American Journal of Physical Anthropology* 23, 149–64

Kierdorf, U. 1994. 'A further example of long-bone damage due to chewing by deer', *International Journal of Osteoarchaeology* 4(3), 209–14

Kierdorf, U. & Becher, J. 1997. 'Mineralization and wear of mandibular first molars in red deer (*Cervus elaphus*) of known age', *Journal of Zoology, London* 241, 135–43

Kirkpatrick, R.D. & Sowls, L.K. 1962. 'Age determination of the collared peccary by the tooth-replacement pattern', *Journal of Wildlife Management* 26(2), 214–17

Klein, R.G., Wolf, C., Freeman, L.G. & Allwarden, K. 1981. 'The use of dental crown heights for constructing age profiles of red deer and similar species in archaeological samples', *Journal of Archaeological Science* 8, 1–31

Klein, R.G. & Cruz-Uribe, K. 1984. *The analysis of animal bones from archaeological sites*. Chicago, Chicago University Press

Krantz, G.S. 1968. 'A new method of counting mammal bones', *American Journal of Archaeology* 72, 286–8

Kratochvil, Z. 1969. 'Species criteria on the distal section of the tibia in *Ovis ammon f. aries* L. and *Capra aegagrus f. hircus* L.', *Acta Veterinaria (Brno)* 38, 483–90

Kratochvil, Z. 1984. 'Veränderung am Gebiss des Rehwilder (*Capreolus capreolus* L.)', *Folia Zoologica* 33, 209–22

Kratochvil, Z. 1986. 'Das Fehlen des 2. Prämolaren beim europäischen Reh (*Capreolus capreolus* L.) aus der jüngeren Steinzeit', *Zeitschrift für Jagdwissenschaft* 32, 248–51

Krupnik, I.I. 1990. 'The aboriginal hunter in an unstable ecosystem: a view from subarctic Pacific', in D.E. Yen & J.M.J. Mummery (eds) *Pacific production systems: approaches to economic prehistory*. Canberra, Australian National University, Occasional Paper in Prehistory 18, 18–24

Kubasiewicz, M. 1956. 'O metodyce badan wykopaliskowych szczatow kostynch zwierzecych', *Materialy Zachodnio-Pomorskie* 2, 235–44

Küpfer, M. & Schinz, H.R. 1923. 'Beiträge zur Kenntnis der Skelettbildung bei domestizierten Säugetieren auf Grund röntgenologischer Untersuchungen', *Denkschriften der Schweizerischen Naturforschenden Gesellschaft* 54, 1–133

Kvaal, S.I. & Solheim, T. 1995. 'Incremental lines in human dental cementum in relation to age', *European Journal of Oral Sciences* 103(4), 225–30

Lasota-Moskalewska, A., Kobryn, H. & Swiezynski, K. 1987. 'Changes in the size of the domestic and wild pig in the territory of Poland from the Neolithic to the Middle Ages', *Acta Theriologica* 32, 51–81

Lauwerier, R.C.G.M. 1983. 'Pigs, piglets and determining the season of slaughtering', *Journal of Archaeological Science* 10, 483–8

Leach, B.F., Davidson, J.M. & Horwood, L.M. 1997. 'The estimation of live fish size from archaeological cranial bones of the New Zealand blue cod *Parapercis colias*', *International Journal of Osteoarchaeology* 7, 481–96

Leader-Williams, N. 1980. 'Dental abnormalities and mandibular swellings in South Georgia reindeer', *Journal of Comparative Pathology* 90, 315–30

Lee-Thorp, J.A. & van der Merwe, N.J. 1991. 'Aspects of the chemistry of modern and fossil biological apatites', *Journal of Archaeological Science* 18, 343–54

Lefèvre, C. 1997. 'Seabird fowling in southern Patagonia: a contribution to understanding the nomadic round of the Canoeros Indians', *International Journal of Osteoarchaeology* 7, 260–70

Legge, A.J. 1996. 'The beginnings of caprine domestication in Southwest Asia', in D.R. Harris (ed.) *The origin and spread of agriculture and pastoralism in Eurasia*. London, University College Press, 238–62

Legge, A.J. & Rowley-Conwy, P.A. 1987. 'Gazelle killing in Stone Age Syria', *Scientific American* 255(8), 88–95

Legge, A.J. & Rowley-Conwy, P.A. 1988. *Star Carr revisited. A re-analysis of the large mammals*. London, Birkbeck College, University of London

Lepiksaar, J. & Heinrich, D. 1977. *Untersuchungen an Fischresten aus der frühmittelalterlichen Siedlung Haithabu*. Neümunster, Karl Wachholz, Berichte über die Ausgrabungen in Haithabu 10

Lesbre, M. F.-X. 1898. 'Contribution a l'étude de l'ossification du squelette des mammifères domestiques', *Annales de la Société d'Agriculture, Sciences et Industrie de Lyon* (7th Series) 5 (for 1897), 1–100

Levine, M.A. 1982. 'The use of crown height measurements and eruption-wear sequence to age horse teeth', in B. Wilson, C. Grigson & S. Payne (eds) *Ageing and sexing animal bones from archaeologial sites*. Oxford, British Archaeological Reports British Series 109, 223–50

Levitan, B.M. 1982a. *Excavations at West Hill Uley: 1979. The sieving and sampling programme*. Bristol, Western Archaeological Trust Occasional Papers no. 10

Levitan, B.M 1982b. 'Errors in recording tooth wear in ovicaprid mandibles at different speeds', in B. Wilson, C. Grigson & S. Payne (eds) *Ageing and sexing animal bones from archaeological sites*. Oxford, British Archaeological Reports British Series 109, 207–14

Levitan, B.M. 1983. 'Reducing the work-load: sub-sampling animal bone assemblages', *Circaea* 1, 7–12

Levitan. B.M. 1985. 'A methodology for recording the pathology and other anomalies of ungulate mandibles from archaeological sites', in N.R.J. Fieller, D.D. Gilbertson & N.G.A. Ralph (eds) *Palaeobiological Investigations. Research design, methods and data analysis*. Oxford, British Archaeological Reports International Series S266, 41–80

Levitan, B.M. 1987. 'Medieval animal husbandry in south-west England: a selective review and suggested approach', in N.D. Balaam, B. Levitan & V. Straker (eds) *Studies in palaeoeconomy and environment in South West England*. Oxford, British Archaeological Reports British Series 181, 51–80

Lewall, E.F. & Cowan, I. McT. 1963. 'Age determination in black-tail deer by degree of ossification of the epiphyseal plate in the long bones', *Canadian Journal of Zoology* 41, 629–36

Lieberman, D.E., Deacon, T.W. & Meadow, R.H. 1990. 'Computer image enhancement and analysis of cementum increments as applied to teeth of *Gazella gazella*', *Journal of Archaeological Science* 17, 519–33

Lieberman, D.E. & Meadow, R.H. 1992. 'The biology of cementum increments (with an archaeological application)', *Mammal Review* 22(2), 57–77

Linsenmayer, T.F. 1991. 'Collagen', in E.D. Hay (ed.) *Cell biology of extracellular matrix*. New York, Plenum Press, 7–44

Lister, A.M. 1996. 'The morphological distinction between bones and teeth of fallow deer (*Dama dama*) and red deer (*Cervus elaphus*)', *International Journal of Osteoarchaeology* 6, 119–43

Long, J.L. 1981. *Introduced birds of the world*. London, David & Charles

Lowe, V.P.W. 1967. 'Teeth as indicators of age with special reference to Red Deer (*Cervus elaphus*) of known age from Rhum', *Journal of Zoology* 152, 137–53

Ludwig, T.G., Healy, W.B. & Cutress, T.W. 1966. 'Wear of sheep's teeth. III. Seasonal variation in wear and ingested soil', *New Zealand Journal of Agricultural Research* 9, 157–64

Luff, R.M. & Moreno-Garcia, M. 1995. 'Killing cats in the medieval period. An unusual episode in the history of Cambridge, England', *Archaeofauna* 4, 93–114

Luke, D.A., Tonge, C.H. & Reid, D.J. 1981. 'Effects of rehabilitation in the jaws and teeth of protein-deficient and calorie-deficient pigs', *Acta Anatomica* 110, 299–305

Lyman, R.L. 1982. ' Archaeofaunas and subsistence studies', in M.B. Schiffer (ed.) *Advances in Archaeological Method and Theory* 5. New York, Academic Press, 331–93.

Lyman, R.L. 1984. 'Bone density and differential survivorship of fossil bone classes', *Journal of Anthropological Archaeology* 3, 259–99

Lyman, R.L. 1994. *Vertebrate taphonomy*. Cambridge, Cambridge University Press

MacGregor, A. 1989. 'Bone, antler and horn industries in the urban context', in D. Serjeanston & T. Waldron (eds) *Diet and crafts in towns*. Oxford, British Archaeological Reports British Series 199, 129–46

Main, M.B. & Owens, R. 1995. 'Estimating mule deer age from measurements of incisor wear', *Northwestern Naturalist* 76, 130–2

Mainland, I. 1995a. 'Dental microwear as evidence for prehistoric diet: the potential of qualitative analysis', in J. Moggi-Cecchi (ed.) *Aspects of dental biology: palaeontology, anthropology and evolution*. Florence, International Institute for the Study of Man, 159–66

Mainland, I. 1995b. 'Reconstructing the diet of archaeological domesticates: the potential of dental microwear analysis', in R.J. Radlanski & H. Renz (eds) *Proceedings of the 10th International Symposium on Dental Morphology, Berlin 1995*. Berlin, M-Marketing, 156–61

Maltby, M. 1983.' Animal bones', in J. Collis, *Wigber Low, Derbyshire: a Bronze Age and Anglian burial site in the White Peak*. Sheffield, University of Sheffield, 47–50

Maltby, M. 1984. 'Animal bones and the Romano-British economy', in C. Grigson & J. Clutton-Brock (eds) *Animals and Archaeology. 4: Husbandry in Europe*. Oxford, British Archaeological Reports International Series 227, 125–38

Maltby, M. 1989. 'Urban-rural variations in the butchering of cattle in Romano-British Hampshire', in D. Serjeantson & T. Waldron (eds) *Diet and crafts in towns*. Oxford, British Archaeological Reports British Series 199, 75–106

Maltby, M. 1993. 'Animal bones', in P.J. Woodward, S.M. Davies & A.H. Graham, *Excavations at Greyhound Yard, Dorchester 1981–4*. Dorchester, Dorset Natural History and Archaeology Society Monograph Series 12, 315–40

Maltby, M. 1994. 'The meat supply in Roman Dorchester and Winchester', in A.R. Hall & H.K. Kenward (eds) *Urban-rural connexions: perspectives from environmental archaeology*. Oxford, Oxbow Monographs, 85–102

Manaseryan, M.H., Dobney, K. & Ervynck, A. 1999. 'On the causes of perforations in archaeological domestic cattle skulls: new evidence', *International Journal of Osteoarchaeology* 9, 74–5

Marshall, J.T. & Sage, R.D. 1981. 'Taxonomy of the house mouse', *Symposia of the Zoological Society of London* 47, 15–25

Martin, P.S. & Wright, H.E. (eds) 1967. *Pleistocene extinctions, the search for a cause*. New Haven, Yale University Press

Matheson, C. 1931. *The Brown and the Black Rat in Wales*. Cardiff, National Museum of Wales

McCartney, P.H. 1990. 'Alternative hunting strategies in Plains Paleoindian adaptations', in L.B. Davis & B.O.K. Reeves (eds) *Hunters of the recent past*. London, Unwin Hyman One World Archaeology, 111–21

McCormick, F. 1988. 'The domesticated cat in Early Christian and medieval Ireland', in G. MacNiocaill & P.F. Wallace (eds) *Keimelia. Studies in medieval history and archaeology in honour of Tom Delaney*. Galway, University Press, 218–28

Meadow, R.H. 1980. 'Animal bones: problems for the archaeologist together with some possible solutions', *Paléorient* 6, 65–77

Meadow, R.H. 1984. 'Notes on the faunal remains from Mehrgarh, with a focus on cattle (*Bos*)', in B. Allchin (ed.) *South Asian Archaeology 1981*. Cambridge, Cambridge University Press, 34–40

Meadow, R.H. 1999. 'The use of size-index scaling techniques for research on archaeozoological collections from the Middle East', in C. Becker, H. Manhart, J. Peters & J. Schibler (eds) *Historiae Animalium ex Ossibus*. Rahden, Verlag Marie Leidorf; 285–300

Miles, A.E.W. & Grigson, C. 1990. *Colyer's variations and diseases of the teeth of animals*. (rev. edn) Cambridge, Cambridge University Press

Millard, A.R. & Hedges, R.E.M. 1995. 'The role of the environment in uranium uptake by buried bone', *Journal of Archaeological Science* 22, 239–50

Miller, F.L. 1972. 'Eruption and attrition of mandibular teeth in barren-ground caribou', *Journal of Wildlife Management* 36(2), 606–12

Mitchell, B. 1967. 'Growth layers in dental cement for determining the age of red deer (*Cervus elaphus* L.)', *Journal of Applied Ecology* 4, 279–93

Mondini, N.M. 1995. 'Artiodactyl prey transport by foxes in Puna rock shelters', *Current Anthropology* 36(3), 520–4

Moore, N.P., Cahill, J.P., Kelly, P.F. &d Hayden, T.J. 1995. 'An assessment of 5 methods of age-determination in an enclosed population of fallow deer (*Dama dama*)', *Proceedings of the Royal Irish Academy* 95B, 27–34

Morales Muñiz, A. 1993. 'Ornithoarchaeology: the various aspects of the classification of bird remains from archaeological sites', *Archaeofauna* 2, 1–13

Morales Muñiz, L.C. & Morales Muñiz, A. 1995. 'The Spanish bullfight: some historical aspects, traditional interpretations, and comments of archaeozoological interest for the study of the ritual slaughter', in K. Ryan & P. Crabtree (eds) *The symbolic role of animals in archaeology*. Philadelphia, MASCA Research Papers in Archaeology 12, 91–105

Morales Muñiz, A., Pecharromán, M.A.C., Carrasquilla, F.H. & von Lettow-Vorbeck, C.L. 1995. 'Of mice and sparrows: commensal faunas from the Iberian Iron Age in the Duero valley (Central Spain)', *International Journal of Osteoarchaeology* 5, 127–38

Morales Muñiz, A. and Rodríguez, J. 1997. 'Black rats (*Rattus rattus*) from medieval Mertola (Baixo Alentejo, Portugal)', *Journal of Zoology, London* 241, 623–42

Moran, N.C. & O'Connor, T.P 1992. 'Bones that cats gnawed upon: a case study in bone modification', *Circaea* 9, 27–34

Moran, N.C. & O'Connor, T.P. 1994. 'Age attribution in domestic sheep by skeletal and dental maturation: a pilot study of available sources', *International Journal of Osteoarchaeology* 4, 267–85

Moreno-Garcia, M., Orton, C. & Rackham, J. 1996. 'A new statistical tool for comparing animal bone assemblages', *Journal of Archaeological Science* 23, 437–53

Morris, P. 1972. 'A review of mammalian age determination methods', *Mammal Review* 2(3), 69–104

Mosimann, J.E. & Martin, P.S. 1975. 'Simulating overkill by Paleoindians', *American Scientist* 63(3), 304–13

Mulkeen, S. & O'Connor, T.P. 1997. 'Raptors in towns: towards an ecological model', *International Journal of Osteoarchaeology* 7, 440–9

Müller, H.-H. 1989. 'Schnittspuren an Wirbeln frühgeschichtlicher Pferdeskelette und ihre Kulturgeschichtliche Interpretation', *Religion und Kult (1989)*, 293–6

Munsell, A.H. 1946. *A color notation*. Baltimore, Munsell Color Company Inc.

van Neer, W., Augustynen, S. & Linkowski, T. 1993. 'Daily growth increments on fish otoliths as seasonality indicators on archaeological sites: the tilapia from Late Palaeolithic Makhadma in Egypt', *International Journal of Osteoarchaeology* 3, 241–8

van Neer, W. & Ervynck, A. 1994. 'New data on fish remains from Belgian archaeological sites', in W. van Neer (ed.) *Fish exploitation in the past*. Tervuren, Annales du Musée Royal de l'Afrique Centrale, Sciences Zoologiques 274, 217–29

van Neer, W. & Morales Muniz, A. 1992. '"Fish middens": anthropogenic accumulations of fish remains and their bearing on archaeoichthyological analysis', *Journal of Archaeological Science* 19, 683–95

Nicholson, R.A. 1992. 'Bone survival: the effects of sedimentary abrasion and trampling on fresh and worked bone', *International Journal of Osteoarchaeology* 2, 79–90

Nicholson, R.A. 1993. 'A morphological investigation of burnt animal bone and an evaluation of its utility in archaeology', *Journal of Archaeological Science* 20, 411–28

Nicholson, R.A. 1996. 'Bone degradation, burial medium and species representation: debunking the myths, an experiment-based approach', *Journal of Archaeological Science* 23, 513–33

Noddle, B.A. 1973. 'Determination of the body weight of cattle from bone measurements', in J. Matolcsi (ed.) *Domestikationsforschung und geschichte der Haustiere*. Budapest, Akademiai Kiado, 377–89

Noddle, B.A. 1974. 'Ages of epiphyseal closure in feral and domestic goats and ages of dental eruption', *Journal of Archaeological Science* 1, 195–204

Noddle, B.A. 1978. 'Some minor skeletal differences in sheep', in D. Brothwell, K.D. Thomas & J. Clutton-Brock (eds) *Research problems in zooarchaeology*. London, Institute of Archaeology Occasional Publications 3, 133–42

Noddle, B.A. 1999. 'The animal bones', in G. Webster, *Wroxeter. Excavation of the Roman baths and macellum 1955–1985. Volume 1 The legionary fortress*. London, English Heritage Archaeological Report 19, 152–4

Noe-Nygaard, N. 1979. 'Problems in quantification of archaeozoological material caused by differences in butchering and marow fracturing techniques', in M. Kubasiewicz (ed.) *Archaeozoology* 1. Szczecin, Agricultural Academy, 109–19

Noe-Nygaard, N. 1983. 'The importance of aquatic resources to Mesolithic man at inland sites in Denmark', in C. Grigson & J. Clutton-Brock (eds) *Animals and archaeology. 2. Shell middens, fishes and birds*. Oxford, British Archaeological Reports International Series 183, 125–42

Northcote, E.M. 1981. 'Size differences between limb bones of recent and subfossil mute swans *Cygnus olor*', *Journal of Archaeological Science* 8, 89–98

Novakowski, N.S. 1965. 'Cemental deposition as an age criterion in bison, and the relation of incisor wear, eye lens weight, and dressed bison carcass weight to age', *Canadian Journal of Zoology* 43, 173–8

O'Connor, T.P. 1982. *The archaeozoological interpretation of morphometric variation in British sheep limb bones*. Doctoral thesis, University of London

O'Connor, T.P. 1986a. 'The garden dormouse *Eliomys quercinus* from Roman York', *Journal of Zoology* 210, 620–2

O'Connor, T.P. 1986b. 'The animal bones', in D. Zienkiewicz, *The legionary fortress baths at Caerleon. Volume II. The Finds*. Cardiff, National Museum of Wales; 223–46

O'Connor, T.P. 1988a. *Archaeological bone samples recovered by sieving: 46–54 Fishergate, York, as a case study. Ancient Monuments Laboratory Report 190/88*. London, English Heritage

O'Connor, T.P. 1988b. *Bones from the General Accident site, Tanner Row. Archaeology of York 15/2*. London, Council for British Archaeology

O'Connor, T.P. 1989. *Bones from Anglo-Scandinavian levels at 16–22 Coppergate. Archaeology of York 15/3*. London, Council for British Archaeology

O'Connor, T.P. 1991a. *Bones from 46–54 Fishergate. Archaeology of York 15/4*. York, Council for British Archaeology

O'Connor, T.P. 1991b. 'On the lack of bones of the ship rat *Rattus rattus* from Dark Age York', *Journal of Zoology, London* 224, 318–20

O'Connor, T.P. 1992a. 'Provisioning urban communities: a topic in search of a model', *Anthropozoologica* 16, 101–6

O'Connor, T.P. 1992b. 'Pets and pests in Roman and medieval Britain', *Mammal Review* 22, 107–13

O'Connor, T.P. 1993. 'Process and terminology in mammal carcass reduction', *International Journal of Osteoarchaeology* 3, 63–7

O'Connor, T.P. 1995. 'Size increase in post-medieval English sheep: the osteological evidence', *Archaeofauna* 4, 81–91

O'Connor, T.P. 1997. 'Working at relationships: another look at animal domestication', *Antiquity* 71, 149–56

O'Connor, T.P. 1998. 'On the difficulty of detecting seasonal slaughtering of sheep', *Environmental Archaeology* 3, 5–11

Ohtaishi, N. 1972. 'A case of congenital absence of the lower second premolars in cattle and a phylogenetic consideration of its origins', *Japanese Journal of Veterinary Research* 20, 7–12

Olsen, S.J. 1960. *Post-cranial skeletal characters of Bison and Bos*. Cambridge, Massachusetts, Papers of the Peabody Museum of Archaeology and Ethnology, Harvard University vol. 35 no. 4

Olsen, S.J. 1979. 'Archaeologically, what constitutes an early domestic animal?', in M.B. Schiffer (ed.) *Advances in Archaeological Method and Theory* 2. New York, Academic Press, 175–97

Olsen, S.J. 1990. 'Was early man in North America a big game hunter?', in L.B. Davis & B.O.K. Reeves (eds) *Hunters of the recent past*. London, Unwin Hyman One World Archaeology, 103–10

Ortner, D.J. & Putschar, W.G.J. 1985. *Identification of pathological conditions in human skeletal remains*. Washington, Smithsonian Institution

Østblom, L., Lund, C. & Melsen, F. 1982. 'Histological study of navicular bone disease', *Equine Veterinary Journal* 14, 199–202

Owen, J.F. & Merrick, J.R. 1994. 'Analysis of coastal middens in south-eastern Australia: selectivity of angling and other fishing techniques related to Holocene deposits', *Journal of Archaeological Science* 21, 11–16

Page, R.C. & Schroeder, H.E. 1982. *Periodontitis in man and other animals. A comparative review*. London, Karger

Panella, G. 1980. 'Growth patterns in fish sagittae', in D.C. Rhoades & R.A. Lutz, (eds) *Skeletal growth of aquatic organisms. Topics in Geobiology* 1, 519–60

Pascoe, J.R., Pool, R.R., Wheat, J.B. & O'Brien, T. 1984. 'Osteochondral defects of the lateral trochlear ridge of the distal femur of the horse', *Veterinary Surgery* 13, 99–110

Pate, F.D. & Hutton, J.T. 1988. 'Postmortem diagenesis in bone mineral', *Journal of Archaeological Science* 15, 729–39

Payne, S. 1969. 'A metrical distinction between sheep and goat metacarpals', in P.J. Ucko & G.W. Dimbleby (eds) *The domestication and exploitation of plants and animals*. London, Duckworth, 295–305

Payne, S. 1973. 'Kill-off patterns in sheep and goats. The mandibles from Asvan Kale', *Anatolian Studies* 23, 281–303

Payne, S. 1975. 'Partial recovery and sample bias', in A.T. Clason (ed.) *Archaeozoological studies*. New York, American Elsevier, 7–17

Payne, S. 1983. 'The animal bones from the 1974 excavations at Douara cave', in K. Hanihara & T. Akazawa (eds) *Palaeolithic site of the Douara Cave and paleogeography of Palmyra Basin in Syria Part III*. Tokyo, Tokyo University Press, 1–108

Payne, S. 1984. 'The use of early 19th century data in ageing cattle mandibles from archaeological sites, and the relationship between the eruption of M_3 and P_4', *Circaea* 2(2), 77–82

Payne, S. 1985a. 'Morphological distinctions between the mandibular teeth of young sheep, *Ovis*, and goats, *Capra*', *Journal of Archaeological Science* 12, 139–47

Payne, S. 1985b. 'Animal bones from Asikli Hüyük', *Anatolian Studies* 35, 109–22

Payne, S. 1987. 'Reference codes for wear stages in the mandibular cheek teeth of sheep and goats', *Journal of Archaeological Science* 14, 609–14

Payne, S. & Bull, G. 1988. 'Components of variation in measurements of pig bones and teeth, and the use of measurements to distinguish wild from domestic pig remains', *Archaeozoologia* 2, 27–66

Payne, S. & Munson, P.J. 1985. 'Ruby and how many squirrels? The destruction of bones by dogs', in N. Fieller, D.D. Gilbertson & N. Ralph (eds) *Palaeobiological Investigations. Research designs, methods and data analysis*. Oxford, British Archaeological Reports International Series 266, 31–48

Perkins, D. jr. 1973. 'The beginnings of animal domestication in the Near East', *American Journal of Archaeology* 77, 279–82

Peterson, R.O., Scheider, J.M. & Stephens, P.W. 1982. 'Selected skeletal morphology and pathology of moose from the Kenai Peninsula, Alaska, and Isle Royale, Michigan', *Canadian Journal of Zoology* 60(11), 2,812–7

Pieper, H. 1982. 'Probleme der Artbestimmung an Knochen des Extremitätenskelettes sowie Bemerkungen zur systematischen Gliederung der Gattung *Aythya* (Aves: Anatidae)', *Schriften aus der Archäologisch-Zoologischen Arbeitsgruppe Schleswig-Kiel* 6, 63–95

Pitts, M. 1979. 'Hides and antlers: a new look at the gatherer-hunter site at Star Carr, North Yorkshire, England', *World Archaeology* 11, 32–42

Plug, C. & Plug, I. 1990. 'MNI counts as estimates of species abundance', *South African Archaeological Bulletin* 45, 53–7

Plug, I. 1990. 'The macrofaunal remains from Mhlwazini Cave, a Holocene site in the Natal Drakensberg', *Natal Museum Journal of Humanities* 2, 135–42

Plug, I. 1993. 'KwaThwaleyakhe Shelter: the faunal remains from a Holocene site in the Thukela Basin, Natal, *Natal Museum Journal of Humanities* 5, 37–45

Plug, I. 1996. 'The hunter's choice: faunal remains from Maqonqo Shelter, South Africa', *Natal Museum Journal of Humanities* 8, 41–52

Plug, I. 1997. 'Late Pleistocene and Holocene hunter-gatherers in the Eastern Highlands of South Africa and Lesotho: a faunal interpretation', *Journal of Archaeological Science* 24, 715–27

Plug, I. & Engela, R. 1992. 'The macrofaunal remains from recent excavations at Rose Cottage Cave, Orange Free State', *South African Archaeological Bulletin* 47, 10–25

Poplin, F. 1981. 'Une probleme d'osteologie quantitative: calcul d'effectif inital d'apres appariements. Generalisation aux autres types de remontages et d'autre materiels archeologiques', *Revue d'Archeometrie* 5, 159–65

Prange, H.D., Anderson, J.F. & Rahn, H. 1979. 'Scaling of skeletal mass to body mass in birds and mammals', *American Naturalist* 113, 103–22

Pratt, C.W.M. & McCance, R.A. 1964. 'Severe undernutrition in growing and adult animals 14. The shafts of long bones in pigs', *British Journal of Nutrition* 18, 613–25

Price, T.D., Blitz, J. & Ezzo, J.A. 1992. 'Diagenesis in prehistoric bone: problems and solutions', *Journal of Archaeological Science* 19, 513–29

Prummel, W. 1986. 'The presence of bones of eel, *Anguilla anguilla*, in relation to taphonomic processes, cultural factors and the abundance of eel', in D.C. Brinkhuizen & A.T. Clason (eds) *Fish and archaeology*. Oxford, British Archaeological Reports International Series 294, 114–22

Prummel, W, 1987. 'The faunal remains from the Neolithic site of Hekelingen III', *Helinium* 27, 190–258

Prummel, W. & Frisch, H.-J. 1986. 'A guide for the distinction of species, sex and body side in bones of sheep and goat', *Journal of Archaeological Science* 13, 567–77

Prummel, W. & Knol, E. 1991. 'Strandlopers op de Brandstapel', *Paleo-Aktueel* 2, 92–6

Quéré, J.-P. & Pascal, M. 1983. 'Comparaison de plusieurs méthodes de détermination de l'age individuel chez le cerf élaphe (*Cervus elaphus* L.)', *Annales des Sciences Naturelles, Zoologie, Paris, 13e Série* 5, 235–52

Quirt-Booth, T. & Cruz-Uribe, K. 1997. 'Analysis of leporid remains from prehistoric Sinagua sites, northern Arizona', *Journal of Archaeological Science* 24, 945–60

Reed, C.A. 1970. 'Extinction of mammalian megafauna in the Old World Late Quaternary', *Bioscience* 20(5), 284–8

Reed, C.A. 1980. 'The beginnings of animal domestication', in H.H. Coles & W.N. Garrett (eds) *Animal agriculture* (2nd edn). San Francisco, W.H. Freeman, 3–20

Reeves, B.O.K. 1990. 'Communal bison hunters of the Northern Plains', in L.B. Davies & B.O.K. Reeves (eds) *Hunters of the recent past*. London, Unwin Hyman One World Archaeology, 168–94

Reher, C.A. & Frison, G.C. 1980. 'The Vore site, 48CK302, a stratified buffalo jump in the Wyoming Black hills', *Plains Anthropologist* 25–88(2), 1–190

Reichstein, H. & Pieper, H. 1986. 'Untersuchungen an Skelettresten von Vögeln aus Haithabu (Ausgrabung 1966–1969)', *Berichte über die Ausgrabungen in Haithabu, Bericht 22*. Neumünster, Karl Wachholz Verlag

Reiland, S. 1978. 'Growth and skeletal development of the pig', *Acta Radiologica Supplement* 358, 15–22

Reitz, E.J. 1982. 'Vertebrate fauna from four coastal Mississippian sites', *Journal of Ethnobiology* 2, 39–61

Reitz, E.J. 1986. 'Urban/rural contrasts in vertebrate fauna from the Southern Atlantic coastal plain', *Historical Archaeology* 20, 47–58

Reitz, E.J. 1994. 'Archaeology of Trants, Montserrat. Part 2. Vertebrate fauna', *Annals of the Carnegie Museum* 63, 297–317

Reitz, E.J. & Ruff, B. 1994. 'Morphometric data for cattle from North America and the Caribbean prior to the 1850s', *Journal of Archaeological Science* 21, 699–713

Rice, L.A. 1980. 'Influences of irregular dental cementum layers on ageing deer incisors', *Journal of Wildlife Management* 44, 266–8

Richardson, C., Richards, M., Terlecki, S. & Miller, W.M. 1979. 'Jaws of adult culled ewes', *Journal of Agricultural Science* 93, 521–9

Ringrose, T.J. 1993. 'Bone counts and statistics: a critique', *Journal of Archaeological Science* 20, 121–57

Ripke, E. 1964. 'Beitrag zur Kenntnis des Schweinegebisses', *Anatomische Anzeiger* 114, 181–211

Roberts, C.A. & Manchester, K. 1995. *The archaeology of disease.* Stroud, Alan Sutton Publishing

Roberts, J.D. 1978. 'Variation in coyote age determination from annuli in different teeth', *Journal of Wildlife Management* 42, 454–6

Rolett, B.V. &d Chiu, M.-Y. 1994. 'Age estimation of prehistoric pigs (*Sus scrofa*) by molar eruption and attrition', *Journal of Archaeological Science* 21, 377–86

Romer, A.S. 1970. *The vertebrate body* (4th edn). Philadelphia, W.B. Saunders

Rowley-Conwy, P. 1995. 'Wild or domestic? On the evidence for the earliest domestic cattle in South Scandinavia and Iberia', *International Journal of Osteoarchaeology* 5, 115–26

Rowley-Conwy, P. 1998. 'Improved separation of Neolithic metapodials of sheep (*Ovis*) and goats (*Capra*) from Arene Candide cave, Liguria, Italy', *Journal of Archaeological Science* 25, 251–8

Rowley-Conwy, P. & Storå, J. 1997. 'Pitted Ware seals and pigs from Ajvide, Gotland: methods of study and first results', in Burenhult, G. (ed.) *Remote sensing vol 1: Osteo-anthropological, economic, environmental and technical analyses.* Stockholm, University of Stockholm Institute of Archaeology Theses and Papers in North European Archaeology 13a, 113–27

Ruddle, J.L. 1996. *An investigation of bone histology as a potential age indicator in roe deer.* PhD thesis, University of London

Rudge, M.R. 1970. 'Dental and periodontal abnormalities in two populations of feral goats (*Capra hircus* L.) in New Zealand', *New Zealand Journal of Science* 13, 260–7

Saavedra, B. & Simonetti, J.A. 1998. 'Small mammal taphonomy: intraspecific bone assemblage comparison between South and North American barn owl, *Tyto alba*, populations', *Journal of Archaeological Science* 25, 165–70

Sanders, W.T. & Price, B.J. 1968. *Mesoamerica: the evolution of a civilisation.* New York, Random House

Scarlett, R.J. 1972. *Bones for the New Zealand archaeologist.* Christchurch, Canterbury Museum Bulletin no. 4

Schmid, E.S. 1972. *Atlas of animal bones.* Amsterdam, Elsevier

Serjeantson, D. 1989. 'Animal remains and the tanning trade', in D. Serjeantson & T. Waldron (eds) *Diet and crafts in towns.* Oxford, British Archaeological Reports British Series 199, 129–46

Shaffer, B.S. & Baker, B.W. 1992. *A vertebrate faunal analysis coding system.* Ann Arbor, University of Michigan Museum of Anthropology Technical Report 23

Shaffer, B.S. & Sanchez, J.L.J. 1994. 'Comparison of ⅛" and ¼" mesh recovery of controlled samples of small-to-medium sized mammals', *American Antiquity* 59, 525–30

Shermis, S. 1985. 'Alveolar osteitis and other oral diseases in *Smilodon californicus*', *Ossa* 12, 187–96

Shigehara, N., Matsu'ura, S., Nakamura, T. & Kondo, M. 1993. 'First discovery of ancient dingo-type dog in Polynesia (Pukapuka, Cook Islands)', *international Journal of Osteoarchaeology* 3, 315–20

Shipman, P. 1979. 'What are all these bones doing here?' *Harvard Magazine* 81, 42–6

Shipman, P. 1981. *Life history of a fossil*. Harvard, University Press

Shipman, P. 1983. 'Early hominid lifestyle: hunting and gathering or foraging and scavenging?', in J. Clutton-Brock & C. Grigson (eds) *Animals and archaeology: 1. hunters and their prey*. Oxford, British Archaeological Reports International Series S163, 31–49

Shipman, P., Foster, G. & Schoeninger, M.J. 1984. 'Burnt bones and teeth: an experimental study of colour, morphology, crystal structure and shrinkage', *Journal of Archaeological Science* 11, 307–25

Siegel, J. 1976. 'Animal palaeopathology: possibilities and problems', *Journal of Archaeological Science* 3, 349–84

Silver, I..A. 1969. 'The ageing of domestic animals', in D.R. Brothwell & E.S. Higgs (eds) *Science and Archaeology*. London: Thames & Hudson, 283–302

Smith, B.D. 1976. '"Twitching": a minor ailment affecting human palaeoecological research', in C.E. Cleland (ed.) *Cultural change and continuity*. New York, Academic Press, 275–92

Smith, P. 1995. 'A regression equation to determine the total length of hake (*Merluccius merluccius*) from selected measurements of the bones', *International Journal of Osteoarchaeology* 5, 93–5

Smith, P. & Horwitz, L.K. 1984. 'Radiographic evidence for changing patterns of animal exploitation in the southern Levant', *Journal of Archaeological Science* 11, 467–75

Smith, R.C., Spirek, J., Bratten, J. & Scott-Ireton, D. 1995. *The Emanuel Point ship: archaeological investigations 1992–1995. Preliminary report*. Florida, Bureau of Archaeological Research, Division of Historical Resources

Smith, R.N. 1956. 'Fusion of the epiphyses of the limb bones of the sheep', *Veterinary Record* 68, 257–9

Smith, R.N. 1969. 'Fusion of ossification centres in the cat', *Journal of Small Animal Practice* 10, 523–30

Sobolik, K.D. & Steele, D.G. 1996. *A turtle atlas to facilitate archaeological identifications*. Orono, University of Maine

Sokoloff, L. 1960. 'Comparative pathology of arthritis', *Advances in Veterinary Science* 6, 193–250

Sokolov, A.A., Gruzdov, A.R. & Pronyaev, A.V. 1996. 'Patterns of cheek tooth wearing in reindeer (*Rangifer tarandus*) from different populations', *Zoologichesky Zhurnal* 75(10), 1,573–80

Spaulding, W.G. 1983. 'The Overkill Hypothesis as a plausible explanation for the extinctions of Late Wisconsin megafauna', *Quaternary Research* 20, 110–12

Spiess, A.E. 1979. *Reindeer and caribou hunters. An archaeological study*. London, Academic Press

Spinage, C.A. 1973. 'A review of the age determination of mammals by means of teeth, with especial reference to Africa', *East African Wildlife Journal* 11, 165–87

Stahl, P.W. 1996. 'The recovery and interpretation of microvertebrate bone assemblages from archaeological contexts', *Journal of Archaeological Theory and Method*. 3(1), 31–75

Stahl, P.W. & Zeidler, J.A. 1990. 'Differential bone-refuse accumulation in food preparation and traffic areas in an Early Ecuadorian house floor', *Latin American Antiquity* 1, 150–69

Stallibrass, S. 1982. 'The use of cement layers for absolute ageing of mammalian teeth: a selective review of the literature, with suggestions for further studies and alternative applications', in B. Wilson, C. Grigson & S. Payne (eds) *Ageing and sexing animal bones from archaeological sites*. Oxford: British Archaeological Reports British Series 109, 109–26

Stallibrass, S.M. 1990. 'Canid damage to animal bones: two current lines of research.', in D.E. Robinson (ed.) *Experiment and reconstruction in environmental archaeology*. Oxford, Oxbow Books

Steele, D.G. 1990. 'Taphonomic provenience and mammoth bone modification', in L.B. Davies & B.O.K. Reeves (eds) *Hunters of the recent past*. London, Unwin Hyman One World Archaeology, 87–102

Steele, D.G. & Baker, B.W. 1993. 'Multiple predation: a definitive human hunting strategy', in J. Hudson (ed.) *From bone to behaviour: ethnoarchaeological and experimental contributions to the interpretation of faunal remains*. Center for Archaeological Investigations, Southern Illinois University at Carbondale, Occasional Paper 21

Stewart, J.R. & Carrasquilla, F.H. 1997. 'The identification of extant European bird remains: a review of the literature', *International Journal of Osteoarchaeology* 7, 364–71

Stewart, W.L. & Allcroft, R. 1956. 'Lameness and poor thriving in lambs on farms in old lead mining areas in the Pennines – I. Field investigations', *Veterinary Record* 68, 723–8

Stiner, M.C., Kuhn, S.L., Weiner, S. & Bar-Yosef, O. 1995. 'Differential burning, recrystallisation, and fragmentation of archaeological bone', *Journal of Archaeological Science* 22, 223–7

Stott, G.G., Sis, R.F. & Levy, B.M. 1982. 'Cementum annulation as an age criterion in forensic dentistry', *Journal of Dental Research* 61, 814–17

Stout, S.D. & Stanley, S.C. 1991. 'Percent osteonal bone versus osteon counts: the variable of choice for estimating age at death', *American Journal of Physical Anthropology* 86, 515–19

Stuart, A.J. 1982. *Pleistocene vertebrates in the British Isles*. London, Longman

Sutcliffe, A.J. 1973. 'Similarity of bones and antlers gnawed by deer to human artifacts', *Nature* 246, 428–30

Sykes, A.R., Coop, R.L. & Angus, K.W. 1977. 'The influence of chronic *Osteotagia circumcincta* infection in the skeleton of growing sheep', *Journal of Comparative Pathology* 87, 521–9

Tabor, R. 1983. *The wild life of the domestic cat*. London, Arrow Books

Tappen, N.C. & Peske, G.R. 1970. 'Weathering cracks and split-line patterns in archaeological bone', *American Antiquity* 35, 383–6

Tchernov, E. 1993. 'Exploitation of birds during the Natufian and early Neolithic of the Southern Levant', *Archaeofauna* 2, 121–43

Tchirvinsky, N. 1909. [The development of the skeleton of the sheep in normal conditions, in conditions of inadequate nutrition, and after early castration of males] (Original in Russian). *Annales de l'Institut Polytechnique de l'Empereur Alexandre II à Kiev 1909*, 1–305

Teichert, M. 1969. 'Osteometrische Untersuchungen zur Berechnung der Widerristhöhe bei vor- und frühgeschichtlichen Schweinen', *Ethnographische-Archäologische Zeitschrift* 10, 517–25

Todd, T.W. & Todd, A.W. 1938. 'The epiphysial union pattern of the ungulates with a note on Sirenia', *American Journal of Anatomy* 63(1), 1–36

Tonge, C.H. & McCance, R.A. 1965. 'Severe undernutrition in growing and adult animals 15. The mouth, jaws and teeth of pigs', *British Journal of Nutrition* 19, 361–75

Trotter, G.W., McIlwraith, C.W., Norrdin, R.W. & Turner, A.S. 1982. 'Degenerative joint disease with osteochondrosis of the proximal interphalangeal joint in young horses', *Journal of the American Veterinary Medical Association* 180, 1,312–18

Tsuda, K., Kikkawa, Y., Yonekawa, H. & Tanabe, Y. 1997. 'Extensive interbreeding occurred among multiple matriarchical ancestors during the domestication of dogs: evidence from inter- and intraspecies polymorphisms in the D-loop region of mitochondrial DNA between dogs and wolves', *Genes and Genetic Systems* 72, 229–38

Turner, A. 1983. 'The quantification of relative abundances in fossil and subfossil bone assemblages', *Annals of the Transvaal Museum* 33(20), 311–21

Turner, A. 1984. 'Sub-sampling animal bone assemblages: reducing the work-load or reducing the information?', *Circaea* 2, 69–75

van der Veen, M. & O'Connor, T.P. 1998. 'The expansion of agricultural production in late Iron Age and Roman Britain', in J. Bayley (ed.) *Science in Archaeology, an agenda for the future.* London, English Heritage, 127–44

Vigne, J.-D. 1995. *Détermination ostéologique des principaux éléments du squelette appendiculaire d'Arvicola, d'Eliomys, de Glis et de Rattus.* Juan-les-Pins. CNRS Fiches d'Osteologie Animale pour l'Archaeologie no. 6

Vigne, J.-D. & Marinval-Vigne, M.-C. 1983. 'Methods pour la mise en evidence de la consommation du petit gibier', in J. Clutton-Brock & C. Grigson (eds). *Animals and archaeology: 1. Early hunters and their prey.* Oxford, British Archaeological Reports International Series 163, 239–42

Vigne, J.-D. & Valladas, H. 1996. 'Small mammal fossil assemblages as indicators of environmental change in northern Corsica during the last 2500 years', *Journal of Archaeological Science* 23, 199–215

Walker, R. 1985. *A guide to the post-cranial bones of East African animals.* Norwich, Hylochoerus Press

Wallace, L.R. 1948. 'The growth of lambs before and after birth in relation to the level of nutrition', *Journal of Agricultural Science* 38, 93–153, 243–304, 367–401

Walters, M. 1980. *Complete birds of the world.* London, Book Club Associates

Wapnish, P. & Hesse, B. 1988. 'Urbanization and the organization of animal production at Tell Jemmeh in the Middle Bronze Age Levant', *Journal of Near Eastern Studies* 47, 81–94

Ward, D.J. 1984. 'Collecting isolated microvertebrate fossils', *Zoological Journal of the Linnaean Society* 82, 245–59

Watson, J.P.N. 1972. 'Fragmentation analysis of animal bone samples from archaeological sites', *Archaeometry* 14, 221–7

Watson, J.P.N. 1978. 'The interpretation of epiphyseal fusion data', in D. Brothwell, J. Clutton-Brock & K.D. Thomas (eds) *Research problems in zooarchaeology.* London, Institute of Archaeology Occasional Publications 3, 97–101

Watson, J.P.N. 1979. 'The estimation of the relative frequencies of mammalian species: Khirokitia 1972', *Journal of Archaeological Science* 6, 127–37

Weiner, S. & Bar-Yosef, O. 1990. 'States of preservation of bones from prehistoric sites in the Near East: a survey', *Journal of Archaeological Science* 17, 187–96

Weiner, S. & Traub, W. 1989. 'Crystal size and organisation in bone', *Connective Tissue Research* 21, 259–65

Wenham, G. & Fowler, V.R. 1973. 'A radiographic study of age changes in the skull, mandible and teeth of pigs', *Journal of Agricultural Science, Cambridge* 80, 451–61

West, B. 1995. 'The case of the missing victuals', *Historical Archaeology* 29, 20–42

West, B. & Milne, G. 1993. 'Owls in the basilica', *London Archaeologist* 7(2), 31–6

West, B. & Zhou, B.X. 1988. 'Did chickens go north? New evidence for domestication', *Journal of Archaeological Science* 15, 515–33

Wheat, J.B. 1972. 'The Olsen-Chubbuck site. A Paleo-Indian bison kill', *Society for American Archaeology Memoirs* 26, 1–180

Wheeler, A. & Jones, A.K.G. 1989. *Fishes.* Cambridge, Cambridge University Press

Wheeler, A. & Locker, A. 1985. 'The estimation of size in sardines (*Sardina pilchardus*) from amphorae in a wreck at Randello, Sicily', *Journal of Archaeological Science* 12, 97–100

Wheeler Pires-Ferreira, J., Pires-Ferreira, E. & Kaulicke, P. 1976. 'Preceramic animal utilization in the Central Peruvian Andes', *Science* 194, 483–90

Wheeler, J. 1984. 'On the origin and early development of camelid pastoralism in the Andes', in J. Clutton-Brock & C. Grigson (eds) *Animals and archaeology: 3. Early herders and their flocks*. Oxford, British Archaeological Reports International Series 202, 395–410

Wheeler, J.C. 1995. 'Evolution and present situation of the South American camelids', *Biological Journal of the Linnaean Society* 54, 271–95

White, E.M. & Hannus, A. 1983. 'Chemical weathering of bone in archaeological soils', *American Antiquity* 48, 316–22

White, T.D. 1992. *Prehistoric cannibalism at Mancos 5MTUMR-2346*. Oxford, Princeton University Press

White, T.E. 1953a. 'A method for calculating the dietary percentages of various food animals utilised by aboriginal peoples', *American Antiquity* 18, 386–98

White, T.E. 1953b. 'Observations on the butchering techniques of some aboriginal peoples no. 2', *American Antiquity* 19, 160–4

White, T.E. 1954. 'Observations on the butchering techniques of some aboriginal peoples nos 3, 4, 5, and 6', *American Antiquity* 20, 254–64

Wild, C.J. & Nichol, R.K. 1983. 'Estimation of the original number of individuals from paired bone counts using estimators of the Krantz type', *Journal of Field Archaeology* 10, 337–44

Wilkinson, P.F. 1976. '"Random" hunting and the composition of faunal samples from archaeological excavations: a modern example from New Zealand', *Journal of Archaeological Science* 3, 321–8

van Wijngaarden-Bakker, L.H. 1987. 'Experimental zooarchaeology', in W. Groenman-van Waateringe & L.H. van Wijngaarden-Bakker (eds) *Farm life in a Carolingian village*. Assen, Studies in Prae en Protohistorie, 107–17

van Wijngaarden-Bakker, L.H. 1996. 'A new find of a European pond tortoise, *Emys orbicularis* (L.) from the Netherlands: osteology and taphonomy', *International Journal of Osteoarchaeology* 6, 443–53

van Wijngaarden-Bakker, L.H. 1997. 'The selection of bird bones for artefact production at Dutch Neolithic sites', *International Journal of Osteoarchaeology* 7, 339–45

van Wijngaarden-Bakker, L.H. & Krauwer, M. 1979. 'Animal palaeopathology. Some examples from the Netherlands', *Helinium* 19, 37–53

van Wijngaarden-Bakker, L.H. & Maliepaard, C.H. 1982. 'Leeftijdsbepaling aan het skelet van het wilde zwijn *Sus scrofa* Linnaeus, 1758', *Lutra* 25, 30–7

Williams, D.E. 1973. 'Flotation at Siraf', *Antiquity* 47, 288–92

Winder, N.P. 1991. 'How many bones make five? The art and science of guesstimation in archaeozoology', *International Journal of Osteoarchaeology* 1, 111–26

Windle, B.C.A. & Humphreys, J. 1890. 'On some cranial and dental characters of the domestic dog', *Proceedings of the Zoological Society* (1890), 5–29

Wing, E.S. 1989. 'Human exploitation of animal resources in the Caribbean', in C.A. Woods (ed.) *Biogeography of the West Indies: past, present, and future*. Gainesville, Florida, Sandhill Crane Press, 137–52

Wing, E.S. & Quitmyer, I.R. 1985. 'Screen size for optimal data recovery: a case study.', in W.H. Adam (ed.) *Aboriginal subsistence and settlement archaeology of the Kings Bay locality, vol 2: zooarchaeology*. Gainesville, Department of Anthropology, University of Florida, Reports of Investigation 2, 49–58

Wolff, R.G. 1973. 'Hydrodynamic sorting and ecology of a Pleistocene mammalian assemblage from California (USA)', *Palaeogeography, Palaeoclimatology, Palaeoecology* 13, 91–101

Wright, H.T. 1977. 'Recent research on the origin of the state', *Annual Review in Anthropology* 6, 379–97

Yalden, D.W. 1995. 'Small mammals from Viking-age Repton', *Journal of Zoology, London* 237, 655–7

Yalden, D.W. 1999. *History of British mammals*. London, T. & A.D. Poyser

Zeder, M.A. 1991. *Feeding cities. Specialized animal economy in the ancient Near East.* Washington, Smithsonian Institution Press

Zeder, M.A. 1994. 'After the revolution: post-Neolithic subsistence in northern Mesopotamia', *American Anthropologist* 96, 97–126

Zeiler, J.T. 1987. 'Exploitation of fur animals in Neolithic Swifterbant and Hazendonk (Central and Western Netherlands)', *Palaeohistoria* 29, 245–63

Zeiler, J. 1988. 'Age determination based on epiphyseal fusion in post-cranial bones and tooth wear in otters (*Lutra lutra*)', *Journal of Archaeological Science* 15, 555–61

Zohar, I., Dayan, T. & Spanier, E. 1997. 'Predicting grey triggerfish body size from bones', *International Journal of Osteoarchaeology* 7, 150–6

Zohary, D., Tchernov, E. & Horwitz, L.K. 1998. 'The role of unconscious selection in the domestication of sheep and goats', *Journal of Zoology, London* 245, 129–35

Zuck, T.T. 1938. 'Age order of epiphyseal union in the guinea pig', *Anatomical Record* 70, 389–99

INDEX

Note that names of sites and of species are not indexed where mentioned only in passing in the text. Species are indexed under both their common and scientific names. Authors are indexed where their work is discussed at some length or in detail.